THE CULTURES OF ECONOMIC MIGRATION: INTERNATIONAL PERSPECTIVES

Studies in Migration and Diaspora

Series Editor: Anne J. Kershen

Studies in Migration and Diaspora is a series designed to showcase the interdisciplinary and multidisciplinary nature of research in this important field. Volumes in the series cover local, national and global issues and engage with both historical and contemporary events. The books will appeal to scholars, students and all those engaged in the study of migration and diaspora. Amongst the topics covered are minority ethnic relations, transnational movements and the cultural, social and political implications of moving from 'over there', to 'over here'.

The Cultures of
Economic Migration
International Perspectives

Edited by

SUMAN GUPTA
The Open University, UK

and

TOPE OMONIYI
Roehampton University, UK

Routledge
Taylor & Francis Group

LONDON AND NEW YORK

First published 2007 by Ashgate Publishing

Published 2016 by Routledge
2 Park Square, Milton Park, Abingdon, Oxfordshire OX14 4RN
711 Third Avenue, New York, NY 10017, USA

First issued in paperback 2016

Routledge is an imprint of th e Taylor & Francis Group, an informa business

British Library Cataloguing in Publication Data
The cultures of economic migration : international
  perspectives. - (Studies in migration and diaspora)
  1. Emigration and immigration - Economic aspects
  2. Emigration and immigration - Political aspects
  3. Emigration and immigration - Social aspects
  4. Emigration and immigration - International cooperation
  I. Gupta, Suman, 1966- II. Omoniyi, Tope
  304.8

Library of Congress Cataloging-in-Publication Data
The cultures of economic migration : international perspectives / edited by Suman Gupta and Tope Omoniyi.
     p. cm. -- (Studies in migration and diaspora)
  Includes index.

  1. Emigration and immigration--Research. 2. Emigration and immigration--Economic aspects. 3. Emigration and immigration--Social aspects. 4. Emigration and immigration--International cooperation. I. Gupta, Suman, 1966- II. Omoniyi, Tope.

  JV6013.5.C85 2007
  304.8--dc22

                                                                    2007000325

ISBN 13: 978-1-138-27360-3 (pbk)
ISBN 13: 978-0-7546-7070-4 (hbk)

Contents

PART III: ASIA

List of Figures and Tables

Notes on Contributors

Efurosibina Adegbija was Professor and Head of the Department of Languages and Mass Communication at Covenant University, Nigeria. He authored numerous articles and books, including *Language Attitudes in Sub-Saharan Africa: A Sociolinguistic Overview* (1994) and *Multilingualism: A Nigerian Case Study* (2003). He passed away in 2005.

Taoufik Agoumy is Professor of Geography at Mohammed V University of Rabat, Morocco, and Vice President of the Association Nationale des Géographes Marocains. He is involved in several collaborative projects: "Atlas 2000 de l'Immigration Maghrébine en Espagne", "The interactions between sea tourism and cultural tourism: the case of Morocco and Majorca (socio-economic and socio-spatial outputs)", "Atlas du Grand Rabat-Salé". His publications include scholarly papers on labour migration, demographic shifts and localities in Moroccan cities, and collective action; he co-edited *La Grande Encyclopédie du Maroc* (1988) and *Global/Local Cultures and Sustainable Development* (2001).

Taghi Azadarmaki is Professor of Sociology at the University of Tehran, Iran. He has published numerous papers and fourteen books on sociology and social matters in Iran, including *Iranian Modernity* (2002) and *The Idea of Modernity in Iran* (2001).

Mehri Bahar is Assistant Professor of Cultural Studies at University of Tehran, Iran. Her research interests are in media and religion in Iran.

Vinay Bahl is Associate Professor of Sociology at the Pennsylvania College of Technology at Williamsport, USA. Her books include the *Making of the Indian Working Class: A Case Study of Tata Iron and Steel Company 1880 to 1945* (1995) and she co-edited *History After the Three Worlds: Post-Eurocentric Historiographies* (2000).

Tapan Basu is Reader in English at Hindu College, University of Delhi, India. His books include *Khaki Shorts Saffron Flags* (1992, co-authored), *T.S.Eliot: An Anthology of Recent Criticism* (1993, edited), *Translating Caste* (2003, edited), and numerous papers on Indian education policy, black American literature, and Indian literature in English. He is currently a Ferguson Fellow at the Ferguson Centre for African and Asian Studies, Open University, UK.

Taieb Belghazi is Professeur de l'enseignement supérieur at Mohammed V University of Rabat, Morocco. His numerous publications include *Actions Collectives: De la mobilisation des ressources à la prise de parole* (2001, with Madani), *The Idea of* *the University* (1997, edited), *Local/Global Cultures and Sustainable Development* (2001, co-edited). He is a Ferguson Fellow at the Ferguson Centre for African and Asian Studies, Open University, UK; a member of the UNESCO International Panel on Literacy; a member of the Rabat Culture and Development Research Unit; and a member of the editorial board of *Time and Society* (Sage).

Subarno Chattarji is Reader in English at the University of Delhi, India. He has authored *Memories of a Lost War: American Poetic Responses to the Vietnam War* (2001), and has edited several books.

Irina Chongarova is Associate Professor in Cultural Studies and Director of the Centre for Languages and Intercultural Communication at the Paissij Hilendarski University of Plovdiv, Bulgaria. Her publications are in semantics, lexicography and cultural studies.

John Eade is Professor of Sociology and Anthropology at Roehampton University, and Executive Director of the Centre for Nationality, Ethnicity and Migration at the University of Surrey, UK. His numerous books include *Community Perceptions of Forced Marriage* (2002, with Samad), *Understanding the City: Contemporary and Future Perspectives* (2002, with Mele), and *Placing London: From Imperial City to Global Capital* (2000).

Suman Gupta is Professor of Literature and Cultural History, and Joint Director of the Ferguson Centre for African and Asian Studies at the Open University, UK, and is Principal Coordinator of the Globalization, Identity Politics and Social Conflict (GIPSC) Project. He is the author of eight single-authored books, including, recently, *The Theory and Reality of Democracy: A Case Study in Iraq* (2006) and *Social Constructionist Identity Politics and Literary Studies* (2007).

Teresa Hayter's numerous books include *Open Borders: The Case against Immigration Controls* (2000), *Exploited Earth: Britain's Aid and the Environment* (1989), *The Creation of World Poverty* (1981) and *Aid as Imperialism* (1974). She has been involved in the campaign to close the Campsfield detention centre in Oxford since 1983, and has been a member of the Barbed Wire Britain network since it was set up in 2000.

Zhivko Ivanov is Vice-Dean of the Faculty of Philology and Professor of Literature at the Paissij Hilendarski University of Plovdiv, Bulgaria. His numerous publications include: *Hristo Smirnenski. Selected works. Volume 1-2* + CD-ROM (2001-2002), *Baj Ganyo. Between Europe and Homeland* (1999), *New Bulgarian Literature 1878-1918* (1998), *Bulgarian Literature from Liberation to the End of World War I* (1989 with Bistra Ganchseva), and *Bulgarian Literature after World War I* (1995).

David Johnson is Senior Lecturer in Literature at the Open University, UK. He is co-editor of the *Historical Companion to Postcolonial Literatures in English* (2005), author of *Shakespeare in South Africa* (1996), and co-author of *Jurisprudence: A South African Perspective* (2001).

Cyril I. Obi is Programme Coordinator of the "Post-Conflict Transition, State and Civil Society in Africa" research programme at the Nordiska Afrikainstitutet in Uppsala, Sweden. His many publications include *The Changing Forms of Identity Politics in Nigeria under Economic Adjustment: The Case of Oil Minorities Movements of the Niger Delta* (2001).

Tope Omoniyi is Professor of Sociolinguistics at Roehampton University, UK. His numerous publications include *The Sociolinguistics of Borderlands: Two Nations, One Community* (2004). He is also a poet, and author of the verse collection *Farting President and Other Poems* (2001).

Yue Daiyun is Professor of Chinese Literature and Comparative Literature, and Director, Centre for Cross-Cultural Studies, at Beijing University, China, and President of the Chinese Comparative Literature Association. She has received numerous awards and honours, including the Honorary Doctor of Letters from McMasters University, Canada. Her many books in English, French and Chinese include *Intellectuals in Chinese Fiction* (1987), *Comparative Literature and Modern Chinese Literature* (1987), *La Nature* (1999), *The Theory of Comparative Literature* (2000), *A Bridge Across Cultures* (2002), *A Course in Comparative Literature* (2003).

Preface

Contemporary migration studies are multi-faceted and complex. Not only do they bisect temporal and geographic boundaries, most pertinently for students of, and researchers into, the movement of people, they cross academic disciplines. At the same time, as the editors of this volume state, 'Migration studies are fraught with socio-cultural anxieties'. These disquiets, diversities and intersections are admirably demonstrated and addressed in this scholarly and ground-breaking book which unites academics from three continents working in such varied territories as Cultural Studies, Economics, English, Geography, Linguistics, Philology and Sociology.

Economic advancement is the dynamic which drives the majority of 'free' migrants, so it is appropriate that that is what was at the source of, and impelled, this volume. However, as in the case of the rational decision-making emigrant, where the economic dimension of the processes of departure, arrival and settlement, is only a part of the experience, so all the contributors to this book proceed from an economic starting point which must, by its very nature, embrace a socio-cultural perspective. On the journey they encounter both real and metaphorical obstacles and boundaries; legacies of xenophobia, nationalism, nation-building and myth come face to face with contemporary reactions to racism, economic hierarchies, spatial reconfigurations and, of course, globalization. The impact of these confrontations are not easy to predict, in some cases the movement from A to B produces nothing more than the rustle of a leaf, in other circumstances it may provoke a typhoon.

Whilst the movement of people is as old as the bible, its study is far more contemporary. Even today, in spite of the burgeoning library of migration literature, there are lacunae to fill. In order to comprehend the process of settlement in an alien environment we need to be informed about the sending societies. In addition, in a globalizing world, it is imperative that we are as knowledgeable about the impact of emigration on the economy and culture of the sending society as we are as to the effect of the incomer on the receiving society. This volume sets out to redress the balance by providing us with a selection of studies of migration, a number of which incorporate the cultural and economic perspective of those left behind as well as those on the receiving line.

In co-editing such an important and informative volume Suman Gupta and Tope Omoniyi have brought together scholarly bedfellows who might forever have remained apart. By so doing they have fulfilled their stated ambition to make a 'definite and considered contribution to migration studies'. I would suggest that they have gone beyond that intention by assembling a volume which is long overdue in its focused yet expansive approach to the study of the movement of people in a global, yet specific, context.

Anne J. Kershen
Queen Mary, University of London
Spring 2007

Acknowledgements

Thanks are due to the British Academy for generously supporting, through a number of grants, the collaborative Globalization, Identity Politics and Social Conflict (GIPSC) Project out of which this book emerged. The editors are grateful for the financial and administrative support given by the Open University, and the encouragement of colleagues therein. The Ferguson Centre of African and Asian Studies in the Open University collaborated in organising a workshop where the foundation for this book was laid. We are grateful for the advice and support given by David Richards, then Director of the Ferguson Centre. Thanks are also due to colleagues and staff at Roehampton University, who contributed in various ways to the process leading up to this collection of papers. We are particularly grateful to Heather Scott, Ferguson Centre, for the hard work she put into finalizing the typescript of this book.

Suman Gupta and Tope Omoniyi
January 2007

Dedicated to Professor Efurosibina Adegbija (1952-2005)

*The editors often didn't agree with him but they admired his
integrity, conviction in open and rational debate and dedication
to research and enjoyed his constant support*

Chapter 1

Introduction:
Socio-Cultural Attitudes to Migration and the Academic Disposition of Migration Studies

Suman Gupta

Faculty of Arts, Open University UK

This volume brings together studies of socio-cultural attitudes toward and perceptions of migration, and the modalities of expression and political implications of these, in different geopolitical contexts. In planning this volume it was felt that 'migration' itself has a myriad of contextually and culturally defined nuances and emphases: in some contexts immigration seems of more moment, in others emigration; in some places internal migration is uppermost in people's minds, in others international; at times the contemplation of migration seems to focus on physical movements and settlements, at others it appears to be constructed in a social imaginary. The authors agreed that space should be left for all these nuances, and that particular emphases would be determined by the geopolitical contexts addressed. However, the authors also felt that this openness might lend itself to a complete diffusion of focus, and that they were keen to focus on contextual views of migration in a way that is free of strong normative preconceptions. A focus on 'economic migration' – with the purposive emphasis of the economic – seemed to serve this purpose well. The materiality of the economic itself seems to promise (and usually does not deliver) a normatively neutral starting point; more importantly it draws away from immediately normatively-charged views that attach to forced migration, asylum or refuge status seeking, conflict-driven movement, and so on. A provisional definition of economic migration for the purposes of this volume was in fact assumed – more of that in due course. The result, the papers that follow this introduction, is diverse and yet coherent. All *contemplate* socio-cultural perceptions and expressions of economic migration, and some *perform* them as well, and, in different ways, most of them are in a continuing conversation with each other from widely dispersed contexts.

This volume was planned with a self-conscious desire on the part of the authors to make a definite and considered contribution to migration studies. That meant that each author was enjoined, in an explicit fashion, to keep the field of migration studies in view when working on their chapters. This could mean interrogating the field, complying with the dominant preoccupations of the field, or trying to give it a new or different bent. I think each chapter of this volume has done this in more or less obvious ways, and from their particular standpoints. In undertaking the task of introducing this volume, it seems to me prudent to start here – to provide in quick strokes a background on the current disposition of migration studies, particularly insofar as the main concerns of this volume, 'social and cultural texts of economic migration', go. This introductory and generalizing background is, naturally, only attempted so that it can be dismantled in the chapters that follow. In the final section of this introduction I give my sense of how that dismantling proceeds.

Public Attitude Surveys and Xenophobia

Migration studies are an area fraught with socio-cultural anxieties. These anxieties are derived from and generated for, or at any rate constantly hover on the fringes of staid academic pursuits, a wider sphere of cultural attitudes and political/media rhetoric. Where resources are expended on taming or exacerbating these anxieties by an industrial production of scholarly information about migration, migration studies consist to a not insignificant degree in the generation of neat figures (how many? from where? why? of what categories? and so on) to reckon with. These figures nourish migration studies, and feed into and upon policy and legislative and media and political and other organizational documents in seemingly measured ways, only tacitly belying or prodding anxieties – they simply open themselves to anxious reckonings.

Public attitude surveys (what do 'our' people think on this issue?) is one of those odd areas within migration studies where the reckonings and the anxieties are themselves turned into neat figures. In contemplating the field of migration studies, it is always worth pausing on this most obvious of sticking points. Public attitude surveys juxtapose the measured quantitative approach on the intractability of anxieties, and reveal a drift. These convey an immediate sense of what migration studies impinge upon and work within and are up against and are in some sense inevitably constituted by. Any (inevitably) random selection of reasonably methodologically-sound surveys speaks for itself. In Canada, a series of Angus Reid surveys of January 1996–October 1998 found that 42 per cent of those surveyed felt that there were too many immigrants and 8 per cent felt there were too few (Palmer, 1999). Surveys in 1996 in Australia (mainly an AGB McNair telephone poll of 1996) showed that 65 per cent of Australians felt that the level of immigration to Australia was too high, while 29 per cent felt it was about right – proportions which generally characterized the period 1990–1996 (Betts, 1996). Examining a range of 1998–1999 surveys Goot found that this had changed, and that in these years the former figure had reduced to 47 per cent and the latter increased to 42 per cent (Goot, 2000), though his interpretation of these data were questioned (Betts, 2000). The South African Migration Project (SAMP) conducted surveys in 2001–2002 which showed that 21 per cent of South African respondents wished to ban the entry of foreigners completely, and another 64 per cent preferred to have strict limits on immigration (Crush and Pendleton, 2004, p. 9). The SAMP report examined comparative figures from other countries and found that the desire to place strict limits on the number of foreigners is very far from uncommon in other countries, though the desire to completely ban foreigners varies widely. A Eurobarometer study of 1997 showed that 70 per cent of surveyed European citizens believed that only a limited number of people of other races, cultures and religions should be admitted to their societies; 65 per cent felt that their countries had reached the limit; and 45 per cent felt that there were too many people of religious and ethnic minority background in their countries (Eurobarometer, 1997, March–April). Subsequent Gallup polls in the USA found that between 2001 (with a sharp increase after 9/11) and 2005 a majority of people felt that immigration levels should be lowered – in early 2005 (3–5 January), 52 per cent were so inclined, while 39 per cent felt it should continue at current levels. Another poll of 2002 (3–9 June) found that 52 per cent of Americans felt that on the whole immigration is a bad thing for the country, against the 42 per cent who felt it was a good thing (Carroll, 2005).

Britain is worth singling out – within Europe the British appear to be more concerned than average about immigration. In 2004, 41 per cent of the British surveyed by Eurobarometer considered immigration to be among the two most important issues facing their country, which was more than twice the figure for any other surveyed country (Eurobarometer, 2004, Spring). A Cabinet Office report of 2001 found, on examining a range of recent surveys, that:

> The British population has a highly erroneous impression concerning the number of ethnic minorities and migrants in the UK. In one poll, the average estimate of the size of the ethnic minority population in the UK was 26 per cent of the population, despite the correct figure being closer to 7 per cent. In another it was 20 per cent. When asked to estimate the proportion of population consisting of migrants and asylum seekers, the modal estimate was 51 per cent plus, despite the real situation being closer to 4 per cent (Saggar and Drean,2001, p. 3).

Overestimation of numbers and anxiety are not necessarily the same thing, of course, but these figures are augmented with others – too numerous to mention here – which show that overestimation is related to negative attitudes towards immigrants and doubts of various sorts about immigration.

All the above-mentioned figures – often aggregates of a large number of surveys conducted independently of each other – are complicated by a range of considerations. Numerous factors play a role in interpretations: the extent and timing of surveys; educational level, age-group, employment and earnings, identity-based convictions and other factors among respondents; modes of conducting surveys (for example in terms of degree of anonymity allowed); the phrasing of questions and the definitions of terms in questions when conducting surveys; local political environment (such as existing government policy, perceptions of extrinsic threat to security, concerns about rising unemployment); the reach of the agency conducting surveys (governmental, academic, media); and so on. Also, often such results come with other public attitude measures which suggest contradictory adherence to principles. Thus, it is occasionally possible for the same survey to show both that a majority feels that there are too many immigrants and a majority feels that immigrants have a positive effect on society, or that a majority wishes that there was more control on immigration and simultaneously a majority maintain that no discrimination should occur in processing immigrants. Despite these caveats, there is a remarkable degree of uniformity in most countries, and over a sustained period, of doubt, anxiety and mistrust regarding immigrants. In countries where there already are significant numbers of immigrants, and which are popular migrant destinations – such as USA, Canada, Britain, South Africa, Australia – generally over 40 per cent of the population, and usually majorities, regard immigration with reserve. Pew Survey figures from 2002 (Pew Research Centre, 2002) showed that immigration is regarded as a problem in almost every country which features there (covering all the continents).

Of course, the field of migration studies is not necessarily, or even significantly, devoted to the quantification and explanation of public attitudes to migration. But this field of study is inevitably within, so to say, the field of public attitudes – however tacitly or unconcernedly – and is necessarily cognizant of the remarkably one-directional *drift* in the latter where its object of study (migration) is concerned. It seems reasonable to infer that migration studies must, however resistantly or unresistingly, construct itself ... cautiously ... circumspectly ... intentionally ... within a social-cultural-political world which is, to be blunt, xenophobic in a widely dispersed and remarkably even fashion. As Robin Cohen, in a wide-ranging study of past and present perceptions and constructions of migration and migrants, has recently observed:

> Despite more guards, more laws and more restrictions, the symbolic and real boundaries that divide societies are eroding. This is a result of ideas, images, money, music, electronic messages, sport, fashion and religions that can move without people, or without many people – forms, if you like, of virtual migration. But nothing is as disturbing to national societies as the movement of people (Cohen, 2006, p. 5).

The Social Construction of Migration Studies

Occasionally, researchers trying to come to grips with public discourses of migration find complicities that emanate from and are immanent within the academic field of migration studies itself. In charting the rise of a new kind of racism centred on migration (primarily with reference to Canada), whereby racism shifts 'from notions of biological superiority to exclusion based on cultural difference' (Ibrahim, 2005, p. 163), Maggie Ibrahim finds herself confronting a set of systemic collusions: 'Due to the assertions of international organizations, states, academics and journalists, migration has become synonymous with a new risk to the liberal world' (Ibrahim, 2005, p. 164). In a related fashion, Btihaj Ajana's reflections (spurred by Michael Howard's anti-immigration 2005 election campaign for the British Conservative Party) on the current political discourse of migration, suggests that its dominant xenophobic bent derives not from academic migration studies per se, but from an extrapolation of forms of argument and rhetoric which have a base in the academic. These distort academic – or more precisely 'expert' or 'specialist' – discourse on migration with immanentist predetermination, while alluding to and drawing upon the authority of academic discourse:

[...] the figurations of immanentist politics are manifested through immigration controls by means of *spatialising, technologising* and *articulating* absolute figures within the political imaginary, giving rise to modes of inclusion and exclusion. Such figurations are problematic insofar as they are deeply ensconced within the determinism of sovereignty in which identity, citizenship, and belonging are reduced to and burdened by the illusive belief in a fixed common substance and the need to sustain a state of self-enclosure (Ajana, 2006, p. 265).

The 'figures' derive from quantitative migration studies ('quotas and numbers are becoming metaphors for dignity and worth', it was clarified earlier [Ajana, 2006, p. 259]), but the allusion/distortion of the academic is not just in drawing upon the production of quantitative 'figures' but also in the 'figuration' thereof, which comes in a distinctly academic-sounding register – '*spatialising, technologising* and *articulating*'.

It would be a mistake, however, to think of migration studies as a passive component in a wider arena of public exchanges about migration, with their anxieties and dominant drift and consequent polarizations. Migration studies also and necessarily and actively responds and intervenes with political intent – this too is a constitutive aspect of the field that locates it within those public exchanges. A familiar play of normative and political advocacy marks the socio-political weight the field carries, and is well worth registering briefly. On the left, migration studies are now powerfully allied with the politics of identity, or the politics of difference. This consists primarily in contesting all forms of xenophobia by elucidating its complicity with global capitalist regimes that breed inequality and injustice. Here it is often persuasively argued that control of labour and markets is facilitated by manipulating existing xenophobic tendencies, and it is maintained that removing border restrictions on immigration and promoting the coexistence of different constituencies in their own terms would lead to a just, fair, equal and economically viable condition. Such arguments take the form of analysing the inequities and oppressions that are engendered by xenophobia in cohort with state-policy (for example, Wrench and Solomos, 1995; Hayter, 2000; Cohen, Humphries and Mynott, 2001; Harris, 2001); examining the historical development of xenophobia in relation to contemporary experiences (for example Taylor, 1993; Jelloun, 2000; Sassen, 2003; Wilder, 2004) and examining the normative principles associated with liberal democracy and human rights in political philosophy terms (for example Dummett, 2001). Such arguments also associate themselves with the salutary contributions of immigrant groups in terms of cultural production and contribution to recipient societies – particularly in, for instance, post-colonial examinations of diasporic texts (King, White and Connell, 1995; Phillips, 1997; Suleiman, 1998; Kumar, 2003). Roughly at the centre of the political spectrum is located an alluring political philosophy strain that examines, in a careworn but well-meaning fashion, the difficulties of pluralism and multiculturalism in liberal democracies. The apprehension of a resistance to accommodating immigrants in so-called liberal democracies, together with the ethical desirability of tolerance and optimism in pluralistic accommodation are here widely debated issues (Gutmann editor, 1994; Kymlicka, 1995; Young, 2002; Benhabib, 2004). Interestingly, the conservative right that presents arguments as favour of immigration control, and regards xenophobia as deriving from rational anxieties based on politically real problems, often derives from and expands on liberal principles too. The problems of reasonable pluralism could easily come to be regarded as insurmountable in liberal democratic rationality: this is amply demonstrated in the initially left-leaning Rawls's struggles to rationalize pluralism leading gradually to the distinctly conservative conception of a 'closed society' (described in Rawls, 1993, p. 12). Neoconservatives take their cue from that Rawlsian move, and present the need for curtailing immigration as the liberal democratic state's duty toward existing citizens, often citing not just (always questionable) economic arguments, but also cultural, security and health considerations (Brimelow, 1995; Taylor et al., 1998; Huntington, 2004). In all these the anxiety about immigration is taken as a priori, is responded to, interrogated or activated.

The Economics of Migration

Socio-cultural anxieties in the public sphere, the demand for and deployment of figures and figurations, the normative and political positions that are assumed in this context all impinge upon the construction and practice of migration studies. Though these are probably not all chartable or explicable in terms of the economic vested interests at stake, migration studies often seem to assume that the economics is the heart of the matter. The general dominant drift toward xenophobia that characterizes attitudes to migration can, all the above-mentioned academic studies ultimately suggest, be explained and defended or countered by a clarification of the economics of migration – by accounting the costs and benefits of migration for all parties, those sending and those receiving migrants. This assumption comes with good reason. If, in trying to discern the general features of migration studies, one cannot but note the impact of the dominant xenophobic drift of socio-cultural attitudes one also cannot overlook the dominant direction of actual migratory movement. Along with the dominant perceptual drift a propos migration there is also a dominant empirical direction of migration.

The dominant direction is the one that is most readily recognized: 'A large majority of international migrants are from less developed countries – not surprising since about 80 percent of world population lives in these countries. [...] Migration flows from the less developed to the more developed countries include the movement from South and Central America to North America, and from North Africa and the Middle East to Europe. The flow from Asia to North America and Australia has also accelerated' (Population Reference Bureau, 2004, p. 12). The dominant direction, described here as a matter of continental flows, devolves along the lines of economic zones into most of the currently in-discussion micro-foci of migration studies: for example, the impact of brain drain in Africa (Oderth, 2001; Donald and Crush, 2002; Physicians for Human Rights, 2004); rural to urban migration in China following recent liberalization of movement (Davin, 1999; Solinger, 1999; Murphy, 2002); the regulation of migration within the European Union with shifting boundaries and phases of accession (Dowd and Wilson, 2003; King, Mai and Dalipaj, 2004; Groenendijk, Guild and Minderhoud, 2005). The economic logic of this dominant direction would seem not to be necessarily congruent with the directions taken by refugees, asylum seekers and other forced migrants. But though most recent studies in this area (such as Dowell, 1996; Nachmias and Goldstein eds. 2004; Tazreiter, 2004; Whittaker, 2005; Nicholas, 2006; Tyler, 2006) emphasize the normative and political nuances of the area, they also suggest that the directions of such movement are largely congruent with the dominant economically determined direction or sieved through similar models of economic analysis.

A complex debate has grown on the identification of effective factors, and on the suitable modes for analysing this economically determined dominant direction of migration. These follow broadly four well-established and linked lines of emphasis. One, following neoclassical theories of analysing international migration in terms of development gaps there are continuing examinations of the relationship between migration and development, both in terms of emigration and immigration (Brown, 1991; Papademetriou and Martin, 1991; Skeldon, 1997; Levy and Foria, 2002; Özden and Schiff, 2006). Two, international migration continues to be assessed in terms of an overarching international order, such as Wallerstein's World-Systems theory, or Samir Amin's dependency theory, or concepts of international capitalism, globalization and neo-imperialism (recently, Mittelman, 2000; Grosfoguel and Cervantes-Rodríguez eds., 2002). Three, in relation to both the above the economics of migration is constantly assessed in international and national policy and consequent regulation/control (Guiraudon and Joppke eds., 2001; Bartram, 2005; Goldin and Kenneth, 2006). Four, relatively recently – following from early 1990s work on world cities and informal economies by Saskia Sassen, Anthony King, and others – a number of focused explorations of the environments within which immigrants conduct businesses and operate informal networks have become available, typically demonstrating that a complex of human, social and cultural capital play with financial capital in these (Rath, 2000; Bauder, 2006).

Each of these approaches to the economics of migration, even when simply presenting and categorizing data, are continuously and necessarily cognizant of socio-cultural attitudes and the consequent politics and ethics attached to the contemplation of migration. Given that the field of migration studies, even with the apparently empirically-led and norm-free aspirations that attach to economic analysis, has to construct itself within a public sphere means that almost nothing can be said that is not inevitably socially and politically affective. The pressures of policy-making and of socio-cultural attitudes render all economic observations and modes of the analysis of migration a gesture of political import, an intervention in the public sphere, and as situated within socio-cultural perceptions. The four linked approaches identified here are, therefore, now all in the cusp of an intermeshing of cultural, social, political and economic factors, increasingly without clear disciplinary prerogatives. They all give in to the implicit need or start out with the explicit desire for ideological advocacy, and political position-taking, and claims of cultural sensitivities and awareness. Nevertheless, a chosen focus on the economics of migration still has something reassuringly tangible about it. It seems to place the less tractable social, cultural and political considerations and anxieties into perspective – and it is widely believed, I suspect almost as a socio-cultural attitude itself, that a proper (whatever that may be) economic approach to the matter will eventually throw up a solution to socio-cultural anxieties and reveal a correct way forward for policy-makers (whatever that might be).

This Book

Out of a dispersed public sphere characterized both by socio-cultural anxieties and high expectations of studying the economics of migration, whereby migration studies is constructed and constituted, emerges the chapters in this volume. The sweeping generalizations above need not be taken further; the chapters that follow bring discrimination by their sense of location and by their predetermined focus on the purposive conjunction of 'economic migration'. The following chapters, as I said at the beginning, dismantle the foregoing introductory generalizations.

The project from which this book largely, but not entirely, emerged is the Globalization, Identity Politics and Social Conflict Project, initiated in 2002 (the website is http://www.open.ac.uk/arts/gipsc). This involved collaboration between researchers from and with interests in a range of African, Asian and European countries and areas. The particular focus on economic migration was built up through a workshop held in London in July 2004,[1] at which early drafts of some of the chapters in this volume were presented and discussed. To initiate this workshop, the following working definition of 'economic migration' was agreed upon:

> Migration refers to the cross-border movement of people from a homeland to a location outside that homeland, with the purpose of taking up employment and conducting a daily existence there for an extended period of time. In principle such movement need be no more than an expression of an individual desire for change or a choice of locale. But as a social phenomenon this usually arises from and reflects on economic inequality or inequality of economic opportunity between politically discrete zones (for example nation-states, provinces within nation-states) – hence economic migration. Such inequalities include differences in workforce requirements, perceptions of differences in standard of living, and perceptions of difference in ideological inclination.

To what extent this working definition has been sustained, questioned, replaced or extended by authors addressing different geopolitical contexts, and to what extent the field of migration studies has been engaged with, are matters that can and should be left open to readers, and to further debates and deliberations. It is, however appropriate in an introduction to draw attention to certain coherences and points of interest that are apparent with hindsight, and to the conversational links between the chapters that follow.

Deeply felt anxiety about migration – *not* in the xenophobic mould, indeed usually anxiety implicitly or explicitly *against* the prevalence and perception of xenophobia – seems to me a consistent thread running through these chapters. The distortions presented by xenophobic anxieties about immigration are addressed particularly by Teresa Hayter and Tope Omoniyi with regard to the British context,

---

1   This was held in collaboration with the Ferguson Centre for African and Asian Studies of the Open University, and was funded by Open University and British Academy grants.

and David Johnson with regard to the South African, and to some extent by Taghi Azadarmaki and Mehri Behar for the Iranian, and Taieb Belghazi in the context of European measures to restrict immigration. Perplexities that immigrants are subject to are discussed in Vinay Bahl's chapter (in this instance, South Asian women immigrants in Britain and North America), narrated in Irina Chongarova's (Russians in Bulgaria), and pondered in terms of literary representations of the East End of London in John Eade's chapter.

Anxieties about emigration receives here a full treatment, and from a range of perspectives. Referring to the impact of emigration from Iran on that country, Taghi Azadarmaki and Mehri Behar assume an optimistic tone and argue against current presumptions and modes of political theorization. Cyril I. Obi's chapter sees Ogoni emigration from Nigeria outwards as an escape from locally enacted but globally orchestrated political repression, and thereby presents a case study of the intricate links between economic migration and political persecution. Pessimistic assessments of the impact of emigrants on their homelands, albeit with markedly contrary ideological orientations and emphases, are apparent in Subarno Chattarji's and Tapan Basu's chapters addressing India, and in Efurosibina Adegbija's presentation of the Nigerian situation. Zhivko Ivanov's chapter about Bulgarian emigration and Taoufik Agoumy's about Moroccan emigration conduct a weighing of pros and cons, and ultimately express, it seems to me, disquiet about the current situation. Taieb Belghazi's consideration of the politics of Moroccan emigration within Morocco and in Europe discerns within this issue the configurations of a positive social movement. Yue Daiyun's unusual take on economic migration as a metaphor for cultural practices in contemporary China, expands some of the associated anxieties of this area toward a broad cultural critique.

Yue Daiyun's metaphoric use of economic migration links to another interesting feature of some of the contributions in this book. It seems to me that many of the chapters test the connotations of economic migration in constructive ways, effectively interrogating the rather strait-laced and familiar working definition that was offered at the beginning of the workshop. This is, to some extent, implicit in the nature of the issue. The contemplation of migration is not only contemplation of social, political and cultural fluidities and movements, but also of connotative fluidities: for example every emigrant from somewhere is an immigrant somewhere else and vice versa. This connotative fluidity is clearly marked in Irina Chongarova's demarcation of vertical and horizontal levels of Russian migration from a Bulgarian perspective. The interrogations of the concept that occur in some of the following chapters are however far more nuanced and sophisticated than my example may suggest. Tope Omoniyi's exploration of the transference of anxieties about physical migration to an area of, so to say, virtual migrations (offshore outsourcing) alludes to conceptual possibilities that have started widening the field only recently. Related to such conceptual considerations, is Zhivko Ivanov's perception of a virtual Bulgaria, built through emigrant websites and electronic fora, and held together by nostalgia. Conceptually, engaging, interrogative and provocative are also Taieb Belghazi's exploration of a social movement that constructs itself around politicized, and intensely symbolically affective, debates about Moroccan emigration; and Teresa Hayter's committed conviction that all border controls should be withdrawn. Yue

Daiyun's chapter not only gives a metaphoric inflection to the idea of economic migration, but also implicitly links it to the cultural effects of internal migrations.

To close this introduction, I would like to draw attention again to what seems to me to be one of the unquestionably salutary aspects of this book. The following chapters are from researchers who are institutionally located in a variety of ostensibly different disciplines – in politics and political economy, sociology, anthropology, cultural studies, literature, linguistics, media studies, geography – or are engaged in the practice of political activism. I regard this volume as proof that for humanistic and social matters such disciplinary boundaries, and divisions between theory and practice, have largely contingent and organizational value and limited intellectual currency. These chapters are all here in productive dialogue with one another.

References

Ajana, B. (July 2006), 'Immigration Interrupted', *Journal of Cultural Research*, **10**(3), 259–273. [DOI: 10.1080/14797580600848104]

Bartram, D. (2005), *International Labour Migration: Foreign Workers and Public Policy* (Basingstoke: Palgrave).

Bauder, H. (2006), *Labour Movement: How Migration Regulates Labour Markets* (New York: Oxford University Press).

Ben Jelloun, T. (2000), *French Hospitality: Racism and North African Immigrants*. Bray, B. (translated by) (New York: Columbia University Press).

Benhabib, S. (2004), *The Rights of Others: Aliens, Residents and Citizens* (Cambridge: Cambridge University Press).

Betts, K. (1996), 'Immigration and Public Opinion in Australia', *People and Press*, **4**, 3. Available at http://elecpress.monash.edu.au/pnp/free/pnpv4n3/betts.htm.

Betts, K. (2000), 'Immigration: Public Opinions and Opinions About Opinion', *People and Place*, **8**(3), 60–67. Available at http://elecpress.monash.edu.au/pnp/free/pnpv8n3/v8n3_7Betts.pdf.

Brimelow, P. (1995), *Alien Nation: Common Sense about America's Immigration Disaster* (New York: Random House).

Brown, L.A. (1991), *Place, Migration and Development in the Third World* (London: Routledge).

Carroll, J. (1 February 2005), *Focus On: Immigration,* ' (Washington DC: Gallup Organization). Downloaded on 6 March 2005 from http://www.gallup.com/poll/content/default.aspx?ci=14785&pw=2/1/2005.

Casciani, D. (5 August 2002), 'Immigration: Fact or Hype?', 'BBC News'. Downloaded on 24 March 2005 from http://news.bbc.co.uk/1/hi/uk/2173792.stm.

Cohen, R. (2006), *Migration and its Enemies: Global Capital, Migrant Labour and the Nation State* (Aldershot: Ashgate).

Cohen, S., Humphries, B. and Mynott, E., eds. (2001), *From Immigration Controls to Welfare Controls* (London: Routledge).

Crush, J. and Pendleton, W.C. (2004), 'Regionalizing Xenophobia?', *Attitudes towards Immigrants, Migrants and Refugees in the SADC, Southern African*

Migration Project (SAMP) (Cape Town: SAMP, and Kingston Ont.: Southern African Research Centre, Queen's University). Available at http://www.queensu. ca/samp/Publications.html.

Davin, D. (1999), *Internal Migration in Contemporary China* (Basingstoke: Macmillan).

Dummett, M. (2001), *On Immigration and Refugees* (London: Routledge).

Eurobarometer (December 1997), 'Racism and Xenophobia in Europe: Eurobaromoter Opinion Poll No. 47.1', (Luxembourg). Downloaded on 15 April 2005 from http:// europa.eu.int/comm/public_opinion/archives/ebs/ebs_113_en.pdf.

Eurobarometer (Spring 2004), 'Public Opinion in the European Union: Annexes', 'T66 (question 27)', Downloaded on 24 March. Available at http://europa.eu.int/ comm/public_opinion/archives/eb/eb61/eb61_anx.pdf.

Goldin, I. and Kenneth, R. (2006), *Globalization for Development: Finance, Aid, Migration and Policy* (Washington: World Bank).

Goot, M. (2000), 'More "Relaxed and Comfortable": Public Opinion on Immigration Under Howard', *People and Place*, **8**(3), 46–60. Accessed on 2 February 2005 at http://elecpress.monash.edu.au/pnp/free/pnpv8n3/v8n3_6Goot.pdf.

Groenendijk, K., Guild, E. and Minderhoud, P., eds. (2005), *Search of Europe's Borders* (Leiden: Brill).

Grosfoguel, R. and Cervantes-Rodríguez, A.M., eds. (2002), *The Modern/Colonial/ Capitalist World-System in the Twentieth Century* (Westport: Praeger).

Guiraudon, V. and Joppke, C., eds. (2001), *Controlling a New Migration World* (London: Routledge).

Gutmann, A., ed. (1994), *Multiculturalism: Examining the Politics of Recognition* (Princeton: Princeton University Press).

Harris, N. (2001), *Thinking the Unthinkable: the Immigration Myth Exposed* (London: I.B. Tauris).

Hayter, T. (2000), *Open Borders: the Case against Immigration Controls* (London: Pluto).

Huntington, S. (2004), *Who Are We: the Challenges to America's National Identity* (London: Simon & Schuster).

Ibrahim, M. (2005), 'The Securitization of Migration: A Racial Discourse', *International Migration*, **42**(5), 163–187. [DOI: 10.1111/j.1468-2435.2005.00345. x]

King, R., Mai, N. and Dalipaj, M., eds. (2004), *Exposing the Migration Myth: Analysis and Recommendations for the European Union, the UK and Albania* (Oxford: Oxfam Academic).

King, R., White, P. and Connell, J., eds. (1995), *Writing across World: Literature and Migration* (London: Routledge).

Kumar, A., ed. (2003), *Away: the Indian Writer as the Expatriate* (London: Routledge).

Kymlicka, W. (1995), *Multicultural Citizenship: A Liberal Theory of Minority Rights* (Oxford: Clarendon).

Levy, A. and Foria, J.P., eds. (2002), *Economic Growth, Inequality and Migration* (Cheltenham: Edward Elgar).

McDonald, D.A. and Crush, J. (2002), *Destination Unknown: Perspectives on the Brain Drain in Southern Africa* (Pretoria: The Africa Institute of South Africa).

McDowell, C., ed. (1996), *Understanding Impoverishment: the Consequences of Development-Induced Displacement* (Oxford: Berghahn).

Mittelman, J.H. (2000), *The Globalization Syndrome: Transformation and Resistance* (Princeton, N.J.: Princeton University Press).

Murphy, R. (2002), *How Migrant Labour is Changing Rural China* (Cambridge: Cambridge University Press).

Nachmias, N. and Goldstein, R., eds. (2004), *The Politics of Forced Migration* (Frederick, MD.: PublishAmerica).

Nicholas, V.H. (2006), *Catching Fire: Containing Forced Migration in a Volatile World* (Lanham, MD.: Lexington).

O'Dowd, L. and Wilson, T.M., eds. (2003), *New Borders for a Changing Europe: Cross-Border Cooperation and Governance* (London: Frank Cass).

Oderth, R. (2001), *Migration and Brain Drain: the Case of Malawi* (San Jose: Writer's Club Press).

Özden, Ç. and Schiff, M., eds. (2006), *International Migration, Remittances and Brain Drain* (Washington: World Bank).

Palmer, D.L. (August 1999), *Executive Summary – Canadian Attitudes and Perceptions Regarding Immigration: Relations with Regional per Capita Immigration and Other Factors*, (Ottawa: Citizenship and Immigration Canada). Downloaded on 2 February from http://www.cic.gc.ca/english/research/papers/perceptions.html.

Papademetriou, D.G. and Martin, P.L., eds. (1991), *The Unsettled Relationship: Labour Migration and Economic Development* (New York: Greenwood).

Pew Research Centre (2002), *What the World Thinks in 2002* (Washington, DC: Pew Research Centre for the People and the Press, Global Attitudes Project. Downloaded on 2 February 2005 from http://www.pewtrusts.com/pdf/vf_pew_global_attitudes.pdf.

Phillips, C., ed. (1997), *Extravagant Strangers: A Literature of Belonging* (London: Faber & Faber).

Physicians for Human Rights (June 2004), 'An Action Plan to Prevent Brain Drain: Building Equitable Health Systems in Africa', (Boston). Downloaded on 24 March 2005 from http://www.phrusa.org/campaigns/aids/pdf/braindrain.pdf.

Population Reference Bureau (March 2004), 'Transitions in World Population', *Population Bulletin* 59:1. Downloaded on 24 March 2005 from http://www.prb.org/Template.cfm?Section=Population_Bulletin1&template=/ContentManagement/ContentDisplay.cfm&ContentID=11692.

Rath, J., ed. (2000), *Immigrant Businesses: The Economic, Political and Social Environment* (Basingstoke: Macmillan / New York: St. Martin's).

Rawls, J. (1993), *Political Liberalism* (New York: Columbia University Press).

Saggar, S. and Drean, J. (June 2001), *British Public Attitudes and Ethnic Minorities* (London: Performance and Innovation Unit, Home Office). Downloaded on 2 February from http://www.strategy.gov.uk/downloads/files/british.pdf.

Sassen, S. (2003), *Guests and Aliens* (New York: New Press).

Skeldon, R. (1997), *Migration and Development* (Boston, MA: Addison-Wesley).

Solinger, D.J. (1999), *Contesting Citizenship in Urban China* (Berkeley: University of California State).

Suleiman, S.R., ed. (1998), *Exile and Creativity: Signposts, Travelers, Outsiders, Backward Glances* (Durham: Duke University Press).

Taylor, J., Francis, S., Rushton, P., Levin, M. and Whitney, G. (1998), *The Real American Dilemma: Race, Immigration, and the Future of America* (Oakton, Va.: New Century).

Taylor, S. (1993), *A Land of Dreams: A Study of Jewish and Afro-Caribbean Migrant Communities in England* (London: Routledge).

Tazreiter, C. (2004), *Asylum Seekers and the State* (Aldershot: Ashgate).

Tyler, I. (May 2006), '"Welcome to Britain": The Cultural Politics of Asylum', *European Journal of Cultural Studies*, **9**(2), 185–202. [DOI: 10.1177/1367549 406063163]

Whittaker, D.J. (2005), *Asylum Seekers and Refugees in the Contemporary World* (London: Routledge).

Wilder, R. (2004), *Bloody Foreigners: the Story of Immigration to Britain* (London: Little Brown).

Wrench, J. and Solomos, J., eds. (1995), *Racism and Migration in Western Europe* (Oxford: Berg).

Young, I.M. (2002), *Inclusion and Democracy* (Oxford: Oxford University Press).

PART I

EUROPE

Chapter 2

Open Borders:
The Case Against Immigration Controls

Teresa Hayter

Author and Activist, Oxford, UK

History of Immigration Controls

It is now considered a matter of common sense that states should have the right to stop people entering their territories, but it was not always so. It was not until the beginning of the twentieth century that immigration controls were introduced in a systematic manner in most European countries and the United States. Previously, nation states had at times expelled people whom they considered undesirable, but they had not attempted to prevent immigration. Britain, for example, expelled all Jews in the thirteenth century, but it was not until 1905 that it adopted laws to keep them out in the first place.

The growth of the culture of human rights has so far failed to assert the right of people to chose where they wish to live, except within the states whose nationality they are born with, or have obtained. Thus, the United Nations' Universal Declaration of Human Rights, adopted in 1948, asserts in its Article 13-1 that: 'Everyone has the right to freedom of movement and residence within the borders of each state', which means the state in which they are officially allowed to reside. Therefore, if, for example, people wish to leave an area of high unemployment and look for work where there is plenty of it, the authorities are not supposed to interfere with this wish provided it is within the boundaries of their 'own' country. The Universal Declaration also states, under Article 13-2, that: 'Everyone has the right to leave any country, including his own, and to return to his country'. When the Soviet Union, East Germany and other states in Eastern Europe prevented their citizens from leaving their countries, sometimes by arresting and even shooting them, and sometimes by building high fences and walls, this was rightly considered shocking.

Less however is said about the walls, fences, razor wire, armed guards and other repressive devices which are supposed to stop people entering rather than leaving territories. The Universal Declaration of Human Rights has nothing to say about the right of people, who are supposed to be free to leave their own countries, to enter another. Historically, states have needed immigration to expand their economies. In the early years of European empire, labour was obtained by varying degrees of force and compulsion. After the Second World War, in the period of reconstruction and boom, most European countries actively engaged in the recruitment of workers from abroad, first from other European countries and then from their former colonies.

But by the early 1970s, with recession and growing unemployment, the European countries which had previously imported labour had all set up controls to stop further immigration for work. By the late 1990s some governments were also increasing their efforts to deport the people who had already come. In France, for example, people who had had more or less automatically renewable 10-year residence permits suddenly found that their permits were not renewed, or were given one-year permits, which meant they had either to go underground and work illegally, or leave the country in which they had lived for many years. They organized themselves as Sans Papiers (undocumented people) to resist. In Britain, the government set targets for deportation, and began to increase random checks, arrests, detention and deportation of long-term British residents who in many cases had jobs, houses, wives and young children.

The Treatment of Asylum Seekers

One, at first legal, route for entry remained. The Universal Declaration of Human Rights, in Article 14, states that: 'Everyone has the right to seek and to enjoy in other countries asylum from persecution'. But, after objections by the British, the declaration did not give them the unqualified right to receive asylum, only to seek it. It is left to the recipient states to decide who they will or will not grant refugee status to, rather than, as was the practice in the nineteenth century, leaving it up to refugees themselves to decide, as they are best qualified to do, whether they need to flee. The 1951 Geneva Convention on Refugees and its 1967 Protocol incorporated a restricted right to asylum. Over the years governments have accepted declining proportions of the number of people who claim asylum, though the number of claims made has remained much the same. In Britain asylum seekers are often attacked as 'bogus', 'abusive' and 'illegal'. Immigration officials, rather than making it their task to examine fairly and objectively a person's case for asylum (which itself is likely to be impossible), take on an adversarial role: like prosecution lawyers, they try to find inconsistencies or inaccuracies in the accounts given by refugees of their reasons for fleeing, which they then say undermine the credibility of their claims. The process is arbitrary. It is influenced more by quotas and targets than by considerations of justice or truth. Governments turn down many asylum claims which meet the criteria set by the international conventions to which they are signatories. They then claim, quite unjustifiably, that this is evidence that most asylum seekers are making false claims and that their real objective is economic betterment (which of course is no reason why they should not migrate). Yet asylum seekers come overwhelmingly from areas in which there are wars and severe political persecution. Many take a large drop in their standard of living, losing jobs, houses and land as well as their families.

Having undermined the right to receive asylum, governments now try to make it harder for people to apply for it. They do this, above all, by imposing visa requirements on the nationals of what they call 'refugee-producing' states, which of course means the states people are most likely to need to flee from. The requirement to obtain a visa means that refugees cannot travel legally to the country they wish to go to. Clearly they cannot apply for a passport to the authorities they are trying to escape from. Supposing they already have a passport, they could in theory go to a foreign embassy to apply for a visa, braving the security guards outside and local employees inside. But if they then asked for a visa to apply for asylum, they would normally be quickly ejected; there is no such thing as a refugee visa. They could in theory apply for a visitor's or student's visa, but this would require documentary proofs and probably some funds, and would in any case constitute deception. The usual course for refugees therefore is to buy false documents. But this is becoming increasingly hard. Under various Carriers' Acts, transport operators are now required to ensure that the passengers they carry have documents, and are fined if they allow them to travel without them. Governments provide technology to enable carriers to detect false documents, and sometimes post agents at foreign airports to check documents. If they succeed, they hand refugees back to the authorities they are fleeing from. Refugees are therefore forced to resort to even more dangerous, clandestine methods of travel. Usually, they have to pay agents to enable them to flee in the holds of ships, in the backs or even in the tyre casings of lorries, underneath trains and even aeroplanes, in often overcrowded and leaky boats. In the process they endure great suffering. Many thousands die each year, of suffocation or drowning. Governments then announce that they will clamp down on the agents and traffickers, for whose existence they are entirely responsible, and have the gall to proclaim concern over their cruelty.

Governments compete with one another to deter applicants by being the most uninviting and the 'toughest'. In Britain, in February 2003, the Prime Minister set a target of halving the number of applications for asylum; the target was met mainly because it was set in relation to the peak in applications, which had itself been almost entirely the consequence of the number of Iraqis fleeing the threat of US-British invasion. But governments appear to believe that the way to reduce the number of refugees is not to refrain from creating the conditions which people flee from, but to make conditions harsher in the countries they are trying to flee to. They lock refugees up in prisons and detention centres, and they reduce them to destitution. The largest numbers imprisoned, in absolute terms, are in the USA. Australia now detains all those who apply for asylum. Britain (but not other west European countries) detains refugees without judicial supervision and without time limit; many have claimed asylum at ports and airports, and are therefore not even technically 'illegal'. Decisions are made by junior immigration officials, who have to give only general reasons, such as 'we believe that the person is likely to abscond'. One official, asked by the writer what evidence he had for believing that a young medical student who subsequently obtained refugee status might abscond, merely replied 'we are not a court of law'. The numbers detained in Britain under immigration laws have quadrupled since the 1970s. They are in prisons and in 'removal centres', the latter surrounded by high fences and razor wire, and mostly run for profit by private security firms whose guards are blatantly racist. The Labour government now imprisons whole families, including young children, babies and pregnant women, sometimes for months at a time; a pamphlet produced by Maternity Alliance, Bail for Immigration Detainees and London Detainee Support Group, entitled *A Crying Shame* (September 2002), gives a harrowing account of the effects of their incarceration.

Most European countries now also deliberately reduce asylum seekers to destitution. Often they are not allowed to work. Increasingly they are denied access to minimal public support, including health services. In several countries, public financial support and accommodation is denied to those who have had asylum claims rejected. In France public support, of a limited nature, is available only after a claim has been lodged, which may take months. In Britain it is not available to those who are deemed not to have claimed asylum immediately on arrival, which is usually difficult or impossible for refugees who are forced to travel clandestinely, and in effect means that two-thirds of new asylum seekers are made destitute. The courts have partially condemned this measure as inhuman and degrading treatment. But many thousands of people, including families, many of whom may subsequently obtain refugee status, have neither the right to work nor the right to receive any form of state support (which is some two-thirds of the sum considered the minimum subsistence level for the rest of the population). Those who are housed are dispersed away from their communities, lawyers and sometimes families. They are given one 'no choice' offer of accommodation, often in sub-standard housing, where they are isolated and vulnerable to racist attacks.

Creeping Fascisisation

Immigration controls thus give rise to some of the worst abuses of human rights in Western societies. Asylum seekers suffer mistreatment of a sort to which the rest of the population is not, so far, subjected. But the abuses threaten to spread, in what the Belgian organization Frontieres Ouvertes described at a rally in Paris in 1999 as creeping 'fascisisation' of European countries. Police surveillance and random checks of immigration status can affect long-term residents who look 'foreign'. These checks have a long history in countries such as France, where residents must carry identity papers or, in some cases, carry proof that they have children born in France, which still protects them from deportation. In Britain, so far without compulsory identity papers, many immigrants already find it prudent to have their papers with them. Asylum seekers have now been issued with 'smart cards' which carry their photograph, finger-prints, and a statement on whether they are allowed to work. And finally, the government has decided that identity cards themselves are to be introduced, and made obligatory at first for foreigners. The Home Secretary David Blunkett was reported in *The Guardian* of 12 November 2003 as saying that, 'An ID card scheme will help tackle crime and serious issues facing the UK, particularly illegal working, immigration abuse, ID fraud, terrorism and organised crime'. Especially since 11 September 2001, the issues of immigration and terrorism are becoming blurred in many countries, most notably the United States. The US Government detains people 'suspected' of terrorist sympathies, indefinitely and in sub-human conditions at Guantánamo Bay, who may never be brought to trial, let alone to public trial with the normal judicial safeguards. In Britain, the government introduced in 2001 an Anti-Terrorism, Crime and Security Act, which gave it powers to detain without trial and indefinitely foreigners 'suspected' of terrorism, some of whom are refugees and cannot be deported. In an even harsher version of what asylum seekers already suffer, they are subjected to judicial procedures which are a mockery of justice, with neither the defendants nor their lawyers having the right to hear what they are being accused of. This extension of detention without trial was denounced in 2004 in the House of Lords, and has (at least for the time being) been abandoned, but house arrest and other control measures, again on the say-so of politicians rather than judges, are being contemplated. An earlier Terrorism Act, introduced in 2000, made it a criminal offence to belong to or support certain 'terrorist' organizations. This means that, for example, Kurdish refugees from Turkey have to choose whether they wish to be prosecuted if they say they are members of the Kurdistan Workers Party (PKK), or fail to obtain refugee status if they do not. Their British supporters have also been prosecuted, and the act has been used to arrest protesters against the arms trade and against the invasion and occupation of Iraq in 2003–2004.

The Need for Workers and 'Managed' Migration

Curiously, the escalation in the repressive apparatus of immigration controls is taking place at a time when European populations are declining, or forecast to decline. These declines, together with the ageing of the population, and the worsening ratios of working to non-working populations, are expected to cause serious economic and social problems in most European countries. The United Nations Population Division, in its document *Replacement Migration* (March 2000), has estimated that to maintain existing ratios of young to old people, European countries would need extra immigration of several million people per year. European governments usually accept that more, rather than less, immigration is needed if their economies are to expand and prosper. Most of them are now back in the business of recruiting foreign workers, especially skilled workers in trades such as computing and health services, but also unskilled workers, mainly in sectors and jobs in which long-term residents are unavailable or unwilling to work and which cannot be transferred abroad, such as agriculture, catering, cleaning and some building work. In Britain, according to Home Office figures, the granting of work permits to employers has nearly doubled since 1998.

It is at first hard to understand why governments are thus recruiting and encouraging foreign workers, and at the same time redoubling their efforts to keep foreigners out; for example, they recruit nurses in Zimbabwe and the Philippines, and imprison nurses who come on their own initiative to seek asylum. The explanation appears to be that they want to 'manage' migration flows. But this too requires elucidation. Some supporters of the free market, including for example the *Wall Street Journal* and at times the *London Economist* and *Financial Times*, argue, with a consistency which is absent elsewhere, that the movement of labour should be free in the same way as the movement of capital and goods is in theory meant to be free. They do not agree that governments should determine the availability of labour to employers or attempt to set quotas according to some estimate of the needs of the economy, and believe recruitment decisions should be left to employers. Harris (2002) and some liberal economists also argue that, like free trade, the free movement of labour across borders would greatly increase prosperity, not only for the migrants themselves but also for the world as a whole. Employers in the United States in particular have called for unrestricted immigration, for the obvious reason that it would suit them to have easier access to the vast reserves of cheap labour that exist outside the rich countries. There is much evidence, now supported for example by research commissioned by the British Home Office (see Glover and Development et al., 2001; Gott and Johnston, 2002), that immigrants make large contributions both to economic growth and to public finances, since they are mostly young, fit and educated at others' expense. Most, if they are legally permitted to and sometimes if they are not, are willing to work for long hours and in poor conditions in jobs which do not require their qualifications.

There is one possible economic rationale for immigration controls, which is that their existence makes immigrant workers insecure or 'precarious', and therefore more exploitable. Most western economies, and especially the United States, are highly dependent on super-exploited immigrant workers, many millions of whom have no legal immigration status. Governments' attitude to illegal working appears to be entirely punitive, designed only to detect and repress it, thus making the situation of the workers even more precarious. Usually the workers admitted on government-issued work permits will have only short-term contracts, tied to particular employers and jobs (in Britain and some other European countries this represents a radical departure from previous labour-importing policies). Whether they are working 'illegally' or on legal, but temporary, contracts, the workers are extremely vulnerable. If they make an attempt to improve their situation, for example by joining a trade union, or try to obtain redress against employers who fail to pay them the agreed amount, sexually harass them or in other ways mistreat them, they can be sacked. For the 'legal' workers, this means having to leave the country or to go underground. Especially for the 'illegal' workers, it may also mean that the police and immigration authorities are called in and that they are then detained and deported. This system of precarious working constitutes what the Sans Papiers of France have called, on many occasions but in particular at the European Social Forum in Paris in 2003, a new form of slavery. The Sans Papiers argue that this is a deliberate policy of neo-liberal governments, designed to ensure that the immigrants provide a model of flexibilization and 'precarization' which can be spread throughout the sectors in which they work and eventually to the economy as a whole. But it is not clear that the policy benefits the economy, and employers, as much as allowing free entry to workers from abroad would. It also does not adequately explain why governments are apparently so anxious to crack down on 'illegal' immigrants, who are the ultimately exploitable work force, and 'illegal' working, and to increase the rate of deportations and deter asylum seekers.

Immigration Controls and Racism

The explanation may be that governments' attempts to prevent the entry of asylum seekers and other clandestine migrants have more to do with political than with economic considerations. Governments appear to believe that the way to defeat the growth of the far right in Europe is to adopt their policies. They believe they must demonstrate that they are adopting 'tough' measures to deter asylum seekers and other immigrants, and that they are doing their utmost to keep them out, or to evict them if they get past immigration controls. Ultimately, the inescapable conclusion is that immigration controls, and government repression of migrants and refugees, are explicable only by racism, or at least by attempts to appease the racists.

Immigration controls have their origins in racism. In Britain, for example, they were first introduced in 1905 as a result of agitation by racist and extreme right-wing organizations, at this time against Jewish refugees. When controls were introduced in 1962 to stop immigration, for the first time, from the former British empire, their introduction again followed agitation by racist and neo-fascist organizations. Up to 1962, the most prominent politicians from all the main parties (quoted for example in Paul Foot's book *Immigration and Race in British Politics*, 1965) had proclaimed that the principle of free movement within the former British empire would never be abandoned. Government reports had found no reason for immigration controls other than the supposed 'non-assimilability' of the new immigrants. The covert aim of the 1962 Commonwealth Immigrants Act was to stop 'coloured' immigration; since the economy still required an expanding labour supply, the legislation was framed to exclude Irish workers from controls and, it was hoped, let in white British subjects from the 'old' commonwealth while excluding black ones from the 'new' commonwealth.

The problem, of course, is that immigration controls do not appease the racists. They merely legitimate racism. And they also embolden the racists to demand more. When politicians lament the recent increase in racism, they fail to acknowledge that it is precisely their own actions, including their constant complaints about the supposed 'abuses' committed by 'bogus' asylum seekers, which explain the rise in racism after a period when it had been in decline. Their actions and their words feed the parts of the media whose political agenda it has long been to stir up racism; these media use information, and phrases, which are often clearly derived from government sources. Governments only very rarely attempt to counter the lies propagated by the media and others. As a consequence, people believe, for example, that the number of immigrants and asylum seekers is far higher than it actually is (see Saggar and Drean, 2001). They fail to realize that asylum seekers, who have become the new object of race hate campaigns and violence, actually constitute an insignificant proportion both of the total number of refugees in the world as a whole, and of the number of other people entering Europe, including visitors, students, the employees of multinational corporations and others with official permission to work. It is hard to understand why governments appear so concerned to reduce the numbers of asylum seekers, rather than of anybody else, unless their purpose is simply to appease the racists and in this way, they hope, win votes.

Immigration controls are inherently racist. Any scheme which tried to make them 'fair' or non-racist must fail. Even if they did not discriminate, as they now do, against black people, east European Roma, the poor, and anybody else who is subject to the current manifestations of prejudice, they would still discriminate against foreigners and outsiders in general. Those who demand tougher controls talk about 'our' culture, whatever that may be, being swamped. But virtually every country in the world is the product of successive waves of immigration. There are few places where there is any such thing as a pure, 'native' culture. European culture, for example, if such a thing exists, is arguably under much greater threat from the influence of the United States, whose citizens have little difficulty in entering Europe, and from its own home-grown consumer excesses, than it is from people who might come from anywhere else. Moreover, 'non-racist' immigration controls, even if these were conceptually possible, would be pointless, since racism is the main reason for their existence. On the contrary, one of the very best ways to undermine the arguments of the racists would be to abolish immigration controls, and to make plain why they are unnecessary.

Equal Rights for Immigrants

For the abolition of immigration controls to make sense, those who migrate must have the same rights as the residents of the countries they migrate to. Proposals that people should have the right to migrate freely in search of jobs but have inferior rights to those of other workers in the same country, would be damaging not only to their interests but to those of many of the existing residents. New immigrants need to have not only the right to work, but all the gains for the working class that exist in the countries they migrate to, including protection against unfair dismissal, the right to join and organize in trade unions, the right to leave their job and look for another one, the right to receive unemployment and sickness benefits and holiday pay, in the same way as everybody else. They should have the right to vote and the right to hold public office, and they should, of course have full access to social provision, including health provision and education for their children. Immigrant workers do not usually take the jobs that might otherwise be available to, or desired by, existing residents. And immigration does not usually lead to any worsening of wages and conditions in the countries immigrants go to (on the contrary there is much evidence that it increases prosperity for all by enabling economies to expand and industries to survive). Nevertheless, if there was any threat to the wages and conditions of the existing work force, it would come from the fact that migrants, if they have no or few rights, can be forced to work in bad conditions and for low wages and cannot fight for improvements without risking deportation. They can come to constitute an enslaved underclass, which employers may hope not only to exploit directly, but to use as a means of weakening the position of all workers. The way to prevent any possibility of this happening is for trade unions, and all of us, to argue for full citizenship rights for all workers and residents, regardless of their nationality or how long they have lived in the country. This was more or less the situation, before 1962, of citizens of the UK and colonies who migrated to Britain; it accounts for their political strength and their militancy in their workplaces. It is, with limitations, the situation of citizens of the European Union who migrate from one EU country to another. It is also of course the situation of United States citizens who migrate between states in the US federation. And it is the situation of people who migrate from one local authority to another within states, and receive the level of public services prevalent in the area they move to.

The Consequences of Free Movement

There are many who say that the abolition of immigration controls is a desirable goal, but that it is politically impossible in a world in which there are severe international inequalities. But the argument that, without controls, there would be 'floods' of migrants who would overwhelm the rich countries is little more than scaremongering. Immigration controls do not work well; if, for example, after years of expensive and painful legal processes, asylum seekers finally have their applications refused, governments often find it impossible to deport them; and with each new, and more vicious, advance in the apparatus of repression, people are forced to find new, braver and more ingenious ways of circumventing it. It is true that if there were no controls there would probably be more migration, since the dangers and cost of migrating would be less; how much more is impossible to estimate. But what is certain is that the fact that there are huge international inequalities in material wealth does not mean that, as neo-classical economists might predict, there would be mass movements of people throughout the world until material conditions and wages equalized.

Most people require powerful reasons to migrate; in normal circumstances they are reluctant to leave their countries, families and cultures. When free movement was allowed in the European Union, some feared there would be mass migration from poorer areas in the South to richer ones in the North. The migration did not happen, to the chagrin of the proponents of flexible labour markets. Similarly, migration from the new accession states in Eastern Europe has been far less than the media predicted. The great desire of many who do migrate is to return to their own countries, when they have saved enough money, or if conditions there improve. Immigration controls mean that they are less likely to do so, because they cannot contemplate the struggle of crossing borders again if they find they need to. In addition, when people migrate from choice, they normally do so because there are jobs to migrate to. For example, when subjects of the former British empire were allowed to enter, settle and work in Britain without immigration controls, and had the same rights as British subjects born in Britain, as was the case until 1962, migration correlated almost exactly with employment opportunities; when job vacancies increased, more people came from South Asia and the Caribbean, and when they declined, fewer did so. Especially for the migrants from South Asia, the pattern was that families sent their young men to do a stint in hard jobs in the factories of northern Britain and then return, perhaps to be replaced by a younger member of the family. When the threat of immigration controls became real, there was for the first time a surge in immigration which did not correlate with job opportunities, to beat the ban; well over half the Indians and about three-quarters of the Pakistanis who arrived in Britain before controls did so in the 18-month period preceding their introduction. Similarly, there is evidence that the harder the US government makes it to brave the razor wire and other obstacles to cross the border into the USA, the more Mexican immigrants find themselves forced to settle in the USA, and give up hopes of return. Finally, if people are extremely poor, they cannot raise the money to migrate, except perhaps to neighbouring countries. People do not or cannot undertake the risks and expense and painful separations of migration, to live in squalor off public funds.

Unless, that is, they are desperate to escape threats of death, imprisonment or torture. It is of course the case that too many people are forced to flee from such threats, if they have the means to do so. Supposing the governments of the rich countries were in reality concerned by the problem of migration, there would be better ways to reduce it than by casting around for yet more brutal ways of enforcing immigration controls. Governments ought to recognize that they themselves often bear direct responsibility, and are nearly always partly responsible, for creating the conditions from which people flee. There is much that they could do, and above all not do: they could refrain from supporting and arming repressive regimes or the opposition to more progressive regimes; they could, as a minimum, not supply weapons to the participants in wars and civil conflicts; and they could cease to engage in armed interventions. The increases in asylum seekers in Europe in the last few years have been mainly from Somalia, former Yugoslavia, Afghanistan and Iraq, all countries where significant military interventions by the West have taken place. In particular, while there was a steady trickle of refugees from Iraq under the Saddam regime, there was a surge in numbers in response to the threat of US/British invasion.

In an ideal world, people would not be forced to migrate. But they would be free to migrate if they wished to.

References

Cohen, S. (2003), *No-one Is Illegal: Asylum and Immigration Control Past and Present* (Stoke-on-Trent: Trentham).

Foot, P. (1965), *Immigration and Race in British Politics* (Harmondsworth: Penguin).

Glover, S. et al. (2001), *Migration: An Economic and Social Analysis* (London: Home Office Research Development and Statistics Directorate).

Gott, C. and Johnston, K. (2002), *The Migrant Population in the UK: Fiscal Effects* (London: Home Office Research, Development and Statistics Directorate).

Harris, N. (2002), *Thinking the Unthinkable: The Immigration Myth Exposed* (London: I.B. Taurus).

Hayter, T. (2000), *Open Borders: The Case against Immigration Controls* (London: Pluto Press).

Saggar, S. and Drean, J. (June 2001), *British Public Attitudes and Ethnic Minorities* (London: Performance and Innovation Unit, Home Office). This can be downloaded at http://www.strategy.gov.uk/downloads/files/british.pdf.

Sutcliffe, B. (1998), *Nacido en otra parte: Un ensayo sobre la migracion internacional el desarollo y la equidad* (Bilbao: Hegoa).

The Maternity Alliance, Bail for Immigration Detainees, London Detainee Support Group (September 2002), *A Crying Shame: Pregnant asylum seekers and their babies in detention,* (London). This can be downloaded at: http://www.maternityalliance.org.uk/documents/crying_shame.pdf.

United Nations Population Division (2000), *Replacement Migration: Is it a Solution to Declining and Ageing Populations?* (New York: United Nations).

Chapter 3

Economic Migrant or Hyphenated British? Writing about Difference in London's East End

John Eade

Sociology and Anthropology, School of Social Sciences, Roehampton University

Introduction

As in many other European Union countries the issue of immigration has recently become even more intense in Britain. Since 9/11 immigration has become embroiled with an anxious debate involving politicians and the media about terrorism, civil rights and the future of multiculturalism. At the heart of this debate is the issue of whether newcomers are to be categorized as economic migrants or as new hyphenated types of citizens (black British or British Asian, for example). The category of economic migrant suggests that people are arriving primarily to make as much money as possible before returning. Hyphenated British indicates a movement from outsider to insider, from temporary resident to permanent settler and from a predominantly homogeneous to an increasingly heterogeneous society. Within this multi-layered debate about immigration there are two other strands which I want to explore in this chapter – a) the ways in which the focus shifts beyond recent events to a history of immigration to Britain, and b) the relationship between Britain and its constituent parts, especially England.

My approach is constructivist in its analysis of the ways in which national and other identities have been ideologically constructed over time (see, for example, Bhabha, 1990; Hall, 1991). I want to investigate how national majorities are constructed through the particular practices of writing (see, for example, Giles and Middleton, 1995) and how boundaries (those performed through social interaction as well as expressed in imaginative communication) between majorities and minorities may weaken or be redefined. The concept of hybridity directs us to explore the various forms of mixing which can lead to new ethnicities as some people come to occupy the liminal space on the boundary. In other words, those arriving as economic migrants may well stay and either they or their descendants develop new identifications with the nation which are shaped by interaction with the majority. Indeed, this process reveals how fraught the process of maintaining a strong boundary between majorities and minorities or insiders and outsiders can be. Post-modern and post-national conditions, shaped by global flows, transnational institutions and regional nationalisms, may be creating a far more fragmentary and contingent situation.

Current debates about economic migrants and new, hybrid ethnicities are bound up with discussions about the break up of Britain (Nairn, 1981, 2000; Crick, 1995) and the growth of regional nationalisms in Scotland and Wales encouraged by political devolution (Crone, 2001). The tension between the image of homogeneous insularity and an active engagement with diverse peoples around the globe was complemented by the long-established tension between British and English national identity. As Kumar (2003) has pointed out, the expression of English nationalism has been complicated by a long-established sense of 'missionary nationalism' which conflated distinctions between England and Britain (at least for many English people as opposed to other inhabitants of the 'British Isles'). The possible development of a revived English nationalism is also being considered (Kumar, 2003).

The recent debates about Britain as a multicultural society have resulted in numerous accounts of the nation's multicultural past. British people are presented as the product of repeated waves of immigration reaching back into pre-Roman times. Against essentialized versions of a pure island race, commentators have talked about a mongrel people whose ancestry can be traced to Celtic, Anglo-Saxon, Viking and Norman settlements. The story of an island open to outsiders is brought to the present day by references to French Huguenot settlers in the late seventeenth century, Irish migration from the eighteenth century, the movement of black slaves from the Caribbean during the 18th and early nineteenth century, East European Jewish settlement in the late nineteenth century, German Jewish arrivals in the 1930s, the post-Second World War settlement of European migrant workers immediately after the Second World War, followed by migration from the British Empire and Commonwealth and more recent flows of refugees, asylum seekers and migrant workers from the East European countries joining the European Union.

What is so striking about the French Huguenot and subsequent migrations is its highly urbanized character. Many Irish and post-1945 European workers found jobs in the countryside but the vast majority of these newcomers became urban residents. The rapid expansion of Britain's urban population during the 19th and early 20th centuries was bound up with industrialization and working class areas in the largest urban concentrations were occupied by large numbers of overseas arrivals. London's prominence within the nation as the seat of government and as both a commercial and industrial powerhouse was underpinned by large-scale immigration from the surrounding countryside as well as by the arrival of overseas migrants. The capital's 'East End' rapidly expanded during the nineteenth century as factories, small trading and dock enterprises drew on the labour of an ethnically and racially diverse working class population. The late Victorian East End was popularly presented as London's dark and dangerous Other where poverty, crime and aliens were gathered. The moral panic surrounding Jack the Ripper in 1888 drew on this popular representation and highlighted the arrival of poor Jews from Poland and Russia.

I focus here on the ways in which immigration has been represented in particular narratives – novels – by those who see themselves or may be seen by others as members of a particular minority. The authors of these novels challenge dominant versions of national identity through their evocation of alternative understandings of the nation. At the same time I explore their marginal position as writers, arguing (along with other commentators) that the very practice of writing separates them from the community they are writing about. My focus is upon two writers in particular, whose writing is not understood as representing a wider body of literature but illustrative of the issues outline above. Finally, I bring together two periods – the 1930s and the present day – to analyse the construction of both British and English identity.

Representing the East End during the 1930s: Simon Blumenfeld and Jewboy

By the end of the 1930s the children and grandchildren of the East European Jews, who had settled in the area during the late nineteenth century, were making their presence felt in numerous ways. They expanded the ethnic niche developed by their elders, not only by entering the garment trade but also developing craft trades and the service sector of small retail and wholesale shops. As the Jewish settlement spread out from the concentrations around Spitalfields and Whitechapel into Stepney and Bethnal Green, the numbers of synagogues and recreational clubs increased and Jews began to make a deep impression on the political and trade union life of the Stepney and Bethnal Green boroughs, in particular. Young (predominantly male) Jews were attracted to the Labour and Communist parties, as well as Zionist groups, and entered the Garment Workers' union (see Kershen, 1997). They were deeply involved in the rent strikes of the 1930s as housing became a crucial resource in an impoverished East End where borough councils and the London County Council were attempting to improve living conditions through slum clearance and the expansion of council housing. They also took a keen interest in political events beyond British shores, particularly the Palestine question, the plight of German Jews after Hitler's accession to power in 1933, and the struggle between Republicans and Nationalists in Spain after 1935.

By the late 1930s the vast majority of the first generation of Jewish settlers were 50 years old and above. Their children and grandchildren had been born and brought up in the East End and some were already moving out eastwards to the vast London County Council estate in Becontree or north towards Golders Green. They had been educated in local elementary schools, while a small proportion proceeded to grammar school and even university. The religious and cultural traditions of East European Jewry were joined by new influences as the second and third generation began to assimilate local working class and national lifestyles. English became the medium through which young Jews reflected on the combination of old and new influences, and the novel – a nineteenth century mode of literary expression – was adopted as the prime means through which these reflections could be mediated.

However, the second generation of Jewish writers wanted to adapt the novel mode to the conditions of the East End. They rejected the dominant model of novel writing, represented by the Bloomsbury group, as 'bourgeois' and pursued a social realist mode which would reflect the realities of East End life. The most well known exponent of this form of writing was Simon Blumenfeld, whose novel *Jewboy*, published in 1935, will be the focus of the following discussion. (Space does not permit consideration of his other novel *Phineas Kahn: The Life of Phineas Kahn* (1937/88) and other writers such as Arnold Levy and John Goldman).

The hero of *Jewboy*, Alec, is, significantly, a second generation Jewish garment worker. The story begins in the heart of the Jewish East End – Whitechapel – and describes his fight for survival in post-First World War London. This struggle involves his job in a garment factory where his trade union enthusiasm leads to him being sacked. It also shapes his emotional and sexual existence, since the continual threat of an unwanted pregnancy and the strain of surviving as a couple from respectable but poorly paid work are important themes of the novel. After a brief involvement with a Jewish girl, he lives with a non-Jewish working class woman, who becomes a West End prostitute after working as a servant in an East End Jewish trader family. His cultural sustenance comes from the famous Artists' Circle meetings and concerts in Whitechapel. Here he is attracted by a young fair haired English middle class woman whom he later meets and who invites him back to her West End flat. After unsuccessful attempts to obtain a visa to work in Soviet Russia the story ends with a political rally in Hyde Park where he meets a black American friend who had appeared at the beginning of the novel.

The novel has a clearly stated political position. Jewish workers are part of an international proletariat exploited by western capitalism. The harsh conditions of East End life are the local manifestation of a structured inequality, which transcends national boundaries. At the same time Blumenfeld acknowledges that nationalism acts to divide workers. When the hero realizes the impossibility of his dream to emigrate to Russia, he resolves to stay in Britain to fight for working class rights across the divisions of religion and race. The high culture of classical music and literature acts as a bridge not only between Jews and their Continental European heritage but also, potentially, between working class and middle class Londoners. His interests contrast with his girlfriend's enthusiasm for popular culture and encourage him to pursue the beautiful middle class woman. She, in turn, is intrigued by his 'exoticism' but her collection of classical recordings cannot compensate for her political conservatism and emotional frigidity. In a powerful passage Blumenfeld describes their mutual exasperation after Alec questions the source of her wealth:

"And where do you get all that money? – Two guineas a week for a flat! Do you work for it?"

She closed the lid of the gramophone sharply.

"I don't have to!" she said. "I have an income from my father. Isn't that good enough?"
"No, it isn't!" he retorted. "It isn't honest. That money comes from us, it's stolen from us, from the workers!"

She became very angry, but she controlled herself rigidly. After all she was a lady. She drew herself up, and her nostrils dilated.

"I'm afraid you've made a mistake," she said aloofly. "My father is a landowner; our money comes from the earth, the English earth, my country. 'Stolen from us!' – Why you should be the last to speak. You and your people are only guests here!" (1986: 254)

Alec, not surprisingly, challenges this dismissal by first describing his father's life as an immigrant and then asserting his birthright:

"But I was born here. This is MY country. Much more than yours. I help to produce its wealth – when I am allowed to do so – And you? What wealth have you ever created? Your country! It's MY country – because I work here – not yours!"

"Now you're talking like a Jew," she answered icily. "One who has no country.'

"But I don't need a country!" he exclaimed. "The whole world is my country! Isn't it time they threw overboard the old superstitions? Up to this line it's my country, beyond this line it's yours. Away with all this mumbo-jumbo. Every country belongs to us! – To the workers. Only to us!" (1986: 255)

In terms of national discourse what is significant about the 1930s is the way in which Englishness was constructed through rural themes and pastoral myths (Kumar, 2003, pp. 229–230). The squalor, overcrowding and noise of the nation's industrial towns and cities was shunned for the 'timeless' life of the English countryside (Kumar, 230). At the same time middle class writers such as Graham Greene, George Orwell and even a member of the Bloomsbury group such as Virginia Woolf reflected a widespread disillusion with England and its political, social and military elites. pre-First World War assertions 'of England's imperial greatness or economic progress were impossible to sustain in the aftermath of an imperialist war or the grinding depression which followed' (Giles and Middleton, 1995, p. 6).

Representing the Contemporary East End: Monica Ali and Brick Lane

As Ken Worpole notes (1983), Simon Blumenfeld's career as a writer illustrates his own marginality to the local community he was trying to portray. Already second generation British Jews were leaving the Jewish East End and significantly Alec becomes deeply involved not with a local Jewish woman but a *shiksa* – an outsider – and he goes to live in Hackney, outside Whitechapel and other densely occupied Jewish neighbourhoods. Monica Ali's recent novel – *Brick Lane* (2003) – has some uncanny parallels with *Jewboy*. It has also been lauded by some reviewers as a convincing portrait of minority and immigrant dilemmas, but the author is even more marginal than her 1930s predecessor.

By the time the Bangladeshi first generation of predominantly male workers settled in the East End, the Jewish community had already disappeared. The newcomers occupied almost the same localities as their Jewish predecessors (Spitalfields and Whitechapel) and gradually spread across to the old Jewish stomping grounds around Stepney. They found work in the same sector as the Jews before them – the garment industry, small shopkeeping, cafes and restaurants. Sometimes they even prayed in the same buildings – the former synagogue on Brick Lane was transformed into the London Great Mosque, while another synagogue on Christian Street (sic) became the *Markazi Masjid* (mosque).

These newcomers came primarily from clusters of villages across one particular district, Sylhet, in north-east Bangladesh. During the 1980s and early 1990s they were joined by their wives and dependants so that by the time *Brick Lane* was published a second and third generation had emerged. These younger Bangladeshis were much engaged with 'mainstream society' and were looking, like the Jews before them, to move beyond the ethnic niche of manufacturing, shopkeeping and catering. They were developing hybrid British Bangladeshi identities and largely looked to a future within Britain rather than returning to Bangladesh (see Eade, 2000; Gardner, 2002; Begum and Eade, 2005).

Brick Lane focuses primarily on the experience of a settler adapting to the rhythms and dilemmas of a new world. The heroine, Nazneen, is born in Bangladesh but comes to London to live with her husband. She brings her two daughters up on a dilapidated council estate near Brick Lane and gradually frees herself from the closed world of a traditional Bangladeshi housewife. She achieves this freedom by joining a small group of Bangladeshi women who, like her, earn some money by homeworking for the local garment industry. She also compensates for the inadequate relationship she has with her husband, Chanu, whose dreams of success are never realized, through a brief affair with Karim, a British Bangladeshi activist, who introduces her to local community politics. The story builds to a climax as secular and Islamist community leaders vie for local control resulting in a riot on Brick Lane which traps Nazneen's daughters.

Tellingly, Nazneen is unimpressed by the struggle between the two community groups and breaks through the police cordon to rescue her daughters. The book ends not with hopes of a glorious socialist future as in *Jewboy* but personal emancipation within a British Bangladeshi women's commune making fashion items for the garment industry. Chanu returns to Bangladesh without Nazneen and the daughters, but Nazneen remains closely in touch with him and ends her affair with the young activist. Freedom is to be gained through working friendships with other Bangladeshi women not in a new relationship with a man. Although the story explores Nazneen's life in London, it also records her close relationship with her sister who remains in Bangladesh. Her sister's life is not a happy one – she runs off with a man from a neighbouring village and after a series of unhappy experiences in Dhaka, she ends up as a servant in Dhanmondi, one of the capital's wealthy neighourhoods. Although her relationships with men fail, she remains determined to follow her heart and not commit suicide like her mother. In the last letter, which she writes to Nazneen before she runs off with her employers' cook, she rejects her mother's act of despair:

> Amma always say we are women what can we do? If she here now I know what she say I know it too well. But I am not like her. Waiting around. Suffering around. She wrong. So many ways. At the end only she act. She who think all path is closed for her. She take the only one forbidden (2003: 363).

Nazneen and her sister's lives may have taken different paths but as women they are united by a personal politics of female agency and liberation. The book ends on this positive note as Nazneen is taken by her daughters and Bangladeshi female friends to Liverpool Street and the City of London for a surprise. They arrive at an ice-rink where her friend, Razia, prepares to skate.

> Nazneen turned round. To get on the ice physically – it hardly seemed to matter. In her mind she was already there.

She said, "But you can't skate in a sari."

Razia was already lacing her boots. "This is England," she said. "You can do whatever you like.' (2003: 413)

This optimism about England as a land of possibility is linked to a more general feminist politics of liberation which may help to partly explain the book's success in both the UK and the USA. In terms of our central theme – economic migrant or hyphenated British – *Brick Lane* shares with *Jewboy* the belief that the newcomers are becoming members of a changing British nation. Their Britishness is mediated through the social and cultural heritage of their country of origin which produces a hyphenated identity through the interweaving of class, gender, generation, religion and language. In *Brick Lane* there is no personal confrontation with a representative of the white middle class as in *Jewboy*.

Monica Ali locates local political conflict within the Bangladeshi community as secular and Islamist activists seek to dominate how their community is represented to the outside world. Whereas Alec in *Jewboy* becomes involved with a white working class woman and lives outside the Jewish heartland, Nazneen lives within her community and only breaks sexual taboos through an affair with a second generation British Bangladeshi. Nazneen is only beginning to develop a hyphenated British identity and it is her daughters – the second generation brought up in the East End – who are engaged in comparing Nazneen's generation with their much more Anglicized peers.

Monica Ali's decision to confine her story primarily to Nazneen and other members of the first generation justifies in many ways this containment within a particular community and locality. Simon Blumenfeld focuses on the second generation in *Jewboy* and in some respects it would be easier to compare *Brick Lane* with *The Life of Phineas Kahn* which tracks the life of a first generation settler in the East End. However, in both novels Blumenfeld is keen to show working class Jews exploring the world beyond the East End. They go on walks outside London, they visit relatives who have already moved to the suburbs, they 'go up west' to London's theatres and cinemas and they keep in touch with their relatives back in Russia. In *Brick Lane* we see the same process at work since Nazneen meets her lover in the West End, maintains close contact with her sister and husband in Dhaka and ends up skating in the City of London. However, characters from the local white working class are few in number and shadowy while London's suburbs and the countryside are unexplored.

What this raises, of course, is the issue of authenticity and the social location of the writer. Monica Ali, like Simon Blumenfeld, occupies a marginal position by the act of writing about 'her community'. Her marginality is also reinforced by her parentage, since her father comes from Bangladesh but from the district of Mymensingh rather than Sylhet (where, as we have seen, the majority of Bangladeshi immigrants originate), while her mother is a white English woman. She was not raised in the East End, and after studying at Oxford she married a white, middle class English man. *Brick Lane* is a work of the imagination informed by her father's tales of Mymensingh countryside and her reading about the lives of Bangladeshi women, such as Naila Kabir's study of the London and Dhaka garment industry, *The Power to Choose* (2000). At the same time, *Brick Lane* has been presented as, to some degree, a realistic portrait of a little known minority and this resulted in considerable criticism of her account. Indeed, the portrayal of Chanu particularly offended leaders of a local Bangladeshi community group, who ominously likened *Brick Lane* to Salman Rushdie's *The Satanic Verses*. Furthermore, Nazneen's adulterous affair was unlikely to recommend itself to those defending conventional notions of the dutiful and respectful Bangladeshi wife.

Conclusion

In this chapter I have brought together two novels written at different periods about minority communities in the same area of London. My aim has been to explore the ways in which they portray the move from temporary economic migrant to permanent hyphenated settler through the marginal position of the writer. What conclusions can be drawn from such juxtaposition?

In *Jewboy* the second generation of settlers are no longer economic migrants and are developing a distinctive identity as hyphenated British. While Simon Blumenfeld is well aware that his characters are brought up within a Jewish community, he emphasizes their membership of a national and international proletariat. He rejects Zionist exclusivism and middle class Jews who wish to be totally assimilated. Alec's upbringing is Jewish but he moves away from the Jewish heartland to live with a non-Jewish former prostitute. His political struggle transcends ethnic and national boundaries and enables him to challenge the insular and racist nationalism of the beautiful middle class woman whose classical musical interests he shares.

In *Brick Lane* we are introduced to the more restricted world of a first generation woman who is settling in London and bringing up two daughters despite her husband's refusal to stay. Monica Ali's story is shaped by contemporary single issue politics and feminist politics in particular where personal freedom is gained not through political parties and community organization but by sharing work and personal experience with other local, non-conforming Bangladeshi women. The economic system of global capitalism is accepted because liberation can be gained through a personal politics of gendered liberation in a country where you have the power to choose. In Dhaka her sister is also able to make choices but the price is poverty and dependence on unreliable men.

Both writers are marginal to the communities they portray. Simon Blumenfeld appears to be a more authentic representative since he was born in the East End and only moved away in adult life. Monica Ali was brought up in a middle class world of mixed identities far away from East London and she relies on texts and imagination just as much as close observation of East End life. At the same time both are writers whose narratives are shaped by the conventions of the English novel where authentic representation has an ambiguous place. Well-known Victorian writers such as Charles Dickens have established some key tropes about London which shape subsequent writing about the city. The East End is presented as a place of poverty, danger, passion and alien exoticism which Simon Blumenfeld and other

1930s working class writers wanted to qualify or reject. Monica Ali's book in many ways appears to confirm the tropes of Dickensian London, which inform other contemporary writers about London's mysterious East End, such as Iain Sinclair and Peter Ackroyd. Bangladeshis appear to be the latest in a long line of impoverished immigrants, whose lives are narrated for the inspection of a suburban white middle class readership.

Yet what redeems these narratives is their insistence on liberation, whether socialist or feminist. The characters retain their dignity and their agency. Furthermore, they act as an inspiration or challenge to other writers who wish to portray 'their community'. What remains to be seen is whether the kinds of censorship demanded by local community leaders after the publication of *Brick Lane* will lead to new forms of 'politically correct' writing, where feminist emancipation is replaced by careful observance of fundamentalist principles. Can the western urban novel survive such a transformation?

References

Ackroyd, P. (2004), *Dan Leno and the Limehouse Golem* (London: Minerva).

Ali, M. (2003), *Brick Lane* (London: Doubleday).

Begum, H. and Eade, J. (2005), 'All quiet on the eastern front? Bangladeshi reactions in Tower Hamlets' in *Muslim Britain: Communities under Pressure*. Abbas, T. (ed.) (London: Zed Books).

Bhabha, H. (1990), *Nation and Narration* (London: Routledge).

Blumenfeld, S. (1986), *Jew Boy* (London: Lawrence & Wishart) first published by Cape, J. 1935.

Blumenfeld, S. (1988), *Phineas Kahn: Portrait of an immigrant* (London: Lawrence & Wishart) first published in 1937.

Crick, B. (1995), 'The sense of identity of the indigenous British', *New Community*, **21**(2), 167–182.

Eade, J. (2000), *Placing London: From imperial capital to global city* (Oxford: Berghahn).

Gardner, K. (2002), *Age, Narrative and Migration: The life course and life histories of Bengali elders in London*, (Oxford: Berg).

Giles, J. and Middleton, T. (1995), *Writing Englishness 1900-1950* (London: Routledge).

Hall, S. (1991), 'New ethnicities' in *Race, Culture and Difference*. Donald, J. and Rattansi, A. (eds.) (London: Sage).

Kabeer, N. (2000), *The Power to Choose* (London: Verso).

Kershen, A. (1997), 'Huguenots, Jews and Bangladeshis in Spitalfields and the spirit of capitalism' in *London: The Promised Land?*, Kershen, A. (ed.) (Aldershot: Ashgate).

Kumar, K. (2003), *The Making of English National Identity* (Cambridge: Cambridge University Press).

McCrone, D. (2001), *Understanding Scotland: The sociology of a nation* (London: Routledge).

Nairn, T. (1981), *The Break-up of Britain* (London: Verso).
Nairn, T. (2000), *After Britain: New Labour and the return of Scotland* (London: Granta).
Sinclair, I. (1997), *White Chapell: Scarlet tracings* (London: Granta).
Worpole, K. (1983), 'Out of the ghetto: The literature of London's Jewish East End', in *Dockers and Detectives*, Worpole, K. (ed.) (London: Verso Books).

Chapter 4

Outsourcing and Migrational Anxieties in Discourse Perspectives

Tope Omoniyi

English Language and Linguistics, Roehampton University

Introduction

I shall begin by establishing a link between anxieties about migration and concerns about outsourcing in the context of the over-arching theme of this volume, 'the cultures of economic migration'. We have defined migration as 'the cross-border movement of people from a homeland to a location outside that homeland, with the purpose of taking up employment and conducting a daily existence there for an extended period of time' (see Gupta's introduction to this volume). This focus on the 'movement of people' locates fraught debates about representation and identity, generated by and about host and guest societies in the economic migration experience, at the centre of an emerging new order of difference. The new order pertains also to a 'movement of jobs'; a new pattern of emigration that has generated similar concerns which are expressed in published individual and institutional correspondences and articles in industry media.

Accordingly, the conventional notion of migration has been significantly expanded to accommodate what could be regarded as a 'reverse migration' within this perspective of the new order of difference. Reverse migration is the movement of people or jobs away from traditional migrant destinations to traditional immigrant sources: urban to rural, North to South, and West to East. Reverse migration of the movement of jobs kind which occurs through outsourcing is the focus of this chapter. To reduce costs and overheads, businesses are outsourcing aspects of, and sometimes, their entire operations, from urban to rural areas, developed North to comparatively less developed South, or from the industrialized West to a less industrialized East. The phenomenon allows people of difference, the Immigrant Other in conventional migration, to share the negative spotlight with the perceived enemies within industry, Western corporate employers who midwife job emigration. In other words, arguably, outsourced jobs have now become the new émigrés and outsourcers the compatriot anti-heroes on the firing line. The 'emigrant' is a job description that is relocated or off-shored to an alternative location in the search for expert yet cheap knowledge, based on the economic logic of optimization of profits within the framework of globalization. In the light of this explanation then, the present discussion can be said to have three main objectives. These are as follows:

1. to identify ways in which outsourcing as a social experience may be accommodated as a subject of interest and within the theoretical provisions of applied linguistics and sociolinguistics;
2. to raise and discuss methodological issues in this relatively new area of research enquiry;
3. to present a sample of data for applied linguistic and sociolinguistic analysis that conveys the anxieties generated by this new dimension of migration.

Outsourcing and Sociolinguistics

To locate outsourcing as reverse migration theoretically within sociolinguistics, it is necessary to first take account of the state of debate on migration generally, especially in applied sociolinguistics. On the balance, macrosociolinguistic concerns (social and political issues around the distribution of language resources) have received relatively less attention than microsociolinguistic concerns (language performance-informed social structures) because the latter assumedly served the deepening of the scientific basis of language study. However, there has been an awakening to the significant contribution that an understanding of social theory can make to a sociolinguistic analysis of social experiences and problems.

Both sociology and anthropology have gone through phases focused on the theme of migration (see Gozdziak and Shandy eds., 2000). Coupland et al. (eds., 2001) and Coupland, (ed., 2003) convincingly argue the need for sociolinguistics to adopt a critical perspective and engage with social theory and particularly with issues raised by globalization as a social phenomenon. Rampton's (1995) seminal work on language crossing detailed the character of interaction in the context of language contact and urban multilingualism, including language crossing because of migration. Kerswill (2004) specifically addressed the impact of migration on urban dialectology within the framework of traditional sociolinguistic variation and change, the principle of which excludes an examination of the ideological issues raised by the process.

Outsourcing (job emigration) generates a different set of concerns from those often reported in traditional migration studies, in that the social and cultural environments of donor and recipient nations of migrants are differently constituted. To some extent the differences are simply due to the fact that the subjects or objects of movement in this particular instance are jobs rather than persons, but the matter, as I shall explain below, goes deeper. They lead in turn to differences in the manifest consequences of movement and therefore in the reactions they generate.

The ongoing debate on the globalization of certain languages, such as English, assumes a new dimension in attending to the analysis of communicative repertoires that have developed around the subject of outsourcing as a social experience. The preference for and proliferation of certain varieties of English in call centre businesses yields new perspectives of looking at the relationship between Englishes in Kachru's (1997) Three Circles model: inner circle (native varieties), outer circle (English as a Second Language) and expanding circle (English as a Foreign Language). The English language schools which have sprung up as an ancillary business to train call centre staff are different from the traditional language schools in their integration of inner circle cultural knowledge. As a community of practice, call centre workers in Mumbai and Bangalore inhabit and encounter a different sociolinguistic environment from other users of English in ESL and EFL contexts. The clients who constitute their interlocutors are mostly inner circle populations.

In this discussion I shall attempt an examination of the discourse of difference around and about outsourcing of jobs, a relatively new social experience of the free market enterprise, at least as a focus of research. Difference has hitherto been theorized along a number of lines, including race, class, gender and sexuality in proffering explanations for structures of inequality, hegemony and discrimination in the distribution of resources in multiracial and multiethnic societies (see Appadurai, 1990). With particular reference to outsourcing, difference may be additionally conceptualized as a basis for discriminating between production and consumption in service industries. In this regard, language constitutes a discriminatory tool in demarcating one from the other.

In the present context, discussions of language behaviour as social practice are already framed within an existing typology that distinguishes formal from informal talk because of the separation of functions between official state languages and other languages within the polity of donor and recipient nations in outsourcing. Not all the discourse is necessarily generated within institutional contexts. A substantial portion of it is constructed by a heterogeneous public. Habermas's (1987) notion of the 'life world' as the totality of social experiences within a specific reality which define human nature covers the changes to ethnoscape and mediascape (Appadurai, 1996) occasioned by the exportation and importation of job cultures. The lifestyles of those who take up outsourced jobs mimic the Western lifestyles of the offshoring society, but with a local toning. Investigating how these practices and tonings are reflected in the communicative repertoires (speech, writing, signs) of those involved reveals the character of glocalisation (Gabadi, 2000, p. 33); the intensifying dialogue and negotiation between the global and the local consists of a set of discursive practices and representative discourse.

Workplace Talk

Workplace interactions have become an interesting area of scholarship in the growing collaboration between social theory and fields like applied linguistics and applied sociolinguistics. Industrial arbitration, employment rights and law, discrimination, harassment and bullying, are some of the issues that analysis of workplace interactions may address. Seminal work by scholars like Holmes and Stubbe (2003) on power and politeness, Mullany (2000) on gender theory and management meetings, Sarangi and Roberts (1999) on talk in institutional settings, especially in the healthcare sector, Cameron (2000) on call centres, and Vine (2004) on power negotiation through discourse in the workplace stand out.

The discourse generated by people affected directly or indirectly by the phenomenon of outsourcing may be classified generally as workplace talk. Workplace talk in the relevant literature is conventionally construed as a practice confined specifically to communicative exchanges between and among employers and employees in a definitive work-space and on official topics. These exchanges include negotiation, complaint, apology, proposal, query, contract and so on. However, Holmes (1995) extended the scope of workplace talk to include informal genres such as corridor chats which occur in the general work environment and form part of the dynamic of relationship negotiation. For instance, if a response to an idle comment made on a corridor outside an office is adjudged to be a cold response then it may be construed by the person being cold-shouldered as signalling a conflict stance and may eventually 'enter' the office space. The data on which my discussion here is based fall into this category of incidental work talk. Particularly in relation to outsourcing and migration one is actually making a case for expanding the category of workplace talk to include on-line commentaries, discussions and arguments produced by workers affected, whether gaining or losing an outsourced job, and similarly within communities, either as beneficiary or victim of migrating jobs. In a sense then, the interactions and the relationships they forge may be understood within the framework of a universe of practice (Bourdieu, 1977) or more appropriately Scollon and Scollon's notion of the *nexus of practice* (2005).

Because outsourcing has an established trend of relocation from the developed to the developing countries, the old subject of North/South inequality fashioned within an ideological framework is invoked and re-worked. Some of the commentaries generated around and about outsourcing corroborate or challenge some of the existing attitudes to the difference between these two bases. The question then is how do language and ideology set outsourcing apart as a unique context of discourse formation? Individual, community and international relations that are impacted introduce ideological perspectives to outsourcing although it is primarily an economic phenomenon.

One clear difference between the traditional workplace and call centres is that in the latter activities including interactions occur in multiple locations and across huge distances, in some cases via information transfer using telecommunications facilities. In spite of this though, they have successfully inherited the same exploitative culture for which the traditional regimes are noted – so much so that call centres have been called the 'factories of the new economy' (*Union Network International* 6 June 2004). The dynamics of language behaviour in this context are bound to be different from those of face-to-face interactions in the conventional workplace. What are the implications of these for sociolinguistic methodology?

Methodology

Arguably, the best approach to the investigation of communicative repertoires pertaining to outsourcing is through recorded interviews and the interactions of people who employ or are employed in outsourced businesses and the clients that they serve. Phone-conferences and conversations, e-mails and other IT talk practices are difficult to observe because of their personal nature, in spite of the fact that they are official transactions. Unless transactions are recorded and such recordings accessed by researchers with the consent of participants there is an ethical problem. Access to these is made more difficult because of both provisions for confidentiality of clients and corporate organizations' desire to protect company secrets from competitors.

Most companies that have outsourced parts or all of their operations are reluctant to accommodate the researcher out of a fear that their weaknesses will be exposed and as a result they could lose their competitive edge. Consequently, indirect ways of accessing and eliciting data need to be explored. In this regard, media publications of the reactions of victims of outsourcing – those whose jobs are outsourced – and the corporate reactions to these constitute a useful corpus to work with.

The data for this discussion derive from four web sources: silicon.com, techsunite. org, washtech.org, and union-network.org. On 17 June 2004 silicon.com, a web-based IT magazine, published an article by Will Sturgeon titled 'UK call centres are rubbish' with the leader 'No wonder firms are off to India', and invited comments from its readership (http://management.silicon.com/careers/0,39024671,39121456,00. htm). Silicon.com's readership comprise mainly of people in industry with a stake of one kind or another in outsourcing. In total, up to 14 July 2004, 26 responses to the original article had been received and published on the site from commentators in five countries: UK (21), Spain (1), India (2), Turkey (1) and New Zealand (1). Together they form the corpus upon which my discussion is based in this chapter. While this sample is open to challenge under a traditional quantitative regime, against the background of the problems earlier highlighted, it still provides us with material to work with in an exploratory study of this nature. The attribution for the comments included country base and in some cases the names of commentators and their occupation. Some of the comments were submitted anonymously (11) including the entries from Turkey and India. We do not know how many of the comments were submitted by the same author, except for one case of two submissions by a Technical Advisor from Sheffield. Anonymity may be an indication that some of the commentators were apprehensive that the views they expressed could have undesirable repercussions.

On the silicon.com webpage we observe the constituting of industry media into a site for the discursive construction of ideologies of national integrity, corporate standards, individual and group employment rights and client attitudes to quality of service or product. Before I proceed, I should make one further observation on methodology. The authentic size of an Internet-based sample is indeterminate because of the endless possibilities that this data elicitation context offers, which fact recommends it as an approach. However, the accompanying possibility for informant and respondent cloning means that a hundred virtual respondents could in reality be no more than one creatively polyphonic obsessive, in which case an additional safeguard might need to be put in place to check this, for instance, tried and tested data sorting resources in forensic and corpus linguistics. For our current purpose we shall make do with exploring qualitative analytical tools.

Data Analysis

Language and Ideology

Blommaert (1999) demonstrates in clear ways the manner in which language serves ideology as its vehicle. The relevance of language and ideology to outsourcing and migration must include the representation of North and South because of the opportunity it creates to revisit the hegemony of Empire and the colonial enterprise. As I shall demonstrate with extracts from the published commentaries that constitute my data, outsourcing may be interpreted from a number of perspectives:

1. exploitative North seeking cheap labour in the South,
2. a considerate North distributing its wealth to the South by sharing jobs as a resource,
3. an emergent South stamping its indispensability on the North by competing and authoring the economic logic to support its intellectual development.

It is obvious from the above that outsourcing means different things to different people or communities and the different perceptions are conveyed in commentaries. Let us examine the areas of ideology covered by the commentaries.

Outsourcing/Offshoring

There is substantial evidence that the migration of jobs is a growing international phenomenon – there are UK, US, and Indian data to corroborate this claim. The scale of these operations can be inferred from the growing number of call centres springing up in offshore locations while onshore ones are closing down in countries like Britain and the USA. The online journal of the Union Network International, *UNI In Depth* (11 February 2004, accessed 6 June 2004) in an article titled 'Offshoring campaign hits Europe and Westminster on same day', reports Datamonitor's prediction that 'there will be 286,000 outsourced European workstations in Eastern Europe, the Middle East and Africa by 2007'. It added, quoting research by the consultants Deloitte and Touche that an expected outsourcing of two million European jobs, mainly administrative and technology-related, would occur by 2008 (*UNI In Depth*, 11 February 2004). Offshore Tracker, a US-based organization, has been monitoring outsourcing activities from media and employee reports and compiling data on the scale of this global operation. It had in its update of 25 April 2005 a list of 495 companies involved in outsourcing although for a few of these there were no data available.[1] Table 4.1 provides information on the outsourcing activities of what Offshore Tracker described as the top 10 'culprits'.

---

1 'The offshore tracker is based upon news accounts and employees. It tracks instances of offshoring beginning in January 2001 and using a list of companies derived from media sources. The tracker is not scientific in determining the precise number of jobs lost, since media reports are not always accurate, we do not have access to all media reports, and many instances of offshoring go unreported. However, this tracker is the only source that accounts for and aggregates the number of jobs lost due to offshoring' (http://www.techsunite.org/offshore/offshoreevents.cfm).

Table 4.1   Top 10 culprits

Company	Most Recent Event Date	Jobs Offshored	Estimated jobs lost
EDS	05 July 2004	20,000	7950
IBM	14 November 2004	15,000	1847
Siemens AG	02 March 2004	15,000	data unavailable
General Electric	20 December 2004	14,250	data unavailable
Convergys	13 December 2003	14,000	100
Accenture	17 November 2004	10,000	90
Keane	01 December 2004	9,000	data unavailable
Computer Sciences Corp	11 September 2003	7,700	5400
Dell	19 January 2005	7,550	5700
MCI	06 June 2004	7,500	800

Source: http://www.techsunite.org/offshore/ accessed 4 May 2005.

Outsourcing and Language

Outsourcing is a subject with multidisciplinary dimensions. Within the tradition of postmodernist sociolinguistic work, that is, one with extensive input from social theory (Coupland, 2003), two approaches immediately offer up analytical and paradigmatic possibilities. The first of these is the *Global English v World Englishes* framework. Although the destination of outsourced jobs is not confined within empire networks, a basic economic principle dictates that production cost should be kept to a minimum to optimize profit. Thus, outsourcing to a nation that shares the same language as an outsourcer nation is bound to be cheaper than outsourcing to one where language barriers exist thus saving on prohibitive training costs and stemming potential losses that may be incurred due to language competence-induced miscommunication. French companies look to African Francophone countries, such as Mauritius and Morocco. Similarly, Latin America provides an obvious offshore location for Spanish companies, whilst Lufthansa, the airline company, has a German-language call centre in Cape Town. In other words, postcolonial English countries are bound to 'profit' by natural selection from economics-determined outsourcing from countries such as the USA and Britain. As a direct consequence of this, native and non-native varieties of English enter into a constant and more intensive dialogue with ideological implications such as the internationalization or tabooing of forms deriving from indigenized Englishes.

However, there is an alternative perspective to the issue of language in outsourcing as a social process. The distinction between languages and varieties of colonial languages presents us with a basis for comparative analysis. This is useful from the point of view of the attitudes that various forms attract. It is difficult to say whether such attitudes are in fact about the people rather than about a language variety. In

Figure 4.1   Poster: 'Congress – if our jobs are at risk ...'

Source: http://www.washtech.org/wt/outsourcing_ad.php

other words, there is a possibility that the expression of negative attitudes towards a particular variety may in reality be an expression of racist attitudes towards the speaker rather than a statement about problems of communication (cf. Davies, 2003).

Choudhary (2002, p. 1) notes, for instance, that 'Most Indians use the phonetic patterns of their mother tongue while speaking English. This "vernacular accent" can be annoyingly unclear to native speakers of English and the lack of clarity becomes acute over the telephone'. In his capacity as the Chief Executive Officer of Competitive Edge Education, an ancillary business to outsourcing operations, we could assume that his criticism is a professional view to be borne in mind in the drawing up of the curriculum for speech training targeted at call centre workers. However, similar criticisms which I shall present in my discussion of ideology and representation in a subsequent section are easily interpretable as reactions to difference.

The second option is to theorize outsourcing in terms of ideology and representation contained in the communicative exchanges between and about its perceived agents and victims. I suggest that reverse economic migration has its associated discourses similar in ways to those we have always identified with conventional economic migration. For instance, there is an emergent 'victim's discourse' in the UK and USA championed by customer service unions (like Union Network International) and organizations such as US-based Offshore Tracker which monitors and records the outsourcing activities of companies. Figure 4.1 is an illustration of how those directly affected by outsourcing discursively construct and convey their reactions.

The working public's recognition of their rights and liberties within the provisions of a liberal democracy is encapsulated in the text of the figure above. American victims of outsourcing remind the US Congress of its duty to defend their rights, which include the right to employment. They choose in this instance to meet the threat to their jobs with a threat to the security of Congress positions by the all-powerful voting public. Its alternative forms include appeals and unionized sanctions. These resistance discourses fit into the liberal protest genre of labour union talk. It is constructed around issues of rights, dignity of labour and so on.

The flip side of this coin is the discursive representation of governments whose policies facilitate incoming outsourced business, the representation of southern nations as providers of knowledge skills to the North against the current of the old order in which knowledge only flowed Southwards. As I pointed out in defining terms and concepts at the beginning however, the flow is not unidirectional. There are intra-South, North/South, South/North and intra-North flows judging by the location of call-centres. It would be misleading to represent outsourcing exclusively as a North-South movement. That this is not so is evidenced by the Indian satellite call-centres now springing up in China as well as one case of reverse offshoring.[2] Additionally, there are call centres of UK IT companies in different locations around the UK, especially in Scotland. There are likely to be differences therefore in the associated discourses because job migration engenders different experiences across different cultural spaces.

One of the misapprehensions surrounding outsourcing is the tendency to explain it ideologically as a *North v South* phenomenon in which developed nations outsource to beneficiary developing nations. *NASSCOM* (The National Association of Software and Services Companies) *Strategic Review* (2003: 84) articulates this reservation suggesting that it is:

> *not just North v South*. It is simplistic to assume that the issue is just a matter of service sector jobs leaving developed countries for developing countries. The country with the largest market in IT outsourced services is in fact Ireland (driven mainly by the development centres of large IT companies such as Microsoft and Dell). India is in second place, but is then followed by Israel and Canada.

---

2   Yilu Zhao writing in the *New York Times* (26 October 2003; Late Edition – Final, Section 3, page 4, Column 1) reports that the Chinese company The Haier Group builds refrigerators in Camden, South Carolina, with an American work force to save on transporting finished products from China and as part of a policy of expanding prestigious overseas markets.

Table 4.2   Ideologies and their associated discourse

IDEOLOGY	COMMENTS
Corporate standards – incompetence	Management rather than call centre is incompetent: (a) 'Management were unapproachable and often absent when a customer wanted to speak to a senior person' Faye, London; (b) 'So if you're going to pick on someone, then pick on the management' Anonymous, Supervisor, Turkey; (c) 'Its the fundamental business structure that is at fault. Managers think that they should provide customer service by email but the truth is that it costs between 3 and 6 times more to deal with an email than a phone call.' R.H., Worcester, UK.
Overt and covert patriotism	British/Indians are better: (a) 'They usually have no more skills than you had to start with' – meaning they are ignorant and lack expertise – CW, Video director, Worthing, UK; (b) 'In all respects the UK beat them'; (c) 'My experience is that quality of service offshore is worse'; (d) 'Give me a British call centre anyday' Anonymous, Systems Engineer, Nottingham, UK; (e) 'I'm glad to be leaving the UK. The attitude problems that are described in the article are quite typical of any Brit ...' JM, IT Consultant, Barcelona; (f) 'I always knew, Indians could do much better than Britons. But for resources crunch and high degree of corruption, Britons are no match for Indians' Anonymous, India; (g) ' Being 'nice' to you to the exclusion of almost everything else (including answering your question). In my experience the Indian and Irish call centres are especially good at [being nice]' Anonymous, UK; (h) '... although the staff in India are well trained and eager you are 3 times more likely to have to phone back at least once more to deal with your problem than with the UK based equivalents' KB, Sheffield, UK; (i) 'I don't like impolite customer service but I also don't see the point of polite service that doesn't solve your problem either' KB, Sheffield, UK; (j) 'And how long before these Indian call centres are infiltrated by organized crime, and phishing takes off using a legitimate business as a front?' BB, Consultant, Stevenage, UK; (k) 'This is symptomatic of any call centre – not just UK.' MS, Winchester, Hants, UK; (l) 'attitudes were beginning to change and that service was being improved as a direct result of customers in the UK wanting to talk to UK based call centres and get dealt with in the first call' KB, Sheffield, UK.
Individual and group rights	Poor working conditions: (a) 'It's a hard, stressful job and one in which you receive little reward or incentive'; (b) 'Who the hell wants to take that kind of shit for £4.00 an hour?' Faye, Account Manager, London; (c) 'Call centres operate just like supermarkets: They employ people that are low in skills and paid badly' CW, Video director, Worthing, UK.

IDEOLOGY	COMMENTS
Language difference	Indian English/British English – challenges notions of the global constituency of English;
	(a) 'The person on the other end could not pronounce the name of my company or Keighley where the equipment is based' Anonymous, Systems Engineer, Nottingham, UK;
	(b) 'After spelling 'Teddington' to the call centre operator he politely told me it did not appear in his listings' Anonymous, Production Manager, UK – implying a lack of place knowledge; Consequently Indian call centres are more expensive for the end user.

While one cannot completely dismiss the *North v South* element, outsourcing discourse comprises several other ideologies which are equally significant and deserving of attention. Table 4.2 is an attempt to capture some of the ideologies associated with outsourcing derived from the set of published correspondences that constituted the data corpus for this study.

The left column lists some of the other ideologies identifiable with outsourcing and in the right column I have provided examples of the language use manifestation of each ideology. The comments that illustrate the ideologies of patriotism and language difference in the table above remind us of those that are often credited to anti-immigration pressure groups as we find in several of the discussions in other chapters in this volume. In a sense therefore, reverse migration and outsourcing are not exactly discontinuous processes from conventional migration. The discourses that characterize both phenomena include that of victimage, patriotism (or fascism), othering, difference and/or diversity and they certainly belong in the same generic class, albeit problematic.

Industry Metaphors, Similes and Sarcasm

One way in which attitudes and opinions are constructed on silicon.com is through the use of metaphors that are peculiar to the industry.[3] Let us look at a selection of extracts.

a) '*... I could have been reporting a fault on a MFI shelf unit and not a Disk Storage Unit* for the amount of knowledge they showed about the fault' (Anonymous, systems engineer, Nottingham, UK);

b) '... Call Centres may actually be able to hold on to skilled, enthusiastic people who have a sense of pride in their work because they are respected as the *essential core of their organization*, rather than being treated *like battery hens*';

c) 'Used car salesmen say new cars too expensive?' – (Anonymous, Md, UK) describing BT;

d) 'BT Welsh (118 400) ... came in third [accuracy stake] at 95 per cent one wonders where that is located, are there many *Welsh speakers in Mumbai*?' – (Anonymous, Md, UK).

---

3   I thank Dr Veronika Koller (Lancaster) for comments on my draft, particularly in relation to the point made here.

The italicized portions of the extracts above exemplify the use of metaphors in outsourcing discourse. In a), a put down of southern call-centre workers is achieved through implying that the latter are ignorant. The acuteness of the level of ignorance is implicit in the claim that hypothetically these workers cannot tell MFI (a UK furniture retailer) shelf units from disk storage units. In sharp contrast with a), extract b) is a positive commentary on call-centre workers in highlighting their indispensability within the industry and making a case for their being regarded with respect rather than like mass-produced battery hens. Extract c) is an attack on British Telecommunication (BT) one of the more recent protagonists of public sector outsourcing in the United Kingdom. In extract d) the commentator employs sarcasm in rhetorical question format to subtly ridicule the claim that a language barrier problem does not exist between clients and call-centre staff. This undermines attempts by call-centre workers to converge towards the perceived speech patterns of their clients. The practice creates a disjuncture between product quality and the stigma attached to their southern production base through disguise.

Use of Solidarity Pronouns and Nominatives

Solidarizing pronouns are inclusive in marking the membership of a speaker in a community that is referenced and excludes the referents in the object complement of the structure they appear in. In outsourcing discourse, employers and employees, and clients and offshore call centre staff are counter-positioned. Nominatives similarly perform the function of establishing and setting apart these same discreet groups. Let us consider the following examples from the data:

e) 'It's unbalanced – Give *us* a major right to reply -Why discriminate *against us* all?' (technical advisor in Sheffield, UK).

f) 'I could have been reporting a fault on an MFI shelf unit and not a Disk Storage Unit for the amount of knowledge they showed about the fault.'

g) 'If *they* provided a good working environment with fair pay, Call Centres may actually be able to hold onto skilled, enthusiastic people.'

h) 'First, I am sick of *people bashing UK call centres* and only getting quotes from *the Indians* whose interests are best served by criticizing *UK call centres.*'

i) 'Second, *Indian call centres* are frequently no better than *UK call centres*, and often worse – *Dell and Three*, hide *your* faces in shame.'

j) 'And how long before these Indian call centres are infiltrated by organized crime, and phishing takes off using a legitimate business as a front?'

The italicized words, phrases and clauses identify the groups that are in opposition in their perception of the desirability of outsourcing. There is an obvious polarization of businesses and their employees, onshore employees (victims) and call centre staff (beneficiaries) in outsourcing discourse. Note that there may be other beneficiaries of outsourcing. For instance, shareholders in publicly owned corporations that outsource their operations could be regarded as beneficiaries of outsourcing but not necessarily agents. Similarly, clients or consumers of outsourced services may be constructed as victims of the process if the alternative provision is deemed inadequate or beneficiaries if it is deemed an improvement on what was previously available.

In extract e) the writer means by 'us' employees in offshore locations who are the subject of all manners of denigration. The use of the imperative here also consolidates the fact that an outgroup addressee is implicit. In extract f), 'they' refers to call centre workers and the criticism is targeted at their expertise. The writer suggests that these workers are incompetent and ignorant. These descriptions are similar to those often used to describe conventional immigrants by their conservative hosts. In contrast, in extract g), the identity of 'they' is corporate business that outsources its operation. The writer alleges that corporate business falls short of providing 'good working environment with fair pay' which is in violation of employment regulations. This may be regarded as taking a Union stance. Extracts h), i) and j) are both attacks on outsourcing generally as well as indirect expressions of nationalism and patriotism achieved by a denigration of India as a beneficiary of outsourcing. In i) the outgroup addressee is made explicit in contrast to the implicit references of the earlier example. Even more interestingly, by this choice of linguistic form the institutional operators of outsourcing are lumped together with the 'foreign' distant beneficiaries of the project.

Conclusion

In the light of the foregoing discussion and analysis, some conclusions may be drawn. First, it is established that outsourcing as a social and cultural experience has sociolinguistic dimensions to it in a broad understanding of the discipline's scope. To the extent that this has only recently begun to attract the attention of academic researchers the wholesale application of theory as it currently exists is obviously problematic. Instead, a need has arisen to modify and adapt paradigms to accommodate the peculiar contexts of communicative interaction associated with the phenomenon.

I have tried to demonstrate that outsourcing as reverse migration in which jobs rather than persons emigrate, especially from North to South nations, generates a different kind of anxiety from that which we often associate with conventional migration. Although both forms of migration attract resistance and negative attitudes among segments of the population in the outsourcing nations, the expressions of these sentiments differ between these two migration contexts. Outsourcing becomes a site of contestation within the industry involving corporate businesses and their employees, and between client consumers and offshore call centre staff. I have presented an emerging discourse of victimage, patriotism, othering, and difference from the perspectives of those who lose their jobs to outsourcing on the one hand and those who gain off-shored jobs. It is observable that these are analogous to existing discourses about migration and migrants.

The data analysis shows how outsourcing may be impacting the character of language politics. With specific reference to the English-speaking world, the various language schools which are established to clone 'native speakers' of English in Indian call centres challenge previously held positions in the World Englishes paradigm. The curriculum operated by these schools has been broadened to include a cultural knowledge of the society from which the clients derive. The traditional curriculum had always indicated a preference for the indigenization of English in the places to which it was transplanted through the Empire project. The association of relatively better educated and better paid call centre staff with British and American accents of English undermines the status of the more popular non-native varieties spoken in offshore communities thus feathering the ideological nest of linguistic hegemony between North and South. Besides, a new social class may be emerging in popular offshore destinations such as Bangalore and Mumbai comprising call centre workers who have more disposable income and therefore more expensive tastes and for whom the preferred and acquired native accents of English become significant social capital. Sagarika Ghosh writing in the *Indian Express* (Wednesday, 4 June 2003) links Westernization to call centres and provides a description of what she calls the 'Call Centre Drawl'. Similarly, *BBC News* (online 14 April 2003) claims that '[e]locution lessons are helping staff working at call centres in India neutralize their accents and make their sales pitch more expensive'. The interesting point to make though is that the article is headlined 'Indians learn to be Brad and Britney', two arguably Western popular culture icons (Brad Pitt and Britney Spears).

I shall close with a methodological observation. The efficacy of web media for the generation of data corpus as a way around the problem of corporate and client confidentiality is established. This solution, as I have pointed out, is fraught with problems such as the anonymity of contributors to web-based discussions on outsourcing or the adoption of pseudonyms in some cases so that we never know for certain if people are who or where they claim they are. Claims based on an analysis of data from these sources must therefore be regarded with caution. This is a limitation that needs to be addressed in the long term. Corporate businesses that outsource their operations must realize that they stand to benefit from facilitating academic researchers' access to recorded interactions for the purposes of critical analysis to better manage the phenomenon of outsourcing.

References

Appadurai, A. (1990), 'Disjuncture and difference in the global cultural economy', *Public Culture*, **2**(2), 1–24.

Appadurai, A. (1996), *Modernity at Large: Cultural Dimensions of Globalization* (Minneapolis: University of Minnesota Press).

Blommaert, J. (1999), *Language Ideological Debates* (Berlin: Mouton De Gruyter).

Bourdieu, P. (1977), *Outline of a theory of practice*. Nice, R. (translated by) (Cambridge: Cambridge University Press).

Cameron, D. (2000), *Good to Talk? Living and Working in a Communication Culture* (London: Sage).

Choudhary, V. (2002), 'Call center training for service representatives'. http://www.expressitpeople.com/200220527/careers1.shtml.

Coupland, N. (2003), 'Introduction: Sociolinguistics and globalization', *Journal of Sociolinguistics*, 7(4), 465–472. [DOI: 10.1111/j.1467-9841.2003.00237.x]

Coupland, N., Srikant, S. and Candlin, C.N., eds. (2001), *Sociolinguistics and Social Theory* (London: Longman).

Davies, A. (2003), *The Native Speaker: Myth and Reality* (Clevedon: Multilingual Matters Limited).

Duszak, A. and Okulska, U., eds. (2004), *Speaking from the Margin: Global English from a European Perspective* (Frankfurt: Peter Lang).

Gabardi, W. (2000), *Negotiating Postmodernism* (Minneapolis: University of Minnesota Press).

Gozdziak, E. and Shandy, D., eds. (2000), *Rethinking Refuge and Displacement: Selected Papers on Refugees and Immigrants* (Vol. VIII) (Arlington, VA: American Anthropological Association).

Habermas, J. (1989), *The Theory of Communicative Action: Lifeworld and System*, Vol. 2. McCarthy, T. (translated by) (Cambridge: Polity Press).

Holmes, J. and Stubbe, M. (2003), *Power and Politeness in the Workplace. A Sociolinguistic Analysis of Talk at Work* (London: Longman).

Holmes, J. (1995), *Women, Men and Politeness* (London: Longman).

Kachru, B.B. (1997), 'World Englishes and English-using Communities', *Annual Review of Applied Linguistics*, **17**, 66–87.

Kerswill, P. (2006), Migration and language in *Sociolinguistics/Soziolinguistik. An International Handbook of the Science of Language and Society*, 2nd edn. Mattheier, K., Ammon, U. and Trudgill, P. (eds.) (Berlin: De Gruyter).

Kielkiewicz-Janowiak, A. and Pawelczyk, J. (2004), 'Globalisation and customer service communication at Polish call centres, in Duszak', A. and Okulska, U. (eds.), 225–238.

Mullany, L. (2000), 'The application of current language and gender theory to managerial meeting discourse', Nottingham Linguistics Circular 15.

Rampton, B. (1995), *Crossing: Language and Ethnicity among Adolescents* (London: Longman).

Sarangi, S. and Roberts, C. (1999), *Talk, Work and Institutional Order* (Berlin: Mouton De Gruyter).

Scollon, R. and Scollon, S.W. (2004), *Nexus of Practice: Discourse and the Emerging Internet* (London: Routledge).

Trudgill, P. (2004), 'Glocalisation and the Ausbau Sociolinguistics of Modern Europe in Duszak', A. and Okulska, U. (eds.), 35–49.

Vine, B. (2004), *Getting Things Done at Work: The Discourse of Power in the Workplace Interaction* (Amsterdam: John Benjamins).

Chapter 5

Economic Satisfaction and Nostalgic Laments: The Language of Bulgarian Economic Migrants after 1989 in Websites and Electronic Fora

Zhivko Ivanov

Philology Faculty, Paisij Hilendarski University of Plovdiv, Bulgaria

Introduction

The objective of this chapter is to trace how the Bulgarian emigrant community speaks and assesses its own position in an alien society, how it formulated its initial goals and to what extent these goals were achieved and reported. The other purpose of the chapter is to examine the different degrees of hidden nationalism that Bulgarian economic emigrants discover in themselves during their residence in the recipient community.

The process of rediscovery of national identity flows with different intensity in two directions: on the one hand, Bulgarian economic emigrants suffer from deepening nostalgia and reassess the quality of life in their homeland; on the other hand, they try to justify more emphatically their choice and perceive any retreat from it as a surrender that will impede their reintegration in the homeland environment.

Background

If we look back to the time (under Ottoman yoke) when the word 'emigrant' did not exist in the Bulgarian language, it is not hard to realize that '… the most famous, the most important people for the formation of the Bulgarian national idea were emigrants for all or most of their lives while actively pursuing political careers and serving the public interests' (Kelbetcheva, 2003). Though the word 'emigrant' had not entered the sociological lexicon of the Bulgarian language at the time, probably because the Bulgarian nation did not exist as an independent political entity yet, there is evidence that emigration was happening in the area. In general, statistical data pertinent to the early phases of emigration from Balkan countries show that rates of return were very high. Seven out of eight people who had emigrated to the USA from Balkan countries at the end of the nineteenth century returned to their homelands (Trajkov, 1993; Kelbetcheva, 2003; see also Alexandrov, 1999). The first

Bulgarian economic emigrants after the Liberation (1878) stayed abroad for one or two years and then returned to their homes only to leave again for longer and longer periods. Anyhow, as a rule of thumb, they did not show any inclination or wish to change their home country and to settle abroad permanently.

Unlike Yugoslavian citizens, between the Second World War and the end of 1989 Bulgarian citizens could not travel and reside abroad without special permission from the Bulgarian Communist Party and state officials. During the 1970s a system had been put in place experimentally in Yugoslavia whereby Yugoslav Federation workers could take up temporary residence in specified countries of Western Europe (mainly Germany, Switzerland, Austria, Sweden). This resulted in legal economic emigration that reached the 1 million mark by the end of the 1970s. Today this number has risen to almost 2 million consisting mainly of Serbians and Croatians (see Todorova, 2000). As a result, in Yugoslavia a well-developed so-called 'gastarbeiter Kultur' (foreign worker, alien employee culture) developed around the long-term work experience of Yugoslavs who went to Western Europe. The impact of those experiences were most visible in literary, entertainment, television and media cultural production. One such 'gastarbeiter' song (Gastarbajterska pesma)[1] presents a brief and clear image of an emigrant worker's life in the foreign country: it is oppressive and monotonous, varied between hard work from Monday to Friday, endless partying with folk songs, rakia, girlfriends on weekends, and subsequent hangovers on Monday mornings. Since Bulgarians did not have the long Yugoslavian tradition of emigrant folklore, I will focus here on other dynamic and steadily expanding forms – websites and electronic fora – in which Bulgarian emigrants' experiences, feelings, reflections and ideas of life abroad and in the homeland are expressed. These data source allows me to claim *tertium non datur* (the third objective position in the binary 'home citizen-homeland').

The Bulgarian situation *a propos* emigration was quite different from the Yugoslavian one. 'Wild', non-institutionalized emigration held the foreground in Bulgaria, usually understood as attempts to achieve a higher standard of living. Only after 1997–1998 did the Bulgarian government initiate certain measures for the civilized structuring of the process of emigration driven by economic goals. Within or outside control, at the beginning of 2004 Bulgaria announced that over 1.250 million of its citizens were choosing a job in a country other than their homeland (National Institute of Statistics, 2004; see also Milanov, 2000). Although somewhat delayed, this wave of emigration continues to expand. Goverment officials unfortunately convey an unclear picture of the phases and scale of emigration from Bulgaria by focusing exclusively on data for the period between 1992 and 2001. They avoid the critical 1989 and 1990 period. It is a curious fact that after the communists received over 55 per cent of the vote in the first democratic elections in1989, some sociologists explained the result as arising from the desire of future emigrants to obtain political

---

1   The song is composed by the Serbian pop group 'Riblja chorba' ('The fish soup') and published in the album 'Ostalo je cutanje' ('The silence is here', 1998). The text of lyrics can be found at http://www.lyricspy.com/2773/Riblja_Corba_lyrics.htm or http://www.lyricspy.com/50974/Riblja_Corba_lyrics/Gastarbajterska_Pesma_lyrics.html

asylum in the USA and other Western countries.[2] The idea was that since communist rule could be thought of as continuing in Bulgaria future emigrants could hope to be received sympathetically in the West. At any rate, the point is that NSI (National Statistic Institute) does not publicize data about emigration between 1989 and 1991, or between 1984 and 2002 insofar as the Turkish exodus goes (NSI, 2004).

Diaspora

Bulgarian emigrants' websites and discussion fora present the interesting process through which the Bulgarian diaspora is increasingly becoming defined by nostalgia. Nostalgia is the bridge between their past and present, closing the geographic gaps between new and old localities. The material I have examined reveals that by and large the initial economic aspirations of emigrants after 1989 have been met, and most feel that they have achieved their initial goals. With this comforting sense of economic fulfilment, the emigrants give rein to nostalgic laments regarding their past in the homeland. Nostalgia, of course, does not restore the past but does provide a new outlook for community networks. If you already have a full fridge (a metaphor of material prosperity) it becomes possible to indulge a form of sophisticated existence, where intellectual and spiritual pursuits take precedence over consumer rules. A set of problems has emerged, in fact, concerning national, ethnic and cultural self-identifications and definitions for Bulgarian emigrants – problems which lie beyond material solutions. It seems to me that these problems are not just pertinent to Bulgarians, but are equally relevant from a wider perspective of ethno-cultural processes at the end of the 20th and beginning of the 21st centuries.

Given the scale and achievement of Bulgarians abroad, it is more appropriate to think in terms of a Bulgarian diaspora than in terms of Bulgarian economic emigration alone. The character of this diaspora has basically changed in the course of the last 15 years from 1990, provoking politicians and researchers to reconsider the status and new dimensions of Bulgarians abroad in relation both to their host countries and to the homeland. It is also worth remembering that this diaspora was not created simply by economic motivations but through complex political processes too. Before 1989 the Bulgarian diaspora had a fragmentary character in cultural and political terms. From May 1989 to December 1989 we witnessed an unprecedented Turkish exodus from Bulgaria due to a coercive, inhuman and shameful event. It produced emigrants, but in fact it was a classic case of ethnic cleansing which infected the region, spreading out to the former Yugoslavia. In 1990, a partial Turkish homecoming began, but along with this a new wave of emigration arose, orientated to two diametrically opposed directions – the Bosporus and the West. This wave was different from the ethnic exodus of 1989, but it started within and over its frame. Between 1989 and 1992, 450,000 Bulgarian Turks left, but then more than 100,000 of them returned within the same period. However another 650,000

---

2   This is based on personal experience rather than textual evidence. At the time the present author was a member of an organization called 'Fair Elections', which organized meetings, speeches, oral analyses and so on following the elections. Such views were aired in that context.

Bulgarian citizens (Bulgarians and Turks, Gypsies, Armenians and others holders of Bulgarian passports) departed to the West on a one-way ticket thereafter.

A large number of research studies maintain that the Bulgarian diaspora is manifested in microcosms, miniature images of Bulgarian society, conserving political views, psychological stereotypes, linguistic and cultural relics. Knowing these people will also help us understand once again what has been lost or what Bulgaria may recover in terms of political, cultural and human potential. However, judging from the material I have examined, it appears that Bulgarians abroad do not simply conserve; for the most part they renew their mentality, creating a new vision of the past in the homeland which is influenced by their perspectives in the present. Moreover, the emigrant's new vision has a tangible impact on the mentality of Bulgarians in Bulgaria. A bilateral process of mutual interrogation unfolds: for Bulgarians abroad it involves asking, 'who am I for my country?'; and for those in Bulgaria it involves considering, 'what are emigrants for me?'.

Wars, natural disasters, environmental degradation, explosive population growth, and the widening gap between rich and poor have resulted in large migratory movements. According to recent estimates there are 175 million people (3 per cent of the world's population) who are international migrants, that is live in a country other than the country of their birth, and that the migrant pool is growing by 5–10 million each year (Population Reference Bureau, 2004, p. 12). This extraordinary level of demographic change is unparalleled in human history, and presents profound challenges to the most basic notions of nation, culture, community, and citizenship (see Statement on Population by World Leaders, signed by 75 heads of government and presented to the United Nations Secretary-General by Indonesian President Soeharto in October 1995 – Grant, 1996, p. 150). The first pictorial survey (Salgado, 2000) to extensively chronicle the current global flux of humanity, follows Latin Americans entering the United States, Jews leaving the former Soviet Union, Africans travelling into Europe, Kosovars fleeing into Albania, and many others. Bulgarians do not seem to figure in this (World Data, 2001). This is primarily because they are more dispersed than many other groups, particularly in USA, Canada and countries of Western Europe, and because they have integrated and adapted their identities in keeping with the civic culture of the West.

I think that the metaphor of the 'unburned bridges' used in the past to define the relationship 'State-Emigrants', does not express the social and cultural disposition of Bulgarian emigration of the 1990s any longer. More precisely, the Bulgarian diaspora now might be imagined as a community network with a defined structure, including within it relationships to the homeland. Further, the biggest exodus of Bulgarians (mainly of young people), which is unfolding before our eyes, confronts us again with extremely complicated problems about changes in their national identity and metamorphosis of their mentality.

Figures

Here are some figures from the Factbook of the National Statistical Institute of Bulgaria (NSI), published at the end of June 2004 (NSI 2004).

Table 5.1   Population at 31 December 2003

Year	All	Male	Female
1990	8,669,269	4,269,998	4,399,271
1995	8,384,715	4,103,368	4,281,347
2000	8,149,468	3,967,423	4,182,045
2001	7,891,095	3,841,163	4,049,932
2002	7,845,841	3,816,162	4,029,679
2003	7,801,273	3,790,840	4,010,433

What is relevant to our dissussion is the trend of decreasing population, in which the annual migration rate is a factor. More precisely, after 1990 the Bulgarian population has decreased by 867,996 individuals. In one year, 2002–2003, the depletion was of 44,568 persons. Emigration rates are not balanced by population growth rates, so the population decrease is due both to negative birth rates and emigration.

Table 5.2   The birth-rate factor – (per 1000)

Year	Birth rate	Growth (per 1,000 peoples)
1990	12.1	-0.4
1995	8.6	-5.0
2000	9.0	-5.1
2001	8.6	-5.6
2002	8.5	-5.8
2003	8.6	-5.7

Since 1990 the process of population decrease has been accompanied by a growing proportion of ageing persons, a consequence of the continuous deterioration of the demographic situation in the country. At present, Bulgaria ranks in the top 10 countries in the world with the largest share of population of age 60 years and over. In this regard the country is placed just after Italy, Greece, Germany, Japan, Sweden and Belgium.

In surveys asking Bulgarian emigrants why they chose to leave their country, 54 per cent declared the reason was to enjoy a higher standard of life, 20 per cent said emigration solved their own and their family's problems, and 9 per cent simply said that 'I don't want to live anymore in Bulgaria'. The main destination of Bulgarian emigrants are as follows: Germany, 23 per cent of all Bulgarian emigrants; USA, 19 per cent; Greece, 8 per cent; Spain, 8 per cent; UK, 6 per cent; Italy, 6 per cent; Canada, 5 per cent; France, 4 per cent. The ethnic composition of emigrants is as follows: Bulgarians, 80 per cent of all emigrants; Turks, 12 per cent; Gypsies, 6 per cent; others, 2 per cent. Figures according to age-group are: 20–39 years, 37 per cent of all emigrants; 40–49 years, 15 per cent; over 50 years, 8 per cent; and 18 per cent of all emigrants have a high level of education (Yanev and Pavlov, 2000). Of related interest, the statistical figures for short term emigration (6 months to 1 year) are: Bulgarians 80 per cent, Turks 12 per cent, Gypsies 6 per cent, others 2 per cent. Of populations involved in long term emigration 81 per cent are Bulgarians, 13 per cent Turks, and 2 per cent Gypsies. Labour migration is divided as follows: 77 per cent Bulgarians, 12 per cent Turks, 8 per cent Gypsies (NSI, 2004).

The data given suggest that the rate of emigration is slowing. Nevertheless, it is undeniable that there is a significant Bulgarian immigrant presence in Western Europe and the USA. As mobility decreases it may be expected that the Bulgarian diaspora will become more coherent and united, and appear more as a distinct community than simply a mass of individuals pursuing higher standards of living, and the comforts of a well-arranged and well-tried social and civic structure, guaranteed security, order and predictable futures.

In 1989, the emigration wave was of an ethnic nature and concerned the Bulgarian Turks. These people were cynically called 'participants in the great trip'. After the fall of the Communist regime we are faced with an entirely new type of emigrants, the majority of whom are economic emigrants. Since 1989 Bulgaria's transition to a market economy has been accompanied by the consequences of a large-scale emigration of primarily young and active people. In the early 1990s emigration from Bulgaria was driven mainly by disparities in earnings and unemployment. People were often willing to accept a job which did not match their education or qualification. According to data of the National Statistical Institute, from Sofia alone emigration has varied between 40 and 70 thousand persons per year in this period. From 1989 up to the present over 750 thousand Bulgarians, that is nearly one in 10 of the national population, have emigrated (see Rangelova and Vladimirova, 2004).

Some of the data available are indicative but uncertain. To demonstrate how doubtful data from Bulgarian newspapers are, I refer to two examples from *The Standart* – a national daily. On 12 January 2004 it was reported that 500,000 Bulgarians abroad brought home 720 million dollars per year; on 24 June 2004 the figures quoted were of 700,000 Bulgarians abroad bringing 1.5 –1.8 billion dollars per year (Standardt News, Internet edition 2004).

In fact, not until the democratic changes of 1992–1993, when The Agency for Bulgarians Abroad (ABA) was founded, did the state start to develop a new and comprehensive policy orientated towards Bulgarians abroad which extended the idea for national unity and approved the concept of Bulgarian unity all over the world. The result of this concept in political terms was the so-called Bulgarian Easter, when all successful Bulgarians were invited to come to the country to meet each other, to discuss and finally to create a program for a new, developed and European Bulgaria.

In about 15 years a Bulgarian Diaspora has emerged abroad with a coherent character and in unprecedented numbers. Neither after the First World War, nor in the late 1920s and early 1930s, or after the Communist takeover have the Bulgarian 'full-fridge seekers' been so numerous.

Nostalgia

As I indicated in my introduction, one of the themes of interest to us in this chapter is the different degrees of hidden nationalism that Bulgarian economic emigrants discover in themselves during their residence in the recipient community. I have commented already that the process of rediscovery of national identity among emigrants flows in contrary directions: on the one hand, Bulgarian economic emigrants suffer from deepening nostalgia and reassess the quality of life in their homeland; on the other hand, they try to justify their choice and perceive any retreat from it as a surrender that will impede their reintegration in the homeland environment. This dual disposition generates both a new devotion toward and a new detestation of the homeland environment, as well as a critical attitude towards the recipient environment.

Most Bulgarian emigrants' Internet narratives are very different from intellectual discourses, especially in terms of their spontaneity, their simplicity, and their deliberately maintained distance from the world of intellectuals and politicians. Most narrators I have come across are 'average' people, who were involved in social and political events while being on the margins of society.

In this context I would like to point to several types of nostalgia that are significant for an emigrant Bulgarian community which networks both with other local communities and people in the homeland at the same time. In the Forum (http://forum.all.bg/) a posting on 31 December 2002 (posted 13: 07) presented an unexpected defence of the national condition of life by pointing to the lower social status of economic immigrants in their recipient communities. It was pointed out that many immigrants are constrained to start from zero and to do work they had never done at home. The posting, '99 Reasons for Staying in the Homeland', reveals the frustration of some emigrants and their disillusionment with rich western societies. This compendium of reasons contains three rhetoric formulas. The first is negative: of the form 'I don't want to wash dishes (and so on)' / 'I hate ...' / 'I dislike ...' – repeated 45 times. The second is affirmative: of the form 'I like to be ...' / 'I love ...' / 'I want ...' / 'I prefer ...' – which occurs 40 times. And the third is declarative, expressed best in number 87: 'I'd like to die for Bulgaria because I'm Bulgarian'. This declaration actually refers to a well-known patriotic poem by the most popular author of nineteenth and twentieth century Bulgaria, Ivan Vazov. He had written the popular line: 'To call myself Bulgarian, such a delight is this for me', in a poem entitled 'I'm Bulgarian' (meaning 'I'm proud to be Bulgarian') ['Az sym bylgarche', 1913]. Such declarations, it seems to me, particularly demonstrate the rising nationalism of Bulgarians living abroad. Together these reasons show a process of rediscovery of the meaning of the national in terms of culture, community, style of living, and hardening distinctions between home and abroad emotionally expressed in terms of 'Like and Hate'. On this Forum some participants regularly criticize those who are writing in Latinate languages, inserting nervously at the end of their posting: 'Write Cyrillic!'

In contrast to '99 Reasons for Staying in the Homeland' appears a posting on 01 March 2003 (posted on 20: 51) which follows a similar structure. The author insists that there are 99 reasons to leave Bulgaria as well. Here there are 52 negative and 47 affirmative statements. In the affirmative part we find statements like: 'I like February too much, when it is time for filling in the income tax form' – which is obviously ironic. However statement 97 has a ring of complicated honesty about it: 'I like to come back because when I'm at home I decide never to come back again'. This has been followed by a new posting entitled '101 Reasons to Come Back, to Work for the Motherland' ... no doubt the exchange will continue. But back to that complicatedly honest statement. This seems to me to express a larger attitude; Bulgarian economic emigrants come to detest the place that feeds them but continue to detest the place that chased them away as well.

Typically, the choice of leaving the homeland is seldom formulated as personal and deliberate, and is usually presented as a coerced decision in which the main pressure comes from the allegorical being of the 'state'. It was through this process that the division between 'homeland' and 'state' was born, and became a battle-cry of the Socialist party during the local elections in autumn 2003. Their leader Stanishev quoted a graffiti message on the wall of the French Language Secondary School in Sofia, which announced: 'I Love the Motherland but I hate the State'. This syllogism is probably embraced by the majority of Bulgarian residents abroad, who blame the state for their own choice. This schizoid situation generates for immigrants a traumatic gap that each tries to fill up with various forms and means of a secondary home-coming. Forums and websites where Bulgarian immigrants unburden their hearts and curse the state have emerged avalanche-like in the past few years (such as, http://ide.li – The Website of Bulgarians All Over the World, containing commentary, opinions, short stories, travel notes, links and so on; or the newsgroup 'Soc.culture.bulgaria' at http://www.bulgaria.com/aba/index.html – Agency for Bulgarians Abroad).

Another dimension of this duality is a useful and essential one. Bulgarians abroad reassess the contents and meanings of a series of stereotypical, trivial and hackneyed national values that had been propagated at school, through the media and by the political class. This reassessment leads to a true understanding of the homeland in its natural and concrete value, which does not have to take recourse to naive and ingenious explanations of national shortcomings, or even apologetic views about past 'shortcomings'. Thus, a large proportion of postings refer to specific elements of the homeland style of living, recalling national memorials and monuments, the climate, mountains and the Black Sea, tripe soup and other untranslatable names of foods, and so on.

As a result of these processes Bulgarian emigrants are gradually occupying a compromise position between their national identity and the standard of living that alienates them from their homeland environment. In the language of the immigrant appears the desire of homecoming under certain conditions, for example the emigrant becomes an exigent and critical Bulgarian who would like to transport the positive in the alien world to his/her homeland space. This desire is apparent in the language of potential emigrants as well, as they 'threaten' the political class and the ruling officials that they will leave the country if conditions of life do not improve.

The compromise between 'Hate and Like' is easily expressed but achieved with difficulty. A young emigrant from the USA wrote (http://forum.all.bg/): 'I dislike the division of "love and hate" because it destroys the differences. I accept basically both points of view regarding Bulgarians, State and country, pro et contra State, so

I will not divide, because union is strength. I'm worried about how to preserve my Bulgarian national spirit ... I'm proud to be Bulgarian but now I'm residing in USA. I was one of those whom President Petar Stoyanov invoked to stay and help the country. The reason I am in USA are our politicians. It is entirely their fault.' Another posting, entitled 'Night for Wailing about Bulgaria' expresses nostalgic sentiments in the following familiar fashion: 'Last night I brought out some photos, I viewed them with my daughter and told her about the people in the photos .... We looked at them and cried'. The Bulgarian diaspora collaborates to find recipes, dairy products, foodstuff, unique delicacies. If they do not find Easter Cake, they use Pannetone instead. 'That is Italian bread with dried fruit and sultanas, it is just amazing, quite like our kozunak (maybe even better)', observes one posting. Another posting informs that in London a Bulgarian café opened called 'Plovdiv, and its address is Green Lane, Haringey, 5 minutes walking distance from Turnpike Lane'. Often we find messages like this one: 'I have a nice life, but nostalgia remains and makes me sad'. This nostalgia is active and creative, offering a sense of rupture and disorientation as well as a sense of suddenly focused presence. The main psychological problem abroad is summarized in the following posted sentiment: 'We live well, in a mixture of comfort and nostalgia, we have our jobs, homes, cars and so on, but our soul is wistful so we all feel some concealed desire to return. I remind myself how you gave me some tips to suppress nostalgia, but it did not work'.

Sometimes expressions of nostalgia turns to the past, extolling the good and brave part of Bulgaria's history: 'Our State is 1300 years old, our origins call us to come back. We are the best, that is why we have survived; look around how many ethnicities and nations have risen and fallen, while we are here and we are alive as a state, a country, a nation, and a community'. It is not ideological, nor national or patriotic but nostalgic discourse which assigns emigrants a key position in this rising community network between them and home. The nostalgically imagined homeland still evokes their sentiments, so that despite being abroad they often become a more dynamic part of the homeland than some social groups inside Bulgaria.

Conclusion

To conclude, I feel that economic emigration after 1990 is shaping a new structure of Bulgarian diaspora, and a new kind of relationship between emigrant and homeland is emerging. What does this emergent schema of emigrant and homeland relations consist of?

First of all, it consists of a unity of local place; second, of a close bond between local communities and homeland; and third, of relationships based on intercommunication. The Bulgarian diaspora also adheres to five basic principles: access for all; mutual interests; openness of mind; no national rivalry, acceptance of their adoptive country's and global values; equality of choice (for example the freedom to stay in Bulgaria is the same as the freedom to leave the homeland). A crucial consolidation of these occurred in 1999–2000. It is evident from the websites and electronic fora observed that since 1999–2000 new discursive trends have appeared, a more positive attempt at building a network which joins the diaspora with the homeland has been undertaken. This network is just emerging, and as yet it is very fragile and unstable. The concrete symptoms of this appear in the form of real estate agencies, air-ticket marketing, websites and fora where more and more postings reflect the real problems of emigrant life, and where a slow and meandering path is being traced from the memorized and imagined homeland to a modern and attractive state. The thin thread that holds diaspora to homeland, through various forms and expressions, is nostalgia. Nostalgia is not only about remembrance but is also a constructive way of realizing a new form of national existence. To be Bulgarian abroad means to be connected in various ways with home. Economic emigrants living abroad discover what patriotism, love of one's country and home, friends and family mean.

Emigration during the period 1989–2004 has changed irreversibly the economic, ethnic and cultural identity of Bulgaria. Often we think about emigrants in term of margins and periphery, with homeland as the core, centre, kernel. Perhaps we are approaching a postmodern transposition of centre and periphery that washes away the idea of only one stable focus. The periphery is centre, the centre is periphery. From the postmodern perspective, modernity was a continuation of the Enlightenment, striving for unity, universality, certainty, and holistic truths. These truths defined a widely-accepted boundary between what was the 'centre' or 'focus' of social existence and what was the 'margin' or 'periphery'. Beginning in the mid to late twentieth century, society became increasingly diverse, pluralistic, and fragmentary. A concern of postmodernism is exploring that fragmentation, and playfully undermining the rigid boundaries between 'centre' and 'margin'. The mass media, web and electronic fora and other forms of virtual cultural production, generate constant re-appropriation and re-contextualization of familiar cultural symbols and images, fundamentally shifting our experience away from 'reality', to 'hyperreality'.

If we adhere to the classical modern perspective, we will have a diaspora that retains its creative energy outside and is non-functional inside. We will have a community abroad strongly divided by all real and imagined boundaries. We will have a lonely and orphaned homeland, isolated and disconnected from the 'other homeland', that which is outside and abroad. Such a narrowly contained and centred homeland has a clear and oppressive future. If such a narrowly contained understanding of homeland is assumed, Bulgarians of the twenty-first century can only pessimistically foresee: an increasingly worsening demographic situation; the continuing flight and draining away of the young; a partial homecoming of emigrants at retirement age. Bulgaria may become, from this sad perspective, a European provincial region, which shall strongly resemble the Roman province of Thrace during the reign of Emperor Trajan and Emperor Claudius. In those times 'retired' legionaries were sent for a well-deserved repose to Bulgarian provinces, which was ironically referred to as 'The Valley of the Dying Elephants'.

References

Alexandrov, E. (1999), 'Bulgarian national policy and the program for Bulgarians abroad' (in Bulgarian), *Bulgaria Today*, **3**, 2 (47), 15-31 January. Retrieved 11 March 2005 from http://www.bulgaria.com/aba/index.html.

Gadzhev, I. (2004), *History of Bulgarian Emigration in USA, 1860-1944* (Sofia: Gutenberg).

Grant, L. (1996). *Juggernaut: Growth on a Finite Planet* (Santa Ana: Seven Oaks Press).

Kelbetcheva, E. (2003), *From Patriotism to Denationalization − the Bulgarian Emigration During the 20th Century,* American University in Bulgaria Database publication. Retrieved on 12 April 2004 from http://home.aubg.bg/faculty/evelina/webmaterials/emigration.doc.

Milanov, E. (2000), 'Local and ethnocultural Bulgarian communities abroad' (in Bulgarian) in *Aspects of the Ethnocultural Situation* (Sofia: Association ACCESS), 117−176.

National Institute of Statistics (2004), 'Statistics of Population'. Retrieved on 22 June 2004 from http://www.nsi.bg/Population/Population.htm.

OECD (Organization for Economic Cooperation and Development) (2001), *Trends in International Migration 2001, Continuous Reporting System on Migration,* Annual report. Retrieved on 22 August 2003 from http://www.oecd.org/dataoecd/21/15/2717624.pdf.

Population Reference Bureau (March 2004), 'Transitions in World Population', *Population Bulletin,* 59, 1. Retrieved on 2 February 2005 from http://www.prb.org/Template.cfm?Section=PRB&template=/ContentManagement/ContentDisplay.cfm&ContentID=11692.

Rangelova, R. and Vladimirova, K. (2004), 'New Bulgaria's Migration: scale, consequences and policy decisions' (Sofia: Institute of Economics Bulgarian Academy of Sciences and University for National and World Economy), *From the Conference de Bruxelles 5-7 May 2004*; Retrieved 22 June 2004, from http://www1.mshparis.fr/reseauemploi/BruxellesColloque/RossitsaBruxelles.html.

Salgado, S. (Photographer) (2000), Migrations: Humanity in Transition, and: Salgado, 2000. The Children: Refugees and Migrants. Retrieved on 30 October 2003 from http://www.amazon.co.uk/exec/obidos/ASIN/0893818917/fototapeta.

Standart News, Internet edition (2004), 'Three Billion Levs Emigrants' Money Circulating in Bulgaria', Thursday, 24 June. Retrieved on 30 June 2004 from http://www.standartnews.com/archive/2004/06/24/english/moneyt/index.htm.

Standart News. Internet edition (2004), 'Three Billion Levs Emigrants' Money Circulating in Bulgaria', Monday, 12 January. Retrieved on 11 June 2004 from http://www.standartnews.com/archive/2004/01/12/english/moneyt/index.htm.

Todorova, S. (2000), 'The Years of Emigration, or Why the West Is the Best for a Large Number of the Young Bulgarians', *NIE Magazine,* 9, 1. Retrieved on 11 October 2003 from http://members.tripod.com/~NIE_MONTHLY/nie9_00/mladej.html.

Trajkov, V. (1993), *History of Bulgarian Emigration to North America: from the beginning of the 19th century to the 1980s* (Sofia: University of Sofia Press).

World Data (2001), 'World Population Data Sheet of the Population Reference Bureau. Demographic Data and Estimates for the Countries and Regions of the World', (Washington: PRB).

Yanev, Y. and Pavlov, P. (2000), 'Worldwide Bulgaria', Sofia: Svetlostruj online publication. Retrieved on 11 May 2004 from http://www.aba.government.bg/bg/pages/Izsledvaniya/WorldBG.html.

Chapter 6

The Immigrating Russian:
The Bulgarian Case

Irina Chongarova

The Paisij Hilendarski University of Plovdiv, Bulgaria

Introduction

The Balkans is a region inhabited by diverse ethnic and religious communities. Such coexistence, combined with the economic backwardness of these communities, makes this region fertile ground for never-ending ethnic and/or religious conflicts. Bulgaria appears to be an island of peace against the turbulent background of the Balkans.

According to the last census from 1 March 2001, Bulgarian ethnicity accounted for 6,665,210 people and constituted 83.9 per cent of the country's population. In the last 8 years, the group's relative share in this population has gone down by 2 per cent, mainly due to emigration. The second largest ethnic group in Bulgaria is the ethnic community of the Turks. In the last 120 years the relative share of the Turks has been constant at about 10 per cent of the Bulgarian population. In the period 1880–1980 about 784,000 Turks emigrated from Bulgaria, and from 1989 to the present they were followed by a further 400,000. Today there are more than 746,000 Turks in Bulgaria who constitute 9.4 per cent of the population. The Gypsies form the third largest ethnic community at about 371,000, that is approximately 4.6 per cent of the population. The greater part of these are Roma. In the last eight years their number has grown by 53, 000 due to their high fertility and relatively low participation in the migration processes. (During the same period the number of Bulgarians decreased by 610,000, and the number of Turks decreased by 42,000). In recent years, a growth in the relative share of Bulgaria's total population has been observed for smaller ethnic groups such as Russians, Armenians, Jews, Greeks, Arabs, Albanians, Ukrainians, who also contribute to the ethno-cultural variety of the Bulgarian population. About 1.5 per cent of the population is from these groups.

The Russian ethnic group, including about 15,595 people (according to the census), is the largest in the category 'others'. Their appearance on Bulgarian territory was first registered in the Middle Ages, but their presence became more established after the Liberation from the Turkish yoke. In 1880, there were only 1,123 Russians in Bulgaria, but their number grew to 10,000 at the beginning of the twentieth century. In 1919, 29,000 (35,000 according to some sources) Russians settled in Bulgaria. The period from 1919 to the 1950s is regarded as the period of the first wave of Russian immigration to Bulgaria, although the first significant settlement of Russians dated as far back as the end of the seventeenth century, when a number of *staroobryadtsi* left Russia discontented with the reforms of Patriarch Nikon, as well as Don Cossacks. There are villages in the Silistra region (alongside the Danube) inhabited by descendants of the Cossacks who settled there as early as the seventeenth century. Post-1950s waves of immigration of the Russian ethnic group to Bulgaria are mainly explained by many mixed marriages with Bulgarians, and after 1989 by the settlement of Russians on the Black Sea coast, mostly in Varna and Burgas.

This chapter offers an analytical review of Russian immigration in Bulgaria for a period covering about 100 years: after the October Revolution of 1917 to the present. We analyse Russian migration on two planes, which we conditionally define as a vertical one – for example description and comparison of the separate waves of settlement of Russians in Bulgaria – and a horizontal one – comparison between the characteristic features of Russian emigration to Bulgaria and Russian emigration worldwide.

Even though Russian immigration in Bulgaria of the last few decades is only part of a more general process of mass emigration from Russia and the formation of a Russian diaspora, the Bulgarian aspect of the phenomenon has some unique features. This chapter discusses the unique features of Russian immigration in Bulgaria and explains the reasons for this specificity (on the horizontal and the vertical planes).

Documentation

Several approaches are explored in this chapter, depending on the period under examination and the type of materials analysed. The first wave of the Russian immigration in Bulgaria became a subject of attention for historians during the 1950s. A relatively closer examination of the first period is possible because of the availability of studies in this area already. The second, and especially the third waves could be thought of as economic migration. We can easily explain the dearth of studies of the latter: the processes involved are too 'hot', and there is no reason for either the immigrants or the institutions in Bulgaria (Bulgarian and Russian ones) to provide detailed statistical information and analysis. Therefore, official statistics, certain texts from electronic and conventional publications on Russian immigration in Bulgaria, and interviews with representatives of the second and third Russian emigration waves, serves as material for our study.

A significant part of the documentation regarding White Russian immigration in Bulgaria (the period 1920s-1950s) is found in Russia, because after the liquidation of the Russian emigration organizations in November 1944 all their records were confiscated by the political representatives of the Third Ukrainian Front. The Bulgarian archives keep only documents referring to the social, psychological, cultural and labour adaptation of the tens of thousands of refugees who emigrated after the October Revolution of 1917 and the first years of Soviet rule, and their contribution to Bulgarian culture, science and all areas of the socio-political and economic life in Bulgaria. A large part of these records is kept in the Central State Archives, which in the beginning of the 1990s accommodated the closed down

Central Archive of the Communist party. The Military Archives in Veliko Turnovo also has a rich documentation fund concerning this issue. One very serious attempt to systematize this archival documentation was the conference 'Bjalata emigratsija v Balgaria' (that is the White Immigration in Bulgaria) organized by the Bulgarian Academy of Science in Sofia in 1996, as well as its concomitant exhibition and catalogue (Kyoseva, 2002).

The First Wave of Russian Immigration to Bulgaria

According to United Nations data (United Nations, 2001), 1.6 million people left Russia after the Revolution. The process of emigration continued until the second half of 1920s, reaching 2.5 million people. At the horizontal plane, therefore, this could be thought of as two waves of Russian emigration: the first immediately after the October Revolution, and the second in the course of the decade following that. At the vertical plane however, because of the numbers involved and the distinctive nature of the experience of Russian emigrants in Bulgaria, the entire period from after the Revolution to the 1950s is generally thought of as the first wave of Russian immigration in Bulgaria.

Most of the political emigrants leaving after the Revolution found a home in the Czech Republic and Poland (about 1 million), in the USA (732,000), Germany (560,000), France (175,000), and Canada (about 100,000). A part of the White emigrants remained on the territory of the former Russian empire (the Baltic region and Besarabia). A big Russian colony was formed in Manchuria, where already before the Revolution about 200,000 Russians engaged in the construction and operation of the Chinese East Railway had settled. Compared to these figures, the number of Russian emigrants recorded for Bulgaria (about 35,000 civilian refugees and disarmed soldiers and officers from the army of General P.N. Vrangel) seems quite insignificant. We should take into account, however, that the overall number of the population of Bulgaria according to the census of 1920 was about 4,850,000 people.

The periodization and chronological framework of Russian immigration in Bulgaria of that first wave (vertically seen) can be correlated to the development of Bulgarian-Russian and Bulgarian-Soviet relations. In an in-depth study of Russian immigration during 1920-1950s, Kyoseva (2002) marks off four separate stages within the framework of this period:

1 The first stage of White immigration covers the period 1919–1923. The policy of the government towards Russian immigration was very inconsistent and contradictory. There was both a tolerant attitude towards certain layers and groups of refugees, and overt persecution and repression of some.

2 The chronological framework of the second stage is determined by the stagnation of Bulgarian-Soviet relations after the coup d'état of 9 June 1923, which lasted till 19 May 1934. The rule of the governments of the Democratic Accord in the period 1923–1930 was a 'golden age' for Russian refugees – in many respects Russians were the most favoured foreign element in the country.

This was an essential prerequisite for a bloom of Russian immigrant culture in Bulgaria as well, and brought Bulgaria considerably closer to Czechoslovakia, which secured the most favourable living conditions for Russian emigrants.

3   The third stage of that first period began with the setting up of Bulgarian-Soviet relations in July 1934, and ended 10 years later on 9 September 1944, when Soviet military units entered and stationed in Bulgaria. The Soviet legation played an essential role in the life of Russian emigrants by recruiting them for intelligence purposes, and plotting a number of provocations with the aim of spreading dissent amongst the emigrants.

4   The fourth stage began on 9 September 1944, and ended in the late 1950s. It was characterized by the Soviet presence in the country, and the policy of turning it into a satellite of the USSR. All Russian schools were closed down, the activities of the Russian immigration organizations were suspended, and their property was confiscated and given to pro-Soviet immigrant citizens in Bulgaria, who were made Soviet citizens. In an attempt to restore its demographic balance, which was disrupted during the War, the USSR granted Russian emigrants who did not cooperate with Nazi Germany Soviet citizenship, and after a filtration process admitted some of them on its territory. Thus, in the mid-fifties the Soviet authorities almost brought to an end the Russian immigration issue in Bulgaria. In September 1954 they allowed the new Soviet citizens to return to the USSR, and work at reclaiming its virgin lands. By the end of 1958 about 5,000 people, which was more than 90 per cent of all Soviet citizens in Bulgaria, left the country. In 1959, there remained about 7,500 'White immigrants' in Bulgaria, some of whom became Bulgarian citizens.

The early Russian emigration stages of the first wave (vertically seen), resulting from the October Revolution, had certain distinctive features. This was characterized by the Russian emigrants' unwillingness to integrate with the local population: they thought of themselves as defenders of the Russian language, Russian culture and mentality, and perceived their stay outside Russia as temporary and not long-lasting. Also of interest here is the acceptance of Russian immigrants in Bulgaria during this period. They were generally received sympathetically by the Bulgarian people and a great part of the Bulgarian governing and political elite, who recognized them as successors of the liberators of Bulgaria from the Ottoman yoke.

The later stages of the first wave, particularly the period following the end of the the Second World War till the late 1950s, was marked by the reshaping the world political map. The sovietization of East Europe and the formation of the socialist block led to the disappearance of the centres of Russian immigration in Berlin, Prague, Belgrade and Warsaw. Beyond the borders of the USSR there remained, according to different sources, about 2–3 million Russians, amongst them prisoners of war, 'Ostarbeiteren', voluntary and non-voluntary aides of the German occupants. Most of the Russians from that period headed to the New World: USA, Canada and Australia. Before the War, about 80 per cent of all Russian emigrants lived in Europe, after the War their number was reduced to 30 per cent.

The transformation of Bulgaria into a satellite of the Soviet Union, on the one hand brought about the repatriation of Russian emigrants, and on the other hand led to their migration to Western European countries and other continents.

The Second Wave of Russian Immigration to Bulgaria

The next and generally new wave of Russian emigration worldwide began in the late 1960s. From the horizontal perspective, this third wave of the Russian emigration falls within the time period of 1968–1985; from the vertical Bulgarian perspective this is thought of as the second wave of Russian immigration in Bulgaria. From the horizontal perspective, it is conditionally called *zastoinaja* (from the Russian word *zastoi* or stagnation, that is the time of the rule of Brezhnev). As far as the direction was the western countries, this emigration was primarily political. Dissidents, 'differently thinking' people, participants in movements to defend rights left or were expelled from the Soviet Union. In this period there also began a process of repatriation of Germans and Jews, and rejoining of Armenian families. Emigrants and repatriates found asylum in countries such as USA, Israel, Germany, Canada, and Australia. Though the repatriates were representatives of the ethnic minorities in Russia, everyone abroad recognized them as Russians.

The immigration of Russians in Bulgaria in this period (the second wave from a vertical perspective) however had an essentially different character from Russian emigration elsewhere. In the 1950s Bulgaria sent hundreds of male adolescents to Russia, who completed their higher education there or were educated in various political schools. After the official authorization of mixed marriages in 1957, many of them returned to Bulgaria together with their Russian wives. Also, thousands of Bulgarian workers went to work in Russia (especially great is the number of the Bulgarians who were engaged in the wood industry in Komi ASSR [Autonomous Soviet Socialist Republic]), married there and returned to Bulgaria (or stayed in Russia) with their wives and children.

It was mainly through marriage that some Russians emigrated to Bulgaria in this second wave.

The Third Wave of Russian Immigration in Bulgaria

The fourth wave of Russian emigrants from a horizontal perspective – which is in fact the third wave for Bulgaria, from a vertical perspective – started with the Perestroika and continues to this day. It is many-sided and varicoloured: involving scientists, businessmen, the jobless, and so on leaving Russia. The reasons for this are also various, but mostly they are of an economic nature.

This fourth wave (horizontally seen) is primarily emigration westwards, and not eastwards. According to the official statistics, there are 717,000 Russian emigrants in Germany, 228,000 in Israel, and just 270 in China (Zajonchkovskaya, 1999). In the early years of this period, the fourth emigration wave was of the ethnic type, as the motherland was left by repatriates: Germans, Jews, Greeks, Finns. Now their share in the overall number of Russian emigrants has been reduced. But the number of people leaving in search of employment and those accompanying repatriates is ever-growing.

The Russian emigrants of the first wave (from the horizontal perspective) aimed at keeping their language and culture. They understood their mission exactly as defenders of the Russian mentality, which they were to bring back to their motherland with their return. That is why their speech was characterized by the peculiarities of Russian language rules of nineteenth century, the speech usage of the 1920–1930s. The language of representatives of the second, third and fourth waves (still with the horizontal perspective) was strongly influenced by the language, culture and mentality of the receiving people, since they tried to integrate as soon as possible into the new society, where they intended to live and bring up their children. As compared to the first wave, which was characterized by anti-assimilative (conservative) behaviour, the subsequent waves bear the mark of strong assimilation, which has an effect on both the language and the culture of emigrant Russians. The influence of local culture and local language is evident.

Since the early 1980s we have also witnessed a growth of research interest (among neurologists, psychologists, ethno- and socio-linguists) in processes of attrition and their extreme manifestation, such as language loss. Researchers in this area have been attentive to the experience of emigrant Russians. Numerous studies have examined various aspects of the process of attrition: its psychological basis, its socio-cultural prerequisites, the structural factors of language alterations on different language levels. Study of immigrant Russian language is an integral part of studies of language contacts, bilingualism and other similar issues. Particularly significant here are works by Andrews (1998) in the context of USA and Protassova (1994, 1998) in the contexts of Finland, Germany and France. Understanding of the later waves of Russian emigration and emigrant-experience is more fruitfully undertaken at present in terms of such research, rather than in terms of political and social history.

With regard to the second and third waves (from a vertical perspective) of Russian immigrants in Bulgaria, such studies of language have only taken place recently (see Baranova, 2002; Derendji, 2000; Merakova, 2001. There is, in fact, a relative dearth of studies on the language of Russian immigrants in Bulgaria. For such research, one may find interesting linguistic material mainly in two types of sources: publications in Russian in the periodicals of the Russian clubs and associations in Bulgaria; and interviews with bearers of the Russian language among first- and second-generation Russian immigrants. I have recently conducted research based on such material.

The results of experiments conducted and observations made by me with regard to children from mixed Bulgarian-Russian families who become first-year students in the University of Plovdiv in the last three years (as a rule, they are children of first-generation Russian emigrants who have arrived to Bulgaria 20 years ago, + or −10 years), demonstrate language interference mainly at the lexico-semantic level and at the semantic-grammatical level. Within an error-analysis framework, such interference features are perceived as mistakes. Thus, several kinds of mistakes are observed in the language usage of informants. Many of these are due to borrowings from Bulgarian language into Russian speech, which in turn lead to a 'violation' of the established norms of usage in Bulgarian. Another feature observed is a deviation from the norms of the Russian language, as a result of generalizations based on the structural similarities between the Russian and Bulgarian languages. Most mistakes occur at the lexical level which is most accommodating of external influences. There is also interference at the phraseological level which is based on false associations, especially in phraseologisms with similar imagery. Inter-language homonymy and paronymy also create problems. In their interactions, as my observations show, bilinguals prioritize communicativeness and information over norms of usage in the Russian language.

Analysis of the Russian press in Bulgaria, mostly of rubrics related to the feedback from readers, such as legal consultations, questions to press editorial boards and so on, demonstrates that those who are arriving in Bulgaria are Russians at a retirement and pre-retirement age who decide to spend their old age in a house near the sea, in a wonderful climate, with low prices and the prospect of Bulgaria's entry soon into the European Union. Actually, choosing Bulgaria as a retirement destination is not limited to Russians. The Bulgarian press published the story of a Japanese family that settled in the Bulgarian village of Shipka.[1] This was followed by other Japanese persons settling in different Bulgarian villages. The price of real estate in Bulgaria (especially near the Black Sea) is growing by 30 per cent per year because of the great interest shown by foreigners. These include Russian emigrants from USA and Israel who prefer to spend their old age in a more peaceful place, which can provide them with a higher quality of life on the retirement pensions that they receive. A re-immigration is expected of the Bulgarians who emigrated abroad in the 1990s.

This fact, as well as the negative growth of the Bulgarian population, requires the Bulgarian state to develop an efficient immigration strategy urgently. As early as 2000 Germany became aware that its ageing population and falling birth rate would inevitably affect the economy adversely. Measures were therefore taken there to attract foreign specialists to work permanently in the country, and changes were made to its immigration laws. The Czech Republic, which in territorial terms is smaller than Bulgaria but has a population of over 10 million, successfully started a pilot project for a controlled attraction of specialists from abroad (initially from Bulgaria, Poland, and Kazakhstan) which would fill the growing gaps in its economy.

It is understandable, given current wages and the state of the economy, that Bulgaria is a desirable destination mainly to citizens from countries which are in a worse economic situation. It is natural for the ethnic Bulgarians from the areas of Bessarabia, Valachia, Banat to be excited by the prospect of living in a member state of the EU, which is also the land of their ancestry. There will no doubt be people from neighbouring countries like Macedonia and Albania who will consider emigration to Bulgaria seriously. The routine emigrant flows will not stop from the Near East, Central Asia and Northern Africa who hope some day to reach further west into Europe.

Another group which looks toward European Bulgaria is the Russians. In addition to the warm sea and the fresh fruits, they acquire safety, well-meaning and friendly people who are nice to converse with, a culture at the European level, an absence of alcoholics and bandits, a possibility for quick adaptation, an understandable language, low prices of real estate, predictable state politics and an inevitable joining

---

1 (http://sedmica.kazanlak.com/?p=view&id=1275 – accessed 31 October 2006.)

of the EU. According to Moscow emigration agencies, with $30,000 a Russian can not only purchase a family home in Bulgaria but also have enough left to start his own business there.

All these considerations mean that Bulgaria needs a state immigration strategy. The absence of serious and responsible solutions by the state can turn Bulgaria into a home for senior citizens – luxurious for the post-retirement immigrants but not for her own elderly inhabitants.

References

Andrews, D.R. (1998), *Sociocultural Perspective of Language Change in Diaspora. Soviet Immigrants in the United States* (Amsterdam/Philadelphia: John Benjamin's).

Baranova, A. (2002), 'Vlianie rodstvennosti russkogo I bolgarskogo jazykov na rodnuju rech russkih v Bolgarii' ('The Influence of the Similarities in Russian and Bulgarian Languages on the Speech of the Russians in Bulgaria') in *Problemy Jazyka Diaspory. Trudy po Slavjanskoj Philologii*. Lingvistika. Novaja serija, (Tartu: New Series of Perspectives of the Language of the Diaspora Works in Slavic Philology), Linguistics 47–54.

Derendji, N. (2000), 'Lexicalna interferentsija ot ruski ezik v rechta na besarabskite bulgari' ('Lexical Interference from Russian Language in the Speech of the Bulgarians from Bessarabia'), in *Proceedings of the International Conference in Sociolinguistics ISOLICO' 2000: Bilingualism and Diglossia*, 22–24 September 2000, (Sofia), 115–21.

Gardner, R.C., Lanonde, R.N., Moorcroft, R. and Evers, F.T. (1987), 'Second language attrition: the role of motivation and use', *Journal of Language and Social Phyhology*, **6**(1), 29–47.

Kouritzin, S.G. (1999), *Face(t)s of Language Loss* (London and Mahwah, N.J.: Lawrence Erlbaum).

Kyoseva, T. (2002), *Ruskata Emigratija v Bulgaria. (The Russian Immigration to Bulgaria)* (Sofia: International Center for Minorities Problems).

Merakova, E. (2001), 'Sledi ot ruskata fonetiko-gramatichna sistema varhu ezikovoto povedenie na ruskini, zhiveeshti v bulgarska ezikova sreda' ('Traces of the Russian Phonetics and Grammar System on the speech behavior of Russian women, living in Bulgarian Language Environment'), in *Proceedings of the International Conference in Sociolinguistics ISOLICO' 2000: Bilingualism and Diglossia*, 22–24 September 2000, (Sofia), 219–24.

Protassova, E. (1994), 'Finsko-russkij bilingvizm I russkij jazyk: Finskij Opyt. K probleme sushestvovanija russkogo jazyka kak rodnogo vne Rossii', ('Finnish-Russian bilingualism and Russian language: The experience of Finland. To the problem of existence of Russian as mother tongue outside of Russia'), *Slavjanovedenie 4, 44–52*.

Protassova, E. (1998), 'Osobennosti russkogo jazyka v Finljandii' (Peculiarities of Russian spoken in Finland'), *Rusistika Segodnja*, **3–4**, 202–209.

United Nations (2001), 'United Nations, Population Division, International migration from countries with economies in transition 1980-2000', Diskette Documentation. ESA/P/WP.166. 8 may 2001, quoted in Denisenko, M. 2001 *Emigraitsia iz Rossii po dannym zarubezhnoj statistiki.* (Emigration from Russia According to Foreign Statsistics) http://www.archipelag.ru/ru_mir/volni/4volna/denisenko/. Retrieved 13 March 2005.

Ushkalov, I. (2000), 'Intelectualnaja emigratsuaj I Bezopasnost', ('Intellectual Emigration and Security') in *Migratsija I Bezopasnost (Migration and Security in Russia).* Vitkovskaya, G. and Panarin, S. (eds.) (Moscow: Interdialect), 100–150.

Vendina, O.I. (2001), 'Russkie za rubezhami Rossii', ('Russians Beyond Russia'), *Geografia* 11–13. This is Available at http://geo.1september.ru/2001/13/8.htm.

Zajonchkovskaya, Zh., ed. (1999), *Migration in the CIS Countries, 1997–1998* (Geneva: IOM). [References here are to the two sections authored by the editor: 'Executive Summary', pp.15–21; and 'Russian Federation', pp.112–132].

PART II

AFRICA

Chapter 7

The Transformative Impact of Transfer Originating from Migration on Local Socio-Economic Dynamics

Taoufik Agoumy

Department of Geography, University Mohamed V – Agdal, Rabat, Morocco

Introduction

In the second half of the twentieth century we have witnessed large scale emigration from Morocco to Europe. This phenomenon has produced an extensive literature and heated debate about the relationship between international migration and development. I focus, in this chapter, on international emigration and its consequences on the urbanization process in the home country. First, I address the different stages of the migration process, then I underline the characteristics and causes of this phenomenon, and, lastly and more specifically, I analyse the direct impact of cash transfers on urbanization. Examples are mostly taken from northeast and south-west Morocco, which depend heavily on cash flow from migrants in Europe.

The emigration of Moroccans to Europe, and to a lesser extent to North America and the Gulf States, has profoundly amplified the process of urbanization in regions where advanced urbanization was under way, and has also triggered a new and unknown mechanism of urbanization in others. The transfer of hard currency by migrants whose origin is linked with the most remote countryside was, and still is, behind the diffusion of micro-urbanization.

International Migration of Moroccans

The Evolution of International Migration

a) History of International Migration

Due to its geographical configuration and history, Morocco has always maintained close relations with Sub-Saharan Africa, the Middle East, and Europe. Early migratory flows arose primarily from individual initiatives, essentially motivated by long distance trade. However, with the colonization of North Africa, particularly Algeria in the first half of the nineteenth century, the nature of Moroccan emigration underwent profound changes.

France, in search of an expanded work force, had started recruiting Moroccan workers at the end of the nineteenth century. The main region affected by this migration, which was seasonal at the outset, was the Eastern part of Rif Mountains and was directed towards Western Algeria, basically as a source of agricultural labour (Bonnet and Bossard, 1973, pp. 23−50; Murray, 1992). The other region affected by early international migration was the south-western part of the Atlas Mountains, for example the Souss region: here, the start of migration was linked with the recruitment of Moroccan troops during the First World War. This was the first time in modern history that Moroccans, in large numbers, experienced contact with European soil. Indeed, the Souss Region was to become the leader in international migration later. Migrations from these two regions were encouraged by the fact that both are mountainous and semi-arid, and *tamazigh* (for example, Berber language speaking).

After independence the seasonal migration that had been directed only to France underwent major changes; emigrants departed for longer periods and explored new European destinations. Hence, at the beginning of the 1960s and with strong economic growth in Europe, major migratory flows of unskilled workers took place, as they were recruited by France and, significantly, other Northern European countries such as, Germany, Belgium and Holland. This shift led to the signing of several agreements between Morocco and certain European countries (Germany, Belgium, France, and Holland) to lay down employment conditions and residency clauses. The most important waves of emigration occurred in the 1961−1973 period (INSEA survey). The rapid increase in this period can not be explained by economic reasons alone; it has to be put in the context of new family reunion policies adopted by some recipient countries.

The economic crisis of the 1970s in Europe triggered a transformation in patterns of Moroccan emigration. It provoked new policies to control work force settlement in Europe, coupled with programs aimed at encouraging immigrants to return to their country of origin. From mid-1970 the nature of Moroccan emigration changed drastically, and has been mainly characterized by family reunion movements, seasonal migration, and clandestine migration since.

In parallel with these flows of migrants to Europe, new western destinations such as Canada, USA and Australia have been selected by Moroccan emigrants, and indeed have gradually come to be regarded as more preferable. Interestingly, emigration to these new destinations can be categorized as a 'brain drain' phenomenon.

b) Recent Trend of International Migration
In the early 1990s international emigration affected some 1.5 million Moroccans, about 80 per cent of whom were established in Europe, 15 per cent in Arab countries, 4 per cent in North America, and the rest (1 per cent) in other countries (CERED, 1990). Today, 2,549,215 Moroccans live outside their country, of whom 82 per cent are to be found in the European Union (Fondation Hassan II, 2002). This scale of international emigration is unprecedented in Moroccan history. Presently, Moroccans constitute the largest non-European community in Belgium, Spain, and Italy, and France hosts a little more than one million Moroccan immigrants. France has been the traditional destination for Moroccan international emigration and still

holds the lion's share with 40 per cent of all Moroccan emigrants. In terms of share of emigrants, France is followed by Italy and Holland, respectively with 11.25 per cent and 10.8 per cent. With the exception of Algeria, Moroccan emigration to the Arab countries is as recent as that to North America. In contrast to the European Union, which 'permits' family reunion, the Gulf States, which do not, attract mainly migrant workers.

Table 7.1   Distribution of Moroccan emigrants by destination

Region or country	1990 (%)	2002 (figures)	2002 (%)
Europe	*80.30*	*2,182,800*	*85.62*
France	43.81	1,024,700	40.19
Holland	9.93	276,600	10.85
Belgium	9.28	214,800	8.42
Spain	5.37	222,900	8.74
United Kingdom (including Gibraltar)	1.41	21,100	0.82
Italy	5.23	287,000	11.25
Germany	4.53	99,000	3.88
Scandinavian countries	0.59	19,800	0.76
Switzerland	0.15	10,500	0.41
Arab Countries	*14.93*	*197,000*	*7.72*
Algeria	6.71	63,000	2.47
Libya	6.04	71,900	2.82
Saudi Arabia	0.74	23,000	0.9
Other Arab countries	1.45	39,100	1.53
North America	*4.37*	*159,300*	*6.24*
Canada	3.02	73,000	2.86
USA	1.34	85,000	3.33
Asian countries	*0.01*	*1,000*	*0.03*
Sub-Saharan Africa	*0.34*	*6,200*	*0.24*
Australia	*0.06*	*2,700*	*0.1*
Total	100	2,549,200	100

Sources: CERED and Fondation Hassan II pour les Marocains Résidents à l'Etranger; INSEE «Recensement de la Population: nationalité», résultat n° 197; OCDE, SOPEMI, 1990; Direction des Affaires Consulaires et Sociales, Ministère des Affaires Etrangères et de la Coopération.

The table above shows that the European share of Moroccan immigration is growing steadily despite new regulations and restrictions on migration. This has to do essentially with clandestine migration. Italy has more than doubled its share, from 5.23 per cent in 1990 to 11.25 per cent in 2002; and over the same period Spain's share went up from 5.37 per cent to 8.74 per cent. It should be stressed that both countries have fallen behind in putting into effect European Community regulations regarding immigration control.

The other noticeable change is the decrease in Moroccan emigration to the Arab countries. Although the Gulf States' share has improved despite the Gulf War, it is the Maghrebi recession which is responsible for the drop, from 14.93 per cent in 1990 to 7.72 per cent in 2002. Reduction in Moroccan emigration to Algeria is linked with internal political turmoil (civil war), in addition to poor relations with Morocco. Libya's economy also suffered greatly from the embargo in the 1990s, and therefore Libya did not hire additional work force. Another factor here is competition from immigrants coming into the country from neighbouring Egypt.

Table 7.2   Growth of Moroccan population in Europe (in thousands)

Year	France	Belgium	Holland	Germany	Italy	Spain	Scandinavia	Total
1968	84.2	21	12.6	18	NV	NV	NV	135.8
1975	260	65.9	33.2	25.7	NV	NV	3.1	387.9
1982	431.1	110	93.2	42.6	NV	30	4.8	7,11.7
1990	653	138.4	184	61.9	78	114	6.1	1,235.4
2002	1,024.7	214.8	276.6	99	287	222.9	19.8	2,144.8

Sources: CERED, 1990 and Fondation Hassan II des Marocains Résidents à l'Etranger, 2002.

Table 7.2 shows that Moroccan nationals in these seven European countries have increased by a factor of 12, the most dramatic increase being the one registered in Holland where the number has increased by a factor of 21. Spain and Italy, which have become the main destinations for Moroccan migrants during the last two decades, do not have reliable data before the 1980s. However, what the 1981 Spanish census suggests (30,000 migrants) seems quite plausible, but at the same time reveals that Spain has remained the main destination over the last two decades (with almost eight times more migrants in 2002 compared to 1982), due largely to the clandestine migration.

Characteristics of Moroccan Emigrants and their Transfer of Hard Currency

a) Demographic and Socio-Economic Characteristics of Moroccan Nationals in Europe
In the beginning, Moroccan international emigration had been limited to a few poor regions – essentially affecting rural areas and a poorly qualified labour force. This was particularly the case for the Souss and Rif regions, which are mountainous

in general, had an old sedentary peasantry, and experienced strong demographic pressure. Thereafter the phenomenon has encompassed other regions to reach the entire Moroccan countryside, with, in the final stage, urban areas suffering from intense rural-to-urban migration, endemic unemployment and significant under-employment. Generally speaking, Morocco was providing Europe with a flexible, cheap, and docile work force. Successive economic crises in Morocco have enticed young unemployed university degree holders and others (satellite television channels have been bringing home the 'European way of life' for over a decade) to migrate in search of a better life.

Thus, the available data showing the distribution of Moroccan nationals living outside the country indicate both population rejuvenation and an increase in the proportion of the female population in recent years.

b) Extensive Financial Flows
Today, it is acknowledged that hard currency transfers carried out by migrants surpass the tourism industry and phosphates export (the main mineral export of Morocco) revenues. But the actual volume of these transfers is not well-known because of the diversity of transfer practices carried out by migrants on the one hand, and the hidden channels of transfers on the other. However, nowadays, increasingly the majority of money transfers is done through official channels.

Table 7.3   Hard currency transfers by emigrants (in millions of Dirhams)

Selected year	Bank notes	Credit transfer	Transfers by post	Total
1970	74.0	35.5	207.5	317.0
1975	331.9	712.3	1,115.4	2,159.6
1980	208.6	2,000.8	1,938.2	4,147.6
1985	909.8	4,592.5	4,229.9	9,732.2
1990	1,568.9	11,706.9	3,261.4	16,537.2

Source: Foreign Exchange Bureau.

The volume of emigrants' transfers evidences an astonishing expansion since 1970, to makes an exceptional scale of contribution to the Moroccan economy in recent years. The comparison between emigrants' hard currency transfers and the revenues from phosphates export shows that the former is 3–4 times larger than the latter, and is around 1.5 times larger than that of tourism.

c) The Transfer of Hard Currency and their Home Impacts
The policy which sustained emigration in the 1960s was due to the fact that the Moroccan government wanted not only to improve the employment situation, but also to allow hard currency flow in the country. Paradoxically, emigrants who live in a precarious situation, for instance those hired on a temporary basis or without

employment contracts, are more likely to transfer their earnings because of the prospect of their returning home. In contrast, those with a regular position in their respective recipient countries are more reluctant to carry out these transfers. Because the latter group chose to live permanently in Europe (and, as result are more and more tempted to invest in their respective recipient countries), their transfers are irregular and less substantial.

The result of international migration is that it triggers and empowers rural-to-urban migration. Though international migration has been facilitated by the family reunion phenomenon abroad in recent years, it has nonetheless contributed to the upsurge of urbanization domestically. By sending money to their relatives who remain at home, emigrants abroad enable them to settle down in neighbouring or other distant cities.

The Impact of International Migration on Urbanization

Most of the studies which address the issue of the impact of international migration domestically have been focusing on its consequences within the rural areas, the main source of emigrants. Yet, emigration from towns has been growing steadily in recent years and has contributed significantly to recent emigration waves. The city is often considered as preferred place of residence in case of a prospective return home, whether temporary or final, even when the emigrant's origin is rural.

The Birth of the First Towns in the Rif

Both the Central Rif (al-Hoceima Province) and Eastern Rif (Nador Province) constitute important centres of work force emigration. The impressive scale of emigration from these areas, mostly of rural origin, has profoundly affected the whole region. With the exception of the Tangier Peninsula all the Rifi towns were the product of the Spanish protectorate, among them al-Hoceima and Nador.

The first evidence of change due to international emigration has been witnessed in the countryside where the weekly rural markets (*suqs*) were given some infrastructure by the state to follow up a massive investment in building by emigrants. Indeed, between 75 and 80 per cent of the dwellings were built by Moroccan emigrants in some cases.

a) The Growth of Towns in Place of Origin
The urbanization phenomenon can be divided into two types, macro and micro urbanization. Whereas the former is nurtured by international emigration and backed by diverse other sources, such as smuggling (with the neighbouring occupied city of Melillia) and cannabis trafficking activities, the latter is basically linked with international emigration combined with state efforts to equip small centres.

This is not the only explanation for the current urbanization. Another explanation is that the capital city, Nador has reached the saturation point, either in the city centre or in the periphery or by speculation on land (Berriane, Hopfinger and Tours, 1999). As a result, there has been a spill-over phenomenon of urbanization beyond the city limit of Nador, with the development of small towns which gave birth to what we call 'Greater Nador'. Small agglomerations such as Bni Ansar, Zeghanghan, Selouane, Al Aroui (now municipality) have almost developed from scratch and became urban centres. Even more recent and smaller entities like Kariat Arekmane, Taouima, Taourirt Boucetta constitute now a second generation of 'cities'.

b) The Extension of International Emigration Effects beyond the Place of Origin
Larger cities like Taza, Tangier, and Fez, in the periphery of Rif and Pre-Rif Mountains, that have not been greatly involved in international emigration, have taken advantage from the latter and have received part of the migrants' investments. In Taza (a city of 170,000 inhabitants according to the last census of 1994), for instance, the emigrants who chose to invest in the city constitute between 14 and 16 per cent of the active population, but their share in housing development was estimated at around 40 per cent, mostly in privately developed estates (Agoumy, 1982, pp. 95–104).

Tangier is the most attractive city for investments by Rifi international emigrants, and at the same time it also attracts emigrants' relatives who have remained in Morocco. The launching of a housing estate named 'Belgium' in 1969 marked the beginning of emigrants' investments in the city.

International Migration and Urbanization in the Rif Region

International emigration triggers or intensifies many flows of internal migration. Given that Rif emigrants of rural origin are inclined to invest in the real estate business and, at the same time, prone to transferring their families from the countryside to regional or extra-regional cities, their contribution to the urbanization process is boosted in regions where international emigration is of a large scale. The part of international emigration in urban growth has been constantly increasing and has been estimated to 26 per cent in the 1960s, 40 per cent in 1970s, 33 per cent in 1980s, and 45 per cent in the 1990s (CERED, 1993).

The tendencies to invest in the real estate business and to move families from the countryside to the city also apply to emigrants who departed through the family reunion process. Hence, a new and unrecorded itinerary in the process of rural-to-urban migration is taking shape which is worth outlining. This is no longer the classical rural-to-urban migration from the countryside to the city whatever its size, direct or indirect, but an abnormal itinerary in which rural-to-urban migration operates through international migration (Lepeltier, 1984, pp. 101–127).

Further, emigrants who return after a long or short stay in Europe usually do not consider return to the countryside, and prefer to move towards the city. Villages (douar) in these regions are more and more deserted. This is not specific to either the Rif region or the Souss region; this occurs wherever the majority of emigrants are of rural origin.

While emigration is motivated by the quest for recognition within the social group, the search for a better life, and the improvement of conditions for emigrants and their offspring, it also functions as a means to seek profitable investments. Therefore, the exacerbation of rural-to-urban migration by international emigration can only lead to expansion in the growth of cities and, moreover, trigger micro urbanization at some distance from the cities and/or in their peripheries.

Investments Confined in One Region, the Souss, Leads to Exacerbation of Urbanization

In contrast to the Rif region, the perception of emigrants' role in the urbanization process in the Souss region is relatively less visible. This is because this region has more economic opportunities than the Rif (sea fishing, tourism, industries, prosperous irrigated agricultural hinterland, important sea port activities). It is, therefore, difficult to detect and sort out the origin of investments occurring here, for example whether it comes from emigrants or from business or from other sources.

However it can be observed that, thanks to the variety of the above mentioned resources, international emigrants' transfers in this region remain, for a greater part, within the region of Souss. Extra-regional investments are reduced to a minimum. If emigrants from this region are attracted by some town or the other it is usually due to some allegiance to the 'native land'. Thus, the choice here is directed by 'affective' and 'socio-familial' motivations, deep-rooted before emigration took place, as well as by economic incentives. As a result, the Souss region combines two elements which explain an even greater degree of urbanization than the Rif, and again largely due to international emigration: economic richness and diversity on the one hand, and ethnic affiliation on the other.

Similar to the Rif region, several surveys in the Souss region have demonstrated that returning migrants prefer to settle in small or medium-sized towns. Among those, Biougra (initially the main regional rural weekly market (*suq*) in the Souss) belongs to the recent phase of urbanization (for example, after the 1970s). According to the 1960 census, the population of Biougra was estimated at 660 inhabitants. In 1971, it reached 1,353 (a growth rate of 105 per cent), in 1982 the centre became 'urban' with 2,460 people (a growth rate of 81.8 per cent), and in 1994 it counted 13,885 inhabitants (a growth rate of 464.4 per cent, or 17 per cent per year). In Biougra the urbanization process was the result of the joining of several villages to each other. The emigrants' investment in building activities in Biougra has attracted a massive immigration of work force, from the poorer Atlantic plains, Anti-Atlas, and High Atlas.

Conclusion

International emigration generates changes in society and within the regional space. These changes are particularly noticeable in rural areas, but also in the process of architectural transformations and modifications in the internal spatial organization of the dwellings in urban areas. The consequences of international emigration are not only due to hard currency transfers, but also to the ideas brought by emigrants. As years go by and under the influence of emigrants' experiences in Europe, a process of creation and restructuring is taking place. The emigrant does not perceive *things* and *reality* in the same way as they did in the past, but they do not renounce pre-migration values.

The investment in real estate business and the exacerbation of urbanization by migrants can be seen as a kind of revenge of the 'forgotten rural world', because of its lack of infrastructure, equipment, and so forth. Of course, the urbanization process is an irreversible phenomenon throughout the world, but in the case of Morocco the gap between urban and rural milieus is being filled by the migrants' initiatives that, at the same time, have largely stimulated the rural-to-urban migration. It is only recently, during the last decade or so, that several development programmes have been carried out specifically designed to equip the countryside and follow up this 'wild urbanization' phenomenon.

References

Agoumy, T. (1982), 'Emigration étrangère et profil commercial de Taza', *Revue de Géographie du Maroc*, **6**, 95–104.

Berriane, M. and Hopfinger, H. (1999), 'Nador, petite ville parmi les grandes', *Villes du Monde Arabe* Vol. 4 (Tours: URBAMA).

Bonnet, J. and Bossard, R. (1973), 'Aspects géographiques de l'émigration marocaine vers l'Europe', *Revue de Géographie du Maroc*, **23**, 5–50.

CERED [Centre d'Etudes et de Recherches Démographiques] (1990), *La migration internationale* (Rabat).

CERED (1993), Migration et urbanization au Maroc (Rabat).

'Direction de la Statistique' (2001), *Annuaire Statistiques du Maroc* (Rabat).

Fondation Hassan II des Marocains Résidents à l'Etranger (2000), *Marocains de l'extérieur* (Rabat).

Fondation Hassan II des Marocains Résidents à l'Etranger (January 2002), *La réglementation de la migration et la protection des migrants marocains* (Rabat).

INSEA [Institut National de la Statistique et de l'Economie Appliquée] (1989), 'Enquête Démographique Nationale à Passages Répétés 1986-88', in *Déplacements et Mouvements Migratoires de la Population au Maroc* (Rabat).

Lepeltier, F. (1984), 'Les investissements immobiliers des travailleurs migrants d'origine rurale dans la ville de Taza (Maroc)', *Etudes Méditerranéennes*, **6**, 101–127.

McMurray, D.A. (1992), 'The contemporary culture of Nador, Morocco, and the impact of international labor migration' (Unpublished Ph.D. dissertation, the University of Texas, Austin).

Troin, J.F. (1967), 'Le Nord-Est du Maroc: mise au point régionale', *Revue de Géographie du Maroc*, **12**, 5–41.

Chapter 8

'Economic Martyrs': Two Perspectives on 'Lahrig'

Taieb Belghazi

Literature and Cultural Studies, Mohammed V University, Rabat, Morocco

Introduction

This chapter discusses two representational modes of engagement with Moroccan and Sub-Saharan underground economic migration since the creation of the Schengen space in 1990. The first mode is deployed by the European Community and Spain on the one hand and by the Moroccan state on the other. This mode makes use of a discourse on underground economic migration that posits immigration as a danger to the security and cohesion of European societies and to the stability of the Moroccan nation, and justifies recourse to repressive institutional strategies to deal with it. It is reflective of a geopolitical vision that highlights the position of both European and Moroccan territory as the object of destabilizing forces that lie outside it. It constitutes a territorializing vision that appears to be at odds with the deterritorializing processes operative in a regional and global context where the denationalization of the economy prevails. This vision, the main objective of which is to reverse the flow of people, is overlooked in approaches that are celebratory of globalization where emphasis is laid on 'time space compression' (Harvey, 1989), the end of 'tyranny of geography' (Blainey, 1966), the move from a world that operates as an island to a world that functions as a cross-roads (Mlinar, 1992), and the logic of flows including the flows of people.

The second mode of representation of illegal migration discussed in this chapter is that of a new social movement mobilized by the families of the victims of underground economic migration and by human rights organization. Through 'The Association for the Defence of the Victims of Economic Migration', the truth of the security discourse wielded by the European states and the Moroccan state becomes a site of struggle and Lahrig as an event is re-narrativized and re-interpreted as the result of an injustice. Furthermore, the discourse of human rights is mobilized to point out the inconsistencies of both Moroccan and European policies and to establish a grass roots transnational solidarity against the securitization of the discourse on migration. The main issue here is the relation between the economic migrants' exit and their friends that transform it into 'voice'. On this reading, illegal migration becomes a mode of resistance rather than a crime; Lahrig, a means of economic survival for the illegal immigrants, becomes central to Morocco's and the region's dynamic of economic, social and political change.

But first, a few words about the phrase 'economic martyrs' and the word 'Lahrig' used in the title, and a general discussion of the phenomenon of Lahrig in the Moroccan context. The phrase 'economic martyr' has been used by a Moroccan candidate for clandestine immigration who has made several attempts to cross to Spain from Morocco via the Straits of Gibraltar to no avail: 'I've tried pateras on three occasions, was arrested once and got drowned twice while six of my companions died. But I'll try again. If I die, I am going to be an economic martyr. All this I do for my family.' (Veerman, 2002, p. 16.) The word martyr has an interesting resonance here, especially in that it is often used by Islamist movements in connection with Islamist suicidal bombers. On this understanding, illegal migration is perceived by those who undertake it as a legitimate cause that is worth dying for. In other words, it constitutes a mode of resistance to the deteriorating economic conditions in the home country's market, indicated by high rates of unemployment among other things.

The word 'Lahrig' is a Moroccan Arabic word which means burning. The word is used in connection with clandestine migrants who sometimes literally burn their ID cards as well as other state-attributed identity documents and enter illegally into Europe. A clandestine migrant is a 'harrag', a 'burner' of steps to social success. He/She burns with desire to reach Europe. There are various categories of burners: a) those who have entered illegally into the host countries and who have no proper documentation that entitles them to reside there; b) those who have entered legally into host countries and who have decided to stay beyond their institutionally ratified period; c) those who work underground during a legal stay; d) those who engage in employment other than the one authorized by their work permit; e) inactive migrants who accompany the above categories.

This chapter focuses on a group of illegal migrants or burners who belong to Morocco and some Sub-Saharan African countries, highly mediatized in recent years, who try to cross the straits of Gibraltar to reach Spain on board of 'pateras' or small fishing boats, called by both the Moroccan and the Spanish press: 'boats of death', 'boats of shame', 'pateras of despair', 'floating tombs', and so on. A number of the passengers of those boats meet their death by drowning and become the subject of much publicity in the Spanish and the Moroccan press. Most often the press gives statistics of these 'non-identity' people arrested by Spanish and Moroccan border patrols. Reports on the number of illegal immigrants arrested or found dead on Spanish and Moroccan coasts highlight the non-identity status of the 'harragas' and enables the construction of their existence as a threat to the security of both Morocco and the EU and a crucial element in international politics captured rhetorically in slogans repeated ad-nauseum in European intergovernmental meetings: 'strategies for an international migration regime', 'global migration management', and so on.

Part I

Despite the fact that Morocco is a source of illegal migration, that a large number of its nationals are legal or illegal immigrants in Europe, and that it is placed in an unequal relationship with Spain and Europe as a country in the Developing World, it appropriates the security discourse on illegal migration deployed by European powers, and implements the policing strategies dictated by these powers, regarding both Moroccan and Sub-Saharan candidates for illegal migration.

Thus, the Moroccan state makes the 'harrag' into the object of representational essentializing or what Arjun Appadurai calls 'metonymic freezing'. The harrag's ambivalent position between being and non-being, 'neither a citizen nor a stranger' (Bourdieu, 1991, p. 9), is given a name/attribute – a harrag – and his/her unmapped itinerant existence is mapped onto the sea and the Spanish and Moroccan coasts. Thus, in the campaign to stop irregular migration from Morocco, television stations broadcast adverts showing a small boat close to a score of corpses. This conveys the picture of a subject literally at sea.

The harrag operates as the object of the security discourse of European Community powers where a clear distinction is made between Europe's inside and its outside. As Anderson has pointed out, this inside as defined by the 1985 Single European Act, and developed in detail by the '1992 programme' insists on

> the four freedoms agreed in principle by the member states with the signing of the Treaty of Rome – freedom of movement of persons, of goods, services and capital. Inter alia, this required the dismantling of the non-tariff barriers to trade embedded in health, safety and industrial standards, professional and trade qualifications, descriptions of goods and administrative procedures (Anderson, 1996, p. 184).

The outside of the European Community is clearly marked by the frontier that operates effectively in the original sense of the term; that is to say, as 'the zone in which one faced the enemy' (Anderson,1996, p. 9). Keen to construct an imagined cultural identity, European states insist on the inviolability of their frontiers since as Stallybrass and White point out, 'Cultural identity is inseparable from limits, it is always a boundary phenomenon and its order is always constructed around the figures of territorial edge' (Stallybrass and White (1988, p. 8). Multicultural agreements such as the Schengen Accords and the other transnational initiatives derived from the Working Group on Immigration constitute procedures aimed at the policing of Europe's external borders and reaffirming Europe's separate and homogeneous identity.

The territorial element centred on borders becomes a crucial element in forging a racialized European identity. A whole range of agencies was set up to ensure the realization of 'inviolable' borders: Ad Hoc Group Migration, clearing centres on asylum and on border crossing (Centre for Information, Discussion, and Exchange for Asylum (CIREA), Centre for Information, Discussion and Exchange on the Crossing of Frontiers and Immigration (CIREFI), and so on). Many of these agencies are secret and contrary to so called democratic systems of accountability (Morrison and Grosland, 2001).

It should be pointed out that it is the creation of a European space of free circulation in 1985, on the model of the Schengen Accords that gave impetus to the establishment of a vast administrative and police arsenal for the closure of European borders. As Mitchell and Russell point out:

The creation of the Single Market has meant that the issues of immigration and asylum are now transnational European problems. Although the Single European act allows for the free mobility of labour only for those holding full citizenship of a EU member state and for the free movement of individuals of those who are either citizens or who are legally resident non-EU nationals, in a situation in which border controls are being progressively reduced, the restriction on the cross-EU mobility of 'illegals' becomes impossible to enforce. It is for this reason that the immigration policy of any single EU member state is now of direct immediate interest to others within the EU (Mitchell and Russell, 1996, p. 55).

The Schengen model has continued to be used as a basis for European unique politics that hierarchized different world territories. A case in point is the document submitted by the Austrian presidency of the European Union entitled 'Strategy Document on the policy of the European Union with respect to migrations and asylum' in the summer-autumn 1998 (CKA-27-ASIM 170, 1 July 1998). The document divides the world into four clearly demarcated concentric circles. Each circle consists of countries that are assigned a particular function within the overall strategy of ensuring the inviolability of the European Union borders. The first circle consists of states which have adhered to the Schengen Accords and which implement the restrictive measures agreed within its framework whose aim is to control access of foreigners to their territories. The second circle consists of neighbouring countries that pursue the same visa policy and control of borders as that of the EU countries. These countries will eventually join the Schengen club. The third circle consists of ex-Soviet Union countries, North Africa and Turkey. The function assigned to them is to control the transit of illegal immigrants through their soil and to act as a 'cordon sanitaire' for Europe. The fourth circle consists of countries of the Middle East, China, and Sub-Saharan Africa whose role is to ensure that the local populations stay in place.

One consequence of this concentric spatial politics is to reify identity by mapping it onto territory. On this construction, Morocco belongs to the third circle. It is located on the outside of the Schengen club, is perceived as a source of illegal migration and constitutes, therefore, a threat to the security of Europe, and assigned the role of combating illegal immigrants, both Moroccan and Sub-Saharans, who use its territory to cross to Europe. It is interesting to note that the Moroccan state, despite its insistence on the need to adopt a global approach to immigration, appears to securitize its own discourse on immigration with respect to its own nationals and to Sub-Saharan immigrants.

We can then speak of continuity between Morocco on the one hand and Spain and the European Union on the other hand with respect to discourse on illegal immigration. But this discourse is also marked by contradictions and discontinuities, closely bound up with economic and political interests, and is operative within a particular historical context. This is why, although clandestine migration existed before the 1980s it is only in recent years that it has been pushed to the forefront of North-South relations. Moreover, despite the fact that, as Marfleet tells us: '[n]umbers of refugees in countries in the Third World are vastly greater than those which have caused refugee 'panics' in Europe and North America in the 1990s' (Marfleet, 1998,

p. 74), Western media give more coverage to illegal immigration from the South, including Morocco.

In Morocco, clandestine migration or Lahrig could be traced back to the period of the protectorate when French entrepreneurs organized it to make up for the shortage in work force. Thus, as Khachani (2003) points out, 75 per cent of the Moroccan labour force working in France in 1950 was composed of clandestine migrants. However, this illegal migration was tolerated because it satisfied the needs of the French economy. Now, the situation is different. Illegal migration from Morocco is not limited to France; it concerns other countries such as Spain and Italy, traditionally known as migration countries. It is perceived as a threat to French and European economy and a threat to social stability.

It should be pointed out that Moroccan illegal migration is less important than the Asian or East European one and that clandestine migration to Spain via ports and airports constitutes 85 per cent of the overall Moroccan clandestine migration. Although clandestine migration into Spain via the Gibraltar Straits is only 15 per cent of the overall number of illegal emigrants (Khachani, 2003, p. 3), it is the latter type of clandestine migration that is given more focus by the Spanish and the European governments, that gets more coverage in Spanish and Moroccan papers and that has gained more prominence in Moroccan policies with its Northern neighbour. This may be explained by the tragic deaths of a huge number of Moroccans in their attempts to cross about 15 km that separate Morocco and Spain on board small boats or pateras.

The following table provided by the Spanish Interior and cited by Belguendouz (2002, p. 44) highlights the increase in the number of tragic death between 1999 and 2000:

Table 8.1   Wrecks of pateras that occurred near Spanish coasts

	1999	2000
Number of Shipwrecks	30	54
Persons who disappeared	23	47
Corpses recovered	29	55
Shipwrecked saved	387	1,037

This table reflects the fact that increasing numbers of Moroccans who are lured by the European Eldorado are opting for the risky sea route on board flimsy boats because less risky possibilities simply do not exist for them. This situation enables various representational strategies on Lahrig: the first one is deployed by the Spanish State and the European Union. It consists in constructing the clandestine emigrants as statistical objects to give some objective support to the various measures taken by Spain and the EU to render access to Europe from the South more difficult. Repeatedly and throughout the year, the Spanish authorities announce arrests of candidates for illegal emigration and display the corpses of drowned harragas on television. These repeated announcements convey the image of huge numbers of Moroccans leaving their country and invading Spain. The effect of this is sometimes to drive some commentators to exaggerate the number of clandestine and legal emigrants from the Maghreb. Thus, Pierre Veerman (June 2002: 1, 16–17) in an article on Maghrebean migration to Europe asserts: 'To this day, the Maghreb's population is 70 million inhabitants; and it is likely that 10 to 15 million Maghrebeans reside in Europe. The ratio for Morocco is 30 million inhabitants, 5 to 7 million of which [sic] live abroad; 100 000 to 200 000 departures each year feed this flow' (Veerman, 2002, p. 1). But as Belguendouz points out: 'There are about 2.5 million Moroccans living abroad, 80 per cent of which [sic] in Europe, 13.5 per cent in Arab countries, 5.5 per cent in North America (Canada and the USA), 1 per cent in the other countries, mainly in Sub-Saharan Africa' (Belguendouz, 2002, p. 44).

The exaggeration and the repeated citing of the figures by North European powers, especially Spain, is mobilized within the framework of a 'security logic'. The repetition and the exaggeration of such figures enable the discursive construction of migration into a threefold danger as it represents a threat to the welfare system, to the public order, and to the cultural identity of the nation and of Europe. This construction involves monitoring of records, engagement with statistical correlations of heterogeneous elements liable to produce illegal migration, and the mobilization of institutions such as the IGC (the Intergovernmental Committee on Migration), a small elitist, informal forum of the members for the exchange of information and the planning of solutions on migration, and the European Action plan on Morocco. Moreover, the deployment of a particular form of knowledge about Lahrig centred on statistics fabricates the latter as a continuing threat to the Spanish nation and to European stability. Thus, the illegal emigrant operates both as a non-entity, a non-being, who is reconfigured as a combination of factors and as a concrete individual to be watched, arrested and sent back home with a fine (300 euros) that the Moroccan Government has to pay.

In this construction, Lahrig is aligned with drugs trafficking and with terrorism and is criminalized in the same way as the latter. As Bigo points out:

> Indeed, not everyone confounds terrorists and immigrants. But a grid of reading asserts itself and enables movement from one label to another without giving the impression that one changes the subject: a conversation that begins on drugs ends naturally on terrorism, asylum seekers, the youth of poor neighbourhoods. It follows one cannot think of the fight on terrorism without reference to the fight against drugs and illegal immigration a (and vice versa) (Bigo, 1996, p. 9).

This mode of representation of illegal migration that links it to terrorism, and so on, is reflected in the manner it is policed. Thus, its control is done in collaboration with the control of drugs, terrorism, and so on. In other words, as Bigo observes:

> Policing is done henceforth through networks: networks of administration where customs, offices of immigration, consulates in charge of the issuing of visas, and even private companies of transport or private companies of surveillance join national police; networks of computer information effected through the setting up of national or European files concerning those who are wanted, those who have disappeared, those banned of residence

or expelled ... networks of liaison officers sent abroad to represent the administration and to allow information exchange, semantic networks through which are elaborated new doctrines and new conceptions concerning conflicts and a political violence (Bigo, 1996, p. 9).

A process of spill-over is at work between the various domains where concepts, modes of operation, and personnel circulate. Everyone deemed to be associated with illegal migration is made to pay, including the families of the victims who have to pay a huge sum of money to recover the corpse of one of their members. The construction of illegal migration as a threat has enabled Spain and the EU to securitize the issue, and to invalidate UN conventions that protect the rights of migrants who break immigration laws to seek asylum in another country (Article 31 of the Geneva Convention) through the adoption of conventions that criminalize such acts, such as the Smuggling Protocol of the 2000 UN Convention on Transnational Organised Crime, which states unequivocally that the 'migrant' should not be viewed as a blameless victim but, rather, as partly complicit in the act of 'illegal migration.' In the current European context, Article 13 of the Universal Declaration of Human Rights, that states that 'each person is entitled to choose his residence and move freely inside a state ... Each person has the right to leave any country including his/her own and to return there', is obsolete.

Spain's and Europe's discursive construction of illegal migration has also provided an ideological cover for the devising of very sophisticated border control systems. One such system is the High Tech Integral System for the Surveillance of the Straits (SIVE), which allows the frontier police to watch any vessel, however small, at any time of night or day. The Surveillance System for the Straits comprises a high-tech surveillance system capable of monitoring a 115-km stretch of coastline (details at http://pajol.eu.org/article626.html). Various inter-European state accords also work to ensure the closure of Spanish borders. Thus, the application convention of the Schengen Accords signed on 19 June 1990 harmonizes the control at external borders through the installation of a uniform visa throughout the territory of Schengen signatories. This is supported by the creation of an automatic police data file, the Schengen Information System, a Europe-wide database to monitor criminals and illegal immigrants, which facilitates the tracking of 'unwanted immigrants' from their first attempt to pass through a border, and prevents them from trying again at another frontier. The Treaty of Maastricht signed on 7 February 1992 had been the occasion for the adoption of the Europol Convention on European police cooperation, and the Eurodac Convention that puts in place a finger print system for asylum seekers. The arsenal of measures adopted by European countries established a closed-door policy towards immigrants. As Marfleet points out, the construction of this cordon sanitaire is 'less a response to requests for asylum than a key aspect of efforts to make a new pan-European identity' (Marfleet (1998, p. 82).

One effect of this policy is that it drives prospective immigrants to risk their lives to gain access to their European Eldorado and to put them at the mercy of a harsh underground economy. As Reyneri puts it:

A formal closed door policy towards immigrants, justified by high domestic unemployment, coupled with a sizeable unauthorised inflows attracted by the underground economy, the lack of a policy of integration coupled with a strong exploitation and stigmatisation of migrant workers employed in the black labour market: this mix is causing more and more vicious effects. Interrupting this cycle is not at all an easy task, but the easy solution of tightening the border controls is without doubt destined to fail (Reyneri (2003, p. 19).

As I pointed out earlier, Morocco has accepted the policing role assigned to it by the European Community. 'The National Strategy for the Fight against Illegal Immigration' is continuous with Europe's strategies of securitizing the issue of immigration. This strategy, set up in 2003, consists of an institutional structure in charge of the control of illegal immigration: 'The Direction of Migration and the Surveillance of Borders' and 'Law 02-03', concerning the stay of foreigners in the Kingdom, was published in the Official Bulletin on 13 November 2003. The Direction of Migration consists of seven regional delegations: Tangiers, Tétouan, Al-Hoceima, Nador, Oujda, Larache Layoun as well as local committees in the other regions of Morocco.

The rationale behind the division of Morocco into regions is to ensure an effective control and surveillance of illegal immigrants who use these regions as places of transit. Law 02–03, prepared by the Ministry of the Interior and adopted by parliament alongside the law on terrorism, falls within this security logic. As Belguendouz points out, its main aim is 'to legalise the expulsion of Sub-Saharan immigrants, to permit the withdrawal of residence permits from those who hold them and to endow Moroccan authorities with judicial instruments that allow an authoritarian and repressive management of everything relating to migration' (Belguendouz, 2003, pp. 33–34). Furthermore, it enables Morocco to comply with the recommendations of the European Community that urge it to stop Sub-Saharan illegal immigrants from entering Spain. Such compliance has always been at the heart of Moroccan policy. This is corroborated by the following statement made by the following statement made by the Moroccan Minister of Interior in front of a French delegation of MPs and cited by Belguendouz:

> The main objective of Morocco consists in being closely associated with Europe's immigration policy after the establishment of Schengen space. Morocco is, in effect, conscious of the community of values of the two parties and of the mutual interests to be defended. At the level of the Mediterranean, we are, because of our geographical position and our economic, cultural and social links, full partners of European security ... [D]efense of European security could only be efficient if Morocco makes its contribution (Belguendouz, 2003, pp. 51–52).

It should be noted, however, that there is a contradiction between this law and the EU recommendations on the one hand, and the International Convention on the protection of the rights of all migrant workers and their families on the other. This convention puts on an equal footing both nationals and non-nationals and establishes as its main objective the suppression of exploitative treatment of migrants including the illegal ones. Furthermore, Law 02–03 is at odds with the Association Agreement between Morocco and the European Union signed on 2 February 1996 that insists among other things on 'the respect of democratic principles and fundamental human rights as proclaimed by the Universal Declaration of Human Rights'. Thus, both

Morocco and Europe are at one in going against their commitments in the area of human rights, especially when immigrants are concerned. Article 39 of Law 02–03 bears this out. It states that Moroccan authorities are entitled to drive out of the country foreigners staying in Morocco legally if they deem them to be a threat to national security.

In line with the repressive strategies of this law on migration and the recommendations of the European Community, Morocco proceeds to regular arrests and trials of Sub-Saharan illegal immigrants. The latter, who seek refuge in hiding places like the forest of Belyounech near Tétouan or the forest of Gourougou in Nador, are subjected to regular attacks by police mounted troops assisted by helicopter flying squads. The Sub-Saharan immigrants are the object of ill-treatment by these forces which have, on a number of occasions, used violence and confiscated food and clothes donated by Immigration and Human Rights NGOs.

The ill-treatment of Sub-Saharan immigrants seems to enjoy an ideological cover in Moroccan media that help racialize the issue. The media usually lay emphasis on the statistical importance of these immigrants and occlude the human tragedies that may have motivated the departures from their home countries. Thus, the Moroccan media speak of 'the proliferation of clandestine Sub-Saharans', ask questions about the ways in which they manage to reach 'our' borders, talk about the problems caused to Morocco's 'national security' by the arrival of the 'huge numbers' of illegal immigrants and the damage done to Morocco's image as a 'good European partner' by this 'Sub-Saharan invasion'.

However, the line Moroccan media adopts with respect to Sub-Saharan immigration is at odds with the rhetoric it deploys in its treatment of Moroccan illegal migration. In the latter case, emphasis is laid on human tragedy and the need for the European Community to think of global solutions to the problem of illegal migration and to help Morocco deal with the push-factors that drive Moroccans out of their country, especially the intolerable economic conditions they endure. On this reading, Moroccan harragas appear to be victims of an unjust economic system and of colonial legacy but are treated differently by the Moroccan press that falls prey to the same racialized security logic that underpins the EU discourse on migration.

It should be noted that, keen to conform to the EU recommendations on illegal immigrations, the Moroccan security also submits harragas of Moroccan origin to a repressive regime. The Moroccans who are arrested at Moroccan borders or on board the pateras in the straits of Gibraltar are tried, fined, and sentenced to prison terms that may be of several years. Morocco has entered the second phase of MEDA agreements and signed the National Index Programme for the period 2002–2004 on 24 January 2002 that contains a project for the control of borders. The overall aims of this project are the following:

- the application of Moroccan law on borders;
- the equipment and training of Moroccan border police;
- effective application of the securitization of borders with a better integration of the national system police;
- deployment of techniques of analysis of risks on a wide scale;
- adequate organization of green and maritime borders;

- the gradual establishment at border crossing points of an effective and speedy control system.

It is clear that this programme applies to both Moroccan and Sub-Saharan harragas. For Morocco, the main thing is to meet the expectations of the EU on the issue of immigration. For this reason, it has accepted to be assessed according to the following performance indicators decided by the EU:

- the number of arrested traffickers;
- efficiency of coordination between the legislations of various countries involved;
- improvement of the fluidity of flow of legal border-crossers.

By accepting the European scheme on immigration, Morocco has confirmed its dependent position in the current global set up. But Lahrig is not merely the reflection of an unequal world system, it is also, I would argue, the occasion for the emergence of a new social movement that has an increasing influence on the political context in Moroccan and in the Mediterranean region.

Part II

The question that needs to be asked here is whether exit or Lahrig and 'voice', as encapsulated in actions or 'L'Association des Familles et des Amis des Victimes de L'Emigration Clandestine' and other immigration organizations and networks, have a rival or a complementary relationship with one another.

Before answering this question, it is important to give an overview of the model presented by A. Hirschman in *Exit, Voice and Loyalty* (1970). The basic concepts of this model are, as the title suggests, loyalty, exit and voice. They are defined as different responses of members of an organization to the degradation of the quality of goods they purchase or the services and advantages they benefit from.

Loyalty refers to the position of a consumer or a member of an organization who, faced with the deterioration of the quality of products and the defects of the structure, remains faithful to the label or to the organization.

Defection or exit is the simple fact of leaving generally because one thinks another enterprise or another structure offers a product, a service or an advantage of higher quality. Therefore, to defect consists in dissociating oneself from a person or an organization. It is generally premised on the availability of choices, the existence of rivals and of well-organized markets. Sometimes, defection may lead the organization that knows some problems to improve its performances.

Voice is the most direct means used to alert the organization to improve the degrading qualities of the services. It consists in complaining or orchestrating the complaint or the protest. It is operative in situations where defection is impossible, costly, or traumatizing.

The basic idea defended by Hirschman is that there is no pre-established link between exit and voice, though most often they tend to neutralize one another.

Indeed, one effect of exit – leaving Morocco – is to undermine voice – participation in political action aimed at bringing about change. However when exit is posited as an achievable aim, despite the sacrifices it may involve, it tends to facilitate voice, in the sense of political expression, and assertive mobilization. The reason for this is that the people concerned with Lahrig feel that getting involved in political action involves fewer risks than the clandestine crossing of borders. While it is correct to say that exit has tended to counter voice, especially when it deprives the latter of its most eloquent members, Lahrig has, at times enabled voice.

The diversity of situations that can be accounted for by this rudimentary model is remarkable. It can be mobilized to give a partial explanation of the absence of a strong social movement in the Moroccan countryside. Exit deprives the geographic unit left behind (the countryside) of its most dynamic activist elements. Rural exodus weakens voice and delays rural reform. Rural exodus was limited at the beginning of the twentieth century when the country used to be the centre of social contestation. In the 1970s it was an important element in the explosion of the urban population. The most dynamic elements – youth and women – left it for the city. Rural exodus concerns mainly the age group between 10 and 24. During the 1980s, defection movement reached extraordinary proportions. According to the results of *L'Enquete nationale demographique a passage repetes de 1986-8* (Direction de la statistique (1993)), some 374,000 left rural areas to live in the city in 1987.

Following this model, it is possible to wonder if emigration or Lahrig has affected voice not only in the country but also in the city. This is, at least, the view expressed by a high-level Moroccan security official to the Spanish newspaper El Pais cited by Belguendouz: 'I am going to be sincere with you. Each Moroccan emigrant who crosses the Straits constitutes one mouth less to nourish, it is one less discontent, and if things go well, she is soon going to be a source for the entry of money that can provide for her family members who have stayed back home' (Belguendouz, 2002, p. 110). Migration to Europe had affected the development of social protest movements before the 1990s. The situation has however changed drastically after the setting up of the Schengen space, which has made migration more costly and more risky.

However, this pendulum movement – the more defection there is the less voice there is – is not enough to explain the complexity of the real. In fact, this model can be complicated by the fact that the observation of the evolution of concrete society and of the political system in action shows that the possibility of exit or Lahrig can consolidate voice. Voice and defection can then be considered as two democratic rights that can be broadened or restrained at the same time. This positive dialectic between multiplication of possibilities of exit and the increased tendency to protest relies on a more complicated picture than that of the pendulum picture. In fact, the acquired liberty to leave opens up new horizons for individuals. With more latitude, they become aware of the wide range of options open to them and are inclined to exploit them. We can then put forward the idea that the development of options of exit can on occasions be combined with more participation and protest and not less.

In recent years, an important social movement has developed in connection with the issue of illegal immigration. It consists of organizations, informal networks, human rights organizations, some of which are based in Morocco and Sub-Saharan countries, but some of which operate in European countries. One of the most active organizations is the Association of the Families and Friends of the Victims of Clandestine Migration.[1] It was formed on 2 August 2001. This association has managed to create a large network of solidarity with clandestine immigrants and has helped re-narrativise clandestine immigration by turning the illegal immigrants' exit into voice. This has been achieved through the organization of events around clandestine migration. The association also gives moral and material support to the Sub-Saharan clandestine immigrants. Because it aims to bring about economic survival for the immigrants in their home countries, it benefits from occasional support from the European Commission and from the Moroccan Government who try to co-opt it. This support has conferred on the movement the characteristic of a consensus movement. But this does not mean it has been co-opted. On the contrary, this consensual dimension has helped exacerbate the discontinuities in the European Union's and the Moroccan state's discourse on illegal migration and undermine the securitizing discourse discussed earlier. Thus, in light of the foregoing remarks, we can say that there exists a complimentarity between the association's voice and the harrag's exit.

References

Anderson, M. (1996), *Frontiers, Territory and State Formation in the Modern World* (Cambridge: Polity Press).

Belguendouz, A. (2002), *L'ahrig du Maroc l'Espagne et l'UE. Plus d'Europe Securitaire* (Kénitra: Boukili Editions).

Belguendouz, A. (2003), 'Le Maroc Non Africain Gendarmed Europe', (Sale: Imprimerie Beni Snassen).

Bigo, D. (1996 October), 'Securite, Immigration et controle local, l'archipel des polices' [Electronic Version], www.monde–diplomatique.fr, p.9.

Blainey, G. (1966), *The Tyranny of Distance* (Melbourne: Sun Books).

Bourdieu, P. (1991), *L'immigration ou le paradoxe de l'alterite* (Bruxelles: de Boeck, Saya).

Harvey, D. (1989), *The Condition of Postmodernity* (Oxford: Blackwell).

Hirschman, A. (1970), *Exit, Loyalty, Voice* (Cambridge, Mass.: Harvard University Press).

Jenkins, B. and Sofos, S.A., eds. (1996), *Nation and Identity in Contemporary Europe* (London: Routledge).

Khachani, M. (2003), 'La Migration Clandestine au Marco'. Retrieved 3 June 2004 from http://www.generiques.org/migrations_marocaines/interventions/khachani_ariticle.pdf.

Kiely, R. and Marfeet, P., eds. (1998), *Globalisation and the Third World* (London: Routledge).

---

1 These are some internet sites where information about the Association of the Families and Friends of the Victims of Clandestine Migration could be found: http://www.afvic.fr; http://www.december18.net/web/contact/start.php?lang=EN&menuID=52. http://www.banlieues.be/themes/textes.asp?theme=6&texte=216.

L'Enquete nationale demographique a passage repetes de 1986–8. (Rabat: Direction de la statistique).

Marfleet, P. (1998), 'Migration and the Refugee Experience' in *Globalisation and the Third World*. Kiely, R. and Marfeet, P. (eds.), 67–89.

Mitchell, M. and Russell, D. (1996), 'Immigration, Citizenship and the Nation-State in the New Europe' in Jenkins and Sofos (eds.) (1996), 54–80.

Mlinar, Z. (1992), *Globalisation and Territorial Identities* (Aldershot: Averbury).

Morrison, J. and Grosland, B. (2001), 'New Issues in Refugee Research: The Trafficking and Smuggling of Refugees: The End Game in European Asylum Policy', Working Paper 39. Can be found at http://www.jha.ac/articles/u039.pdf, 1–88.

Reyneri, E. (2003), 'Illegal Immigration and the Underground Economy [Electronic version]'. Centre Paper 68. http://www.anu.edu.au/NEC/reyneri.pdf (1–21), retrieved 6 March 2005.

Stallybrass, P. and White, A. (1988), *The Politics of Transgression* (London: Methuen).

Veerman, P. (June 2002), 'En Guise d'Avenir, l'Exil: Les Marocains rêvent d'Europe', *Le Monde Diplomatique*, 1(16–17).

Chapter 9

The Cultural Consequences of Economic Migration from Nigeria to the West

Efurosibina Adegbija

Modern Languages and Linguistics, Ilorin University, Nigeria

Our age is one of transition, and transitions are often difficult and painful. In the territories of the former Soviet Union, in the increasing Western European federalism, … also in the struggles of peoples in North and South America, in the debates about multicultural accommodations in the new-world "receiving" societies (Canada, Australia, the USA) – we see contexts in flux, identities up for re-negotiation, languages in contact or conflict, "small" cultures attempting to resist larger ones, and so on (Edwards, 2001, p. 48).

Introduction

As of 1998, 20,000 Nigerian academics were employed in the United States, 700 Ghanaian physicians were practicing there also, and more than 300 Ethiopian physicians were working in Chicago, USA, alone. According to research reports, Africa loses 20,000 intellectuals yearly. A new report broadcast by the BBC says Africa has lost one-third of skilled professionals in recent decades, costing the continent $4 billion dollars a year to replace them with expatriates from the West. By contrast, rich countries like the US save $26 billion dollars, which should have been spent to train 130,000 highly qualified physicians (Ashanafi, 2002). South Africa and Nigeria are the biggest losers of professionals to the West.

Speaking to the Nigerian Academy of Science, Peter Okebukola, the Nigerian Universities Commission Executive Secretary, quoted the 2000 and 2002 World Science Report as concluding that most of the countries of Africa represent perhaps the most scientifically backward countries in the world in terms of basic input and output (see Okebukola, 2004). Africa's input seems negligible when examined by such science and technology indicators as enrolment in secondary schools, vocational and tertiary institutions; national spending on education in these areas; national research and development spending by universities and other institutions; and institutional infrastructure. Okebukola conjectured that Nigeria occupies about the top 25 per cent within this ignoble group. Patents, scientific publications and major technological innovations are painfully thin on the ground. Quoting statistics from the National Manpower Board, he said Nigeria would need for the petroleum sector alone 6,200 petroleum engineers, geologists, civil engineers, technicians over the next 5 years. There are 2,300 of them in the country at the moment. For the agricultural sector, Nigeria needs 28,200 agronomists and other specialists over the same 5-year period. At the moment, some 12,950 of them exist. It is from such a perspective of lack of experts that the economic migration from Nigeria to the West must be understood. My focus in this chapter, however, is not on the economic consequences, grave as these may be, but on the cultural consequences.

Immigration is a powerful force in generating subcultures in societies. When groups of different cultural backgrounds come into contact in one society, but are prevented from fully assimilating into the national culture, ethnically based subcultures tend to develop (Taylor, 2001, p. 402, citing Yinger, 1960). Most writers, despite different theoretical positions, agree that subcultures tend to arise in societies characterized by 'social differentiation based on factors such as age, gender, ethnicity, class or other structural variables, combined with social, political, and/or economic marginality which promote different patterns of interaction and collective identity' (Taylor, 2001, p. 403). Migration usually brings members of two divergent cultures together. When two divergent cultures come into contact either willingly or by force, it is natural for an imprint of one form or the other to be left in the lives of those involved on both sides.

In the case of economic brain drain, the normal pattern is for large numbers of professionals, sometimes non-professionals, to move from their homelands to the developed countries with the primary goal of earning a better living or securing a better and more hopeful future. This chapter investigates the cultural consequences of this kind of economic migration. Specifically, it focuses on Nigerians that have emigrated to the West mainly for economic reasons. Methods adopted for the study include observation of a sample of those involved; informal interviews with those who have emigrated and those who desire to but have not been able to do so; and an analysis of information collected through a general email questionnaire (see Appendix at the end of this chapter) on the cultural consequences of economic migration, completed by some of the emigrants.

Definitions of Culture

Culture is viewed from many different angles. Asked for the definition of culture, one of the respondents to the questionnaire who had lived almost 7 years away from Nigeria, with intermittent visits, says culture is: 'The range of activities and beliefs of a set of people at a given point in time.' He identifies the following as its main ingredients: 'religious beliefs, social activities, language, norms, outlook to life, and so on'. Another person defines culture as: 'The way of life of people, traditional values of the people, beliefs and norms of the people,' adding, 'It is passed on from one generation to another'. Offering an omnibus definition, she says: 'Culture can therefore be defined as the total way of life, traditional values, beliefs and norms of people in a particular community that is passed on from generation to generation'. Yet another person defines culture as the 'belief, tradition, rules, norms, outlook, way of dressing by which a people are characterized'. Some of these lay definitions of culture are certainly very close to some of the academic definitions found in the literature. One view is that: 'culture is a wider umbrella under which we find marriage, naming habit, music, dance and a host of other ways of looking at life generally' (Omotoye, 2002, p. 16). Tyler (1871), cited in Jekayinfa (2002, p. 42), defines culture as: 'a configuration of institutions and modes of life', 'that complex whole which includes knowledge, beliefs, art, morals, law, custom and any other capabilities and habits acquired by man as a member of society'. Forster (1962), also cited in Jekayinfa (2002, p. 420), defines culture as: 'the common learned way of life shared by members of society, consisting of the totality of facts, techniques, social institutions, attitudes, beliefs, motivations and systems of values of a group'. Obayan (2003, p. 15) provides what she calls a simple definition of culture as follows: 'things a stranger needs to know when in a new place. Culture consists of all of those things that people have learned to do, believe, value and enjoy in their history. It is the ideals, beliefs, customs, skills, tools, and institutions into which each member of a society is born'. She also cites Pederson (1991) who defines culture as: 'a shared pattern of learned behavior that is transmitted to others in a group'.

All accept that culture is learned through personal interaction, emulation, and socialization and through deliberate indoctrination or teaching. It is dynamic and transmittable from one generation to another. Learning culture is a life-long process, beginning from the cradle and going on to the grave (Jekayinfa, 2002). The content and substance of culture varies from society to society, but the fact that man is able to adapt to learning a new culture makes it possible for those who emigrate to a new society to be able to learn a new culture easily. Taylor (2001, p. 401), for instance, emphasizes 'the diversity of norms and values to be found in heterogeneous societies'.

A Broad Typology of Culture

Culture may be divided into several broad categories, including the following: the core and peripheral; and the material and non-material.

A propos core and peripheral culture:

- The core culture refers to basic or central cultural categories. It would involve aspects of culture such as ethnicity, language, customs, traditions, superstitions, beliefs and values. We are influenced by all of these in our personality make up, our philosophical leanings, and in our response to culture and contribution to the production of culture.
- The peripheral culture refers to the non-basic, outer-edge cultural categories. It would include aspects such as age, gender, interests, educational background, lifestyles, socio-economic status, residential area, and so on which constitute the total make up of a person as a member of a particular community or society. These also influence us in different complex and dynamic ways.

Material and non-material culture would include the above two categories. Many aspects of the material and non-material culture belong to the core cultural category. Specifically:

- Material culture refers to the products of man's industry or works of art. Elements like carving, food, paintings, dress, pottery, weapons, cloths, houses, and so on, which are peculiar from one society to another, and which are made from the materials available from the surrounding or environment, are involved. They meet certain crucial needs within the particular culture concerned.

- Non-material culture refers to abstract entities that are not palpable but nevertheless are important in defining a particular group of people, as well as individuals within the group, and in charting their cultural and personality identity. This would include language, dance, music, religion, morals and values relating to issues such as freedom, love, beauty, justice, accountability, honesty, and beliefs.

Each person grows up being socialized or acculturated into a particular cultural mode. Contact with another culture, therefore, often implies a need for re-socialization into a different cultural mode, the addition of new cultural paraphernalia, the subtraction of old ones or the blending of the old with the new. It is a recreation, reconstitution, remodeling or renegotiation of the cultural essence. Such exposure of a person to a new culture can thus result in that person becoming clothed in a new cultural garb, in a hybridization or overlap of culture and the sharing of cultural identity and essence. The more the number of new and different cultural groups to which a person is exposed, the greater will tend to be overlap and the demands for re-socialization, re-acculturation, intercultural tact, and the recreation of a new or metamorphosed cultural essence. Table 9.1 illustrates some of the elements involved in our broad and somewhat fluid classification of culture:

Table 9.1   Some broad classifications of culture

Material culture	Core culture	Peripheral culture	Non-material culture
Products of man's industry: • works of art, • carving, food, • dress, clothes, • pots, paintings, • weapons, • houses	• ethnicity • language • customs • traditions • superstitions • music • beliefs • values	• Age • Gender • Interest • Educational background • Lifestyles • Socio-economic status • Residential area	Abstract entities: • language • dance • religion • literature • the media • morals and values such as freedom, justice, honesty, love, beauty • names and naming practices

Factors that Influence Culture

Several factors exert influence on our perception of culture and the creation of our cultural essence, multicultural reality and identity. These include parental upbringing and socialization; social, political, economic, historical and religious context; type of educational exposure; place of residence; social network; individual and societal attitudes. These interact with cognitive, affective and connative, observation and introspection; exposure to and contact with other cultural, ethnic and linguistic groups; and the idiosyncratic sub-culture to which one is exposed when participating in a larger culture, physical environment, and so on. All these crucially impact our cultural constitution, influence us in one-way rather than another and affect the understanding, perception and imbibing or nurturing of our cultural essence. Figure 9.1 illustrates some of the factors that affect the nurturing of our cultural essence.

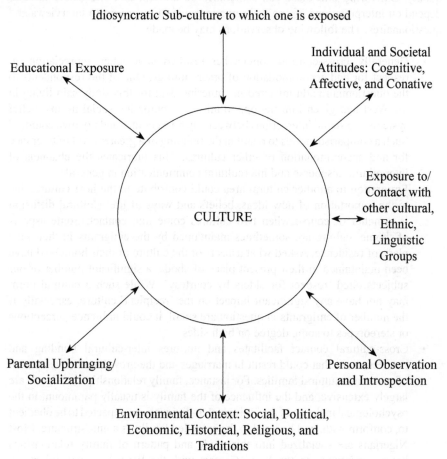

Idiosyncratic Sub-culture to which one is exposed

Educational Exposure

Individual and Societal Attitudes: Cognitive, Affective, and Conative

CULTURE

Exposure to/ Contact with other cultural, Ethnic, Linguistic Groups

Parental Upbringing/ Socialization

Personal Observation and Introspection

Environmental Context: Social, Political, Economic, Historical, Religious, and Traditions

Figure 9.1   Cultural influences – some predisposing factors

Types of Cultural Influence

Cultural influences naturally impact on and through a person's discourse patterns,philosophy of life, outlook and personality. Because, as indicated above, several aspects of culture can be material or non-material, and several factors predispose us to being influenced in one-way rather than another, the influence of a particular culture on a person can also be material or non-material, overt or non-overt, determinate or indeterminate.

Nigerians who have emigrated to the West reflect these different kinds of cultural influences upon their lives. While the material consequence of culture is visible and palpable, the non-material is often invisible and of a somewhat ethereal quality. Burrowing into these can sometimes be difficult and one would have to depend on interpretations of one's observations and of responses to interviews and questionnaires. The following observations may be made:

- Generally, cross-cultural contact has resulted in a better appreciation of, respect for and accommodation of other cultures. One of the respondents to the questionnaire administered in gathering data for this study said living in the West had given him the opportunity of 'comparing social norms, belief systems and social interactions between my host country and my own country.' Such a comparison tends to result in the building of a greater level of tolerance for and accommodation of other cultures. This lubricates the channels of intercultural discourse and intercultural communication in general.
- Emigration to another cultural area could contribute to the host culture, due to the importation of new ideas, beliefs and ways of life. Cultural diffusion is a matter of course when two cultures come into contact. Some aspects of 'home' culture are sometimes maintained by the emigrants in their new place of residence. Asked what aspects of the culture of their homeland have been maintained in their present place of abode, a significant number of our subjects cited 'respect for elders by courtesy'. While such a cultural norm may not have any significant impact on the 'recipient' culture, especially if the number of emigrants in question are small, it could influence perceptions or stereotypes to some degree on both sides.
- Cross-cultural contact facilitates and nurtures inter-cultural bonding and connectedness that could result in marriages and the growth and development of new cross-cultural families. For instance, family relationships in Nigeria are largely extensive, and the influence of the family is usually paramount in the psychological make up of the individual. Individuals are expected to be obedient to, conform with, and be loyal to the extended family as a unit/structure. Most Nigerians are socialized into this mode and pattern of family relationships before emigrating to the West. Contact with the West, however, initiates a different kind of awareness of family relationships, where the emphasis is on the individual as an independent, sophisticated and self-sufficient entity (cf. Idowu, 1985; Obayan, 2003, p. 18). The complexion and dynamics involved in these different socialization patterns could sometimes generate cultural and identity clashes – for example, between the desire to be an individual (as is the case in the West) and the need to still associate with the extended family (as is the case in Nigeria). The cultural centripetal and centrifugal loyalty pulls exerted by these two forces can sometimes trigger off a divided personality, a dual personality, a confused personality, or what one might refer to as a chameleon-like cultural personality – behaving in Nigeria as Nigerians want you to behave and in England as the English want you to behave.

Before Migration

As regards the factors that play a role in predisposing thoughts, shaping attitudes, decision-making and internal preparation before and leading up to emigrating, the following observations can be made:

- Admiration for target culture: One predisposing factor seems to be that all those who migrate to the West have some prior measure of admiration for the target culture as being able to offer something better than is available in their own culture. At least economically, it is expected that life as a émigré will offer better opportunities. This admiration normally results in finding out more information about the target culture from individuals, books, the media; getting interested in issues relating to the target culture; and conducting informal interviews with those who have already emigrated to the target culture. Those contemplating emigrating often listen to the radio or watch television programmes of the target culture, gather information on different aspects of life therein, and engage in a form of self-education as prior preparation for emigrating. Applications for employment or placement of one kind or the other may also commence at this early stage.
- The media discourse on a particular country often plays a major role in decisions to emigrate or not to emigrate. Reportage on various manifestations of political and social stability and instability have a significant impact on choice of target culture and decisions to emigrate. Similarly, media images and narratives suggestive of affluence and freedom in a particular cultural context, often works as a powerful incentive for emigration in that direction. This also depends on what kind of media access is available in the home culture, and what sort of media coverage occurs therein.
- Interpersonal interactions and contacts with those already in the target culture also form part of the cultural discourse and knowledge that play a dominant role in final decisions to emigrate. Some of the interpersonal contacts may indeed be the support anchor for settling down in the host community immediately after emigration. Interpersonal contacts serve as an information source, sometimes as an initial economic support group, as a guide on social and cultural life in the host community, and as counsellor to the new emigrant.
- By the time a decision has been made, some form of vicarious experiencing of the target culture has commenced. Intense anticipation of when the emigration will finally occur begins. Expectations about what life would be like when emigration has occurred begin. Initial cognitive acceptance of aspects of the culture in the new place of abode takes place. This tends to engender a generally positive attitudinal posture and positive discourse orientation with regard to the target culture. Some of these initial feelings, hunches, orientations, internalizations and vicarious enjoyments and experiences of aspects of the target culture are eventually either confirmed or disconfirmed, reinforced or jettisoned, after emigration has actually occurred (see Heffernan, 1996, p. 189 for a similar observation).

After Migration

A lot hinges on the predisposing factors and attitudes that become perceptually salient in the emigrant after arrival at the recipient country and culture. The following observations are relevant here:

- Cultural diffusion often results in cultural rejuvenation, rebirth or regeneration. Asked the question: 'What aspects of the culture of your present place of abode would you say have influenced you most?', emphasis was laid by respondents on the simplicity and 'less expensive nature of most ceremonies like naming a child, weddings, burials, and so on'. In essence, a new order of difference in thinking of re-socialization, which can impact on attitudes of the home culture upon return begins to emerge and crystallize. Ashanafi (2002) observes, relevantly in this context, that the movement of intellectuals like university lecturers and researchers from one national setting to another, ranging from permanent relocation to short-term visits or exchange programs, facilitates the dissemination of knowledge and the broadening of cultural horizons.
- Language loss is another major cultural casualty of economic migration to the West. As Gunnarsson rightly points out:

> Language is an important part of the national culture and identity, and language patterns at different levels are closely related to cultural patterns and to societal conditions. It has long been known that vocabulary reflects society. Less well-known is the fact that textual patterns are culture-specific (Gunnarsson, 1996, p. 157).

While some of those who have migrated succeed in keeping their home languages with its different textual patterns, others do not. Some do not even want to. Instead, they want to pick up the accent of the language of those in their new place of residence. In many cases, the children of the emigrants do not speak the home or native languages of their parents. Gunnarson (1996, p. 158) also points out findings that reveal that our knowledge of native text patterns is consciously transferred to texts written in a foreign language, observing that studies have shown 'how culture-bound our text expectations and interpretations are'. The languages of the West seem to predominate in some of the homes of the emigrants, but some continue to speak the home language even in the foreign land. In homes where the languages of the West are dominant, Western language patterns, modes of interpretations and cultural nuances are also more evident. In such homes, there is little intergenerational transmission of language, culture, textual modes and discourse patterns. The converse of language loss, language gain or addition, may also occur after migration. The new circumstances usually constitute a high and strong motivation for learning the language in the new place of abode. In most instances where there is some measure of prior competence in the language of the larger community, enhanced competence in the complex nuances, discourse modes and patterns and peculiar idiosyncrasies and cultural secrets of the language tends to occur after emigration has taken place.

- Economic migration often results in the migration of expertise intellect and the consequent loss of the intellectual culture that emigrants have exported. For instance, Philip Emeagwali, reported to be one of the most searched person on the Internet worldwide, is a Nigerian. His intellectual culture is being used to enrich the West while his own country stays intellectually impoverished. When Nigeria had to launch a satellite in September 2003, 15 Nigerian scientists had to be trained abroad, whereas there are many Nigerian space scientists in the West. The same is true of other professionals that have emigrated to the West. This shift of intellectual capital from Nigeria to the West is a major loss attributable to economic migration to the West. Francis Obikwelu, a naturalized Portuguese citizen born in Nigeria, is reported to have won second place in the 200 meters race of the 24th European championships. It is only the second silver medal for Portugal in such a game and the best-ever result for a Portuguese athlete in short distance races (Malheirs, 2004). The home cultural values sometimes become extinct, when faced with competition from the culture of the West, particularly among the offspring of emigrants.

- Reinterpretation of different aspects of one's home culture tends to occur – with regard to, for example, a taboo like not looking straight in the eye of an elder, giving out something using the left hand, greeting patterns, and prior value placed on cultural institutions like marriage, kinship, naming ceremonies, and other cultural festivals. One respondent said, for instance: 'in my homeland, we seem to spend a lot of time and precious resources on ceremonies. I would not say I have missed this aspect of my culture. I really love being away from such practices – at least for the time being!' So, the time and expenses invested on such festivals and ceremonies are now reinterpreted as an unnecessary waste by many of the emigrants. In Nigeria, taboos have a strong impact on the thinking patterns of individuals. As Obayan observes:

certain behavior modes are often prescribed or proscribed by the culture. Among most cultural groups in Nigeria, for example, it is rude to look at an older person directly in the eye even during conversation. One finds that the younger person usually has eyelids averted during the conversation. On the contrary, however, in the West, not maintaining eye-contact during conversation may be interpreted to mean having something to hide, or having a low self-esteem (Obayan (2003, p. 19).

Such cultural taboos tend to be easily reinterpreted after migration. Thus, even though after migration, many migrants still value cultural aspects of life like respect for elders, they tend to easily jettison or devalue aspects of culture that are freshly reinterpreted as unnecessary.

- A reengineered mindset, belief and attitude system is naturally evident in most Nigerians that have emigrated to the West. Naming and marriage practices, values, norms and previous modes of entertainment tend to be devalued or completely obliterated. Most cherish and adore the freedom in their new society. In fact, one respondent, when asked 'what kind of adjustment problems have you had since you came to your present place of abode', responded, 'None really. This is a free society by and large'. In the West, they have the freedom to take decisions, behave and act as they think proper without having to consult father, mother, or any member of the extended family, even for what would be regarded as crucial family decisions like getting married across racial divides, for instance. They are free to take such a decision without feeling that anyone would encroach on their prerogatives to make up their minds in their own way. On the contrary, in Nigeria, marriage is essentially a family affair, and quite often, family sanction and support is required before any marriage can be regarded, from the cultural perspective at least, as having been properly contracted. Asked what kind of adjustment problems frequently occur when the home land is visited, one respondent answered: 'I find it a bit difficult adjusting to the demands on my resources: time, money, need to attend elaborate ceremonies, and so on'. What such a response indicates is that the mindset has been reengineered to value time, a culturally important aspect of life in the West, to downgrade traditional ceremonies, culturally important in Nigeria, and to manage money as something personal, rather than something meant for taking care of the entire extended family, which is the attitude and mindset of most Nigerians still living in Nigeria.

• A reorientation of attributive patterns also generally tends to occur after emigration. While, in Nigeria, causality, particularly in negative episodes, generally tends to be other-directed, or attributed to divine (usually devilish) motifs (for example calamities, deaths, failure, and so on), in the West there seems to be a greater emphasis on taking individual responsibility for events in life instead of looking for a scapegoat for one's misfortunes and mishaps. In the Nigerian cultural context, causality is externally attributed, particularly if the event is negative. It is easy to accuse the enemy, some person, object or event, a witch, as being responsible. In many Nigerian obituaries, for instance, the enemy is sometimes accused as having 'done their worst', by bringing about the death of the deceased, while succour is taken in God, who has the responsibility for the future happenings of the family concerned.

• The loss of the connection, bonding and embeddedness provided by the extended family context in Nigeria often tends to result in a devaluation or reinterpretation of domestic and personal ethical norms. Family and marriage norms upheld by some of the emigrants often tend to align with those of the new place of abode, thus resulting in attitudes to family moral values, divorce, and so on which would be taboo in Nigeria. Thus, in the new place of residence, married couples seem to be freer to divorce and marry someone else when the relationship is unsatisfactory. It is reported that one in every four marriages ends in divorce in the United Kingdom, whereas in Nigeria, divorce is still somewhat a taboo, particularly in traditional communities. Whereas the cultural attitude in the West seems to be that divorce is a personal affair, the attitude in Nigeria is that it is a family and societal affair. Many emigrants tend to lean more towards the former attitude. In Nigeria, culturally idiosyncratic behaviour such as men plaiting their hair, wearing earrings, ladies smoking, unconventional modes of dressing are in fact quite common in certain circles. Some of such practices have become permissible or, rather, are tolerated. Respect for elders among the youth seems to be waning in cities like Lagos, which are frequented by migrants. Contract marriages for convenience, without investigation of family compatibility and background, have become commonplace also in cities. Human trafficking especially of young girls who are then lured into prostitution once abroad has also become a major concern for Nigeria. Some commentators have attributed this to the impact of Western liberalism. It has been so serious that many of the Islamic northern states, after declaring the Sharia law within their states, have devised punishment even for adultery in addition to effecting the Constitutional provisions on prostitution. Although prostitution is illegal throughout the country, the law enforcement agencies tend to turn a blind eye. This cultural attitude to sex and sexuality is completely different from that in many Western countries where prostitution has, in fact, been legalized and prostitutes are recognized as other legal workers who must pay tax to the government.

• As a result of all the above, a hybrid culture sometimes develops, which is neither totally the home culture, nor that of the recipient culture. In some cases, émigrés succeed in blending with the host culture and with their own culture when they pay visits to their homeland. One respondent, when asked how he would characterize himself presently in terms of cultural identity, responded: 'Honestly, I do not have any cultural identity crisis as such. I practice the best of my own culture as well as the best of the culture in my temporary place of abode'. This kind of attitude, no doubt, is bound to result in cultural enrichment and a broadened cultural horizon that would be good for both the recipient culture and the home culture of the emigrant.

Conclusion

Heterogeneity is the distinguishing feature of culture in today's world. Heterogeneous populations result in great numbers of subcultures, created in a dynamic mix and combination of age, gender, ethnicity, class, religion, place of residence, and region. These create 'a diversity of subcultures in modern, industrialized and complex societies, all with somewhat differing norms and expectations of conduct .... Individuals may also participate in several subcultures simultaneously and to different degrees' (see Taylor, 2001, p. 402).

Migration results in 'new paths of shared identity and global circulation' (Malheirs, 2004) as it brings different cultures into contact. Thus, instead of thinking of identity as an accomplished fact, represented by the new cultural practices, 'identity should be thought of as a "production", which is never complete, always in process, and always constituted within, not outside, representation'. As Hall rightly points out, this view problematizes the very authority and authenticity of the term 'cultural identity' (Hall, 1990, p. 22), cited in Omoniyi (2003, p. 365). The question then arises as to what the authentic cultural identity is, especially with regard to the changes that characterize globalization (Omoniyi, 2003, p. 365). Economic migration tends to hasten globalization and the cultural influences it engenders.

One culture's meat can be another's poison. When two cultures come into contact in the lives of people, there is usually some form of mutual renegotiation of cultural essence, mutual gain and loss, both at the individual and societal levels. Contact of two cultures puts both on the cultural credit and deficit account at one and the same time. This is often true societally and individually. The cultural ledger book may go completely in the red when the presence of a particular cultural group becomes a menace to the dominant community. Balancing the cultural account to maintain some level of mutual renegotiation of cultural essence is where the challenge lies, and it is a big one because devising a coordinated effort to direct cross-cultural pollination is not an easy task.

References

Adegbija, E. (2004), *Multilingualism: A Nigerian Case Study* (Trenton, N.J.: Africa World Press).

Akanji, M.A., ed. (2002), *Leading Issues in General Studies: Humanities and Social Sciences* (Ilorin: General Studies Division).

Ashanafi, G. (November 2002), 'Causes and Consequences of Brain Drain – How Long should Africa Tolerate This?'. http://chora.vurtualave.net/brain-drain.7.htm.

Edwards, J.R. (2001), 'Multiculturalism and Language', *Concise Encyclopedia of Sociolinguistics* (Amsterdam: Elservier), 48–50.

Forster, E.B. (1962). 'A Historical Study of Psychiartric Practice in Ghana'. *Ghana Medical Journal* 1. 15–18.

Gunnarsson, B.-L. (1996), 'Text, Discourse Community and Culture: A Social Constructive View of Texts from Different Cultures' in Hickley and Williams (eds.) (1996), 157–169.

Gupta, S., Basu, T. and Chattarji, S., eds. (2003), *India in the Age of Globalization: Contemporary Discourses and Texts* (New Delhi: Nehru Memorial Museum and Library).

Hall, Stuart (1990). 'Cultural Identity and Diaspora'. In J. Rutherford ed. (1990), *Identity* (London: Lawrence & Wishart). 7–23.

Heffernan, P.J. (1996), 'The Intercultural made Explicit in the Teaching of Cultural Content in a Bilingual, Multicultural Country' in Hickey and Williams (eds.) (1996), 188–195.

Hickey, T. and Williams, J., eds. (1996), 'Language, Education and Society in a Changing World', (Dublin /Clevedon: IRAAL/Multilingual Matters Ltd).

Idowu, A.I. (1985), 'Counseling Nigerian Students in United States Colleges and Universities', *Journal of Counseling and Development*, **63**, 506–509.

Jekayinfa, A.A. (2002), 'The Effect of Culture-Contact on the Contemporary Nigerian Life' in Akanji, M.A. (ed.), 42–49.

Malheirs, J. (2004), 'Migration Information', Centra des Etude, Geographicos-Universidad de Lisboa, http://www.migrationinformation.com/feature/.

Mathuna, L.M. (1996), 'Integrating Language and Cultural Awareness Components in Irish-Language Teaching Programmes' in Hickey and Williams (eds.) (1996), 179–187.

Nye, D.E. and C. Pederson (1991). *Consumption and American Culture* (Rotterdam: Uitgeverij).

Obayan, A.O. (2003), 'Family Systems, Cultural Dynamics and Counseling

Outcome–The African Paradigm', a public lecture presented at the Covenant University on Wednesday 9 July 2003.

Okebukola, P. (2004), 'Challenges before the Academy of Science', *Guardian*, 10 June 2004.

Omoniyi, T. (2003), 'Culture and Identity Shifts Via Satellites and Virtual Reality in the Era of Globalization' in Gupta, B. and Chattarji (eds.) (2003), 353–398.

Omotoye, R. (2002), '*The Practice* of Religion in Relation to African Culture' in Akanji, M.A. (ed.) (2002), 16–32.

Ouane, A., ed. (2003), *Towards a Multilingual Culture of Education* (Hamburg, Germany: UNESCO Institute for Education).

Taylor, R.L. (2001), 'Subcultures and Countercultures' in *Concise Encyclopedia of Sociolinguistics* (Amsterdam: Elsevier), 401–407.

Tyler, E.B. (1871). *Primitive Culture Vol. 1* (London: John Murrary).

Von Gleich, U. (2003), 'Multilingualism and multiculturalism in Latin America: Matters of Identity or obstacles to modernization' in Ouane (ed.) (2003), 261–298.

Yinger, J. Milton (October 1960). 'Contraculture and Subculture'. *American Sociology Review* 25. 625–35.

Appendix

Questionnaire on the Cultural Consequences of Economic Migration

I am Professor Efurosibina Adegbija, at Covenant University, Ota, Ogun State, Nigeria. I am conducting research into the topic above and would be grateful if you could kindly spare some of your time for me.

Kindly complete the attached questionnaire as fully as you possibly can. It is meant for research purposes only and is an aspect of my data-gathering instrument. I am grateful for your time and appreciate your assistance in conducting the research. There are 10 open-ended items on the questionnaire. Kindly complete the questionnaire on time and send it to me through my email address as follows: efuroade@yahoo.com.

I would be grateful if you could kindly email the questionnaire to close friends from your homeland presently living in the same country with you who would be willing to assist in completing it.

1. How long have you lived in your present place of abode?
2. How would you define culture, and what would you consider its main ingredients?
3. Do you ever have opportunities to use your home language in your present place of abode? If you do, in what contexts?
4. What would you consider to be the major cultural impacts or consequences of your having left your homeland to settle in another country?
5. What aspects of the culture of your homeland have you maintained in your present place of abode?
6. What aspects of the culture of your present place of abode would you say have

influenced you most?

7. What aspects of life/culture in your homeland have you missed most since you settled in your present place of abode?

8. In terms of cultural identity, how would you presently characterize yourself?

9. What kinds of adjustment problems have you had since you came to your present place of abode?

10. What kind of adjustment problems do you commonly have when you visit your homeland?

Thank you very much for your assistance.

Chapter 10

From Homeland to Hopeland?
Economic Globalization and Ogoni
Migration in the 1990s

Cyril I. Obi
Nigerian Institute of International Affairs, Lagos, Nigeria

For the first time in our history, we have become a migrant population as a direct result of the effect of international trade. (Owens Wiwa, 2001)

Introduction

Since the end of the Cold War in the late 1980s, globalization has accelerated the rate at which information, capital and people move across borders from one end of the globe to another. The paradoxical dimension to globalization, where openings in some spaces lead to closures in other spaces, forms one of the critical concerns in this chapter. It has also been observed that greater globalized penetration of the poorer countries has largely contributed to the outflow of people from poor to the rich countries (Akokpari, 2000, p. 72).

While insisting on the opening up of economies of poor countries, the rich countries are closing their doors to migrants from these countries (Okome, 2003). Even for most of those who gain entry and decide to stay permanently (migrants), the harsh realities of underemployment, racism and exploitation sours the expected sweetness of their new homes in the West. Some however find succour in diasporic communities built up over the generations by waves of migration and a determination to thrive in their new home.

This chapter explores the linkages between the economic globalization, represented by oil multinationals operating in Nigeria's oil-rich Niger Delta, and Ogoni resistance and the migration of Ogoni victims of environmental conflict and military repression in the 1990s. It establishes the connection between the pressures and contradictions unleashed by corporate (oil) globalization in an oil-rich locale, and the Ogoni search for another life outside of Nigeria's borders – represented by the metaphors of 'protest', 'escape', 'refuge', and 'hope'. In this context, trans-territorial movement assumes the form of Ogoni people fleeing from a hegemonic economic regime – global oil, backed by a brutal military dictatorship.

Globalization

Globalization lends itself to several definitions, all of which are connected to the acceleration of trans-border flows as a result of the compression of time and space (Olukoshi, 2003). Another critical aspect of globalization is the transcendence of state borders, and the undermining of the power and authority of states as power flows into the hands of regional supra-state groupings, multilateral organisations and multinational corporations. Free from any real form of global regulation, and not being accountable to the citizens of the countries in which they operate, multinationals have sought to optimize extraction of profits without much regard for the rights of the people whose resources they exploit. Globalization is fundamentally about a restructuring of global economic relations in which power over the world's resources, markets, and capital is being speedily accumulated by the world's most powerful economic actors controlled by citizens from the advanced market economy countries. Thus, globalization has in most parts of Africa served to worsen existing crises, while the continent is further marginalized from the mainstream of global commerce and growth (Aina, Chachage and Annan-Yao eds. 2000; Assefa, Rugumamu and Ahmed, 2001).

Migration

The notion of migration is synonymous with the movement of people across space(s) and time(s) to settle outside their homeland. Migrations are a part of human history and in the past reflected the quest of a people for survival, freedom, an identity and security. Akokpari (1999, p. 75) differentiates between internal migration within a country, and international migration across national borders. In his view, involuntary migration is linked with people 'who are forced by factors or circumstances beyond their control to seek sanctuary in other parts of the country or beyond the borders of their country of residence'. Such migration has usually been identified with economic, political, and environmental factors. It is within this perspective that Ogoni migration to the West is framed

Globalization, Oil, Ogoni Resistance, and Migration

Ogoni land is about 404 square miles in size. It is located in the Niger Delta, Nigeria's oil rich belt, where petroleum was discovered by Shell in 1958. In the early 1990s the Ogoni, an ethnic minority group of about 500,000 people, began a well-organized local and global campaign under their umbrella organization, the Movement for the Survival of the Ogoni People (MOSOP). Ogoni resistance had its roots in the alienation from their lands and waters, and the proceeds from oil production. Oil production has also polluted the farmlands and forests and waters, destroying the environmental basis of Ogoni livelihoods: fishing, farming, hunting and trading. As Naanen argues: 'Ogoni represents the paradox of capitalist accumulation – as the poorest and most industrialized enclave in Nigeria' (Naanen, 1995, p. 65). It must be noted that this paradox is the direct consequence of the expropriation of oil-rich land as a result of a creation of growing global hunger for cheap oil, and corporate globalization.

The control of global oil by Oil Multinationals is inextricably tied to the survival, power and global hegemony of the G-7, led by the US. In the hierarchy of Oil Multinationals, Shell is a foremost global player. With operations in over 140 countries, spanning refining, chemicals, energy, plastics and retail service stations that bring in profits exceeding a hundred billion dollars annually (Doyle, 2002). Shell, therefore, is a major global economic power, earning much more than the Petro-states with which it does business and wielding enormous influence as a globalizing economic force. It was therefore hardly surprising that Nigeria's Niger Delta from which Shell got about 10 per cent of its global oil production would also be a site of pollution. Given that the Niger Delta is Africa's largest wetlands with a fragile ecosystem supporting a wide biodiversity and subsistence activities, oil pollution had a particularly devastating impact that threatened the survival of the people of the region. The location of the Ogoni in the Delta also meant that they were both host to Shell, one of the world's most powerful economic players, and victims of its exploitative and polluting activities.

MOSOP picked on Shell as the most visible and oldest operating oil multinational in the Niger Delta. Also, Shell was believed to have considerable leverage over the federal government, and had a lot to lose by being shamed in its own backyard in Europe and the US as a violator of human and environmental rights. In this regard the Ogoni presented the Nigerian Government with the Ogoni Bill of Rights (OBR) very much in the tradition of the American Civil Rights Movement. The subsequent non-response of the federal government to the OBR then led to the intensification of MOSOP's protests, and its internationalization of the struggle.

Thus, conceptually, Ogoni resistance in the 1990s was a direct response to corporate (oil) globalization. It sought to block oil production in Ogoniland as a way of drawing attention to the plight of the Ogoni people, and force the Nigerian state and Shell to respond to the demands of the Ogoni people. In response, the Nigerian state and corporate power was deployed in repressing Ogoni resistance to global oil. Apart from seeking to remove what was seen as a challenge to their control of oil, it was also felt that setting the Ogoni as an example would stop other oil minorities in the Niger Delta from contemplating any form of resistance to the 'oil alliance'. This unleashing of massive violence against the Ogoni reached a peak under the General Abacha-led military regime, and then fed into migration as a modality of escape from a local site of oil production that had become a site of violence, persecution and destruction (Idemyor, 2004; Wiwa, 2004).

An Anatomy of Ogoni Resistance and Migration

The Ogoni adopted the Ogoni Bill of Rights on 26 August 1990, and sent it to the Federal Government of Nigeria. Its main demands were: political autonomy for the Ogoni within Nigeria, the right to control and use a fair proportion of Ogoni economic resources for Ogoni development, and the right to protect the Ogoni environment and ecology from further degradation (OBR, 1990; Obi, 2001a). Within a year, the

Movement for the Surival of Ogoni People was formed to struggle for the objectives of the OBR. In 1992, MOSOP produced an addendum to the OBR, making specific demands for local autonomy, compensation for pollution, reparations for unpaid royalties to the people, on the Nigerian government and Shell. This was also ignored as tensions in the Niger Delta continued to mount with the Nigerian military adopting a carrot and stick policy in the oil producing communities of the region.

On 4 January 1993, about 300 Ogoni were mobilized to protest against the state-Shell alliance. The demonstration, one of the largest of its kind, was reported widely locally and internationally. After the protests, and in the face of its success in drawing attention to the plight of the Ogoni, the attempt to repress MOSOP began in earnest. On 30 April 1993, Nigerian soldiers forcefully dispersed Ogoni villagers protesting against the bulldozing of crops in their farms by an oil service contractor Willbros clearing land on behalf of Shell. In the incident a farmer, Karalolo Kogbara, was shot in the arm. While Shell insisted it got the land legally, and therefore invited the military that forcibly dispersed the protesters, MOSOP insisted that Shell did not negotiate with its representatives (Human Rights Watch, 1995, p. 6). In August, an invading force from a neighbouring group, the Andoni, slaughtered about a hundred Ogoni villagers. This was followed by similar attacks by other neighbouring communities, the Okrika in December 1993, and the Ndoki in April 1994. In these attacks many Ogoni villages were destroyed and looted, and hundreds of villagers were killed, and thousands were injured or displaced. While the state and Shell explained these attacks as communal conflict (Boele, 1995), MOSOP blamed them on Nigerian security forces. A Human Right Watch Report based on an investigation of the attacks and killing of the Ogoni did confirm the involvement of members of Nigerian security forces in the attacks against the Ogoni, based on eyewitness accounts and interviews conducted with Nigerian Army personnel in Ogoniland (Human Rights Watch, 1995, pp. 7–10; Rowell, 1996). It was also alleged later that Shell had provided some logistic support for the operations of the military forces in Ogoniland – transportation, allowances and light weapons (Ghazi and Duodu, 1994; Ake, 1996; Duodu, 1996; Lock and Rienner, 2000, pp. 5–6).

In spite of the state terror unleashed against it, MOSOP continued with its protest, forcing Shell to leave Ogoniland in May 1993. Shortly after MOSOP itself was torn apart by factional struggles within its leadership. One group was led by then President of MOSOP Dr Garrick Leton, who felt the organization was becoming too militant and unrealistic in its demands, and also being overshadowed by Saro-Wiwa's personal ambitions and radical youth supporters, while the other group felt that MOSOP had to be radical to succeed and viewed the others as conservative elements that were (pro-government and pro-Shell) 'sell outs' or 'vultures'. During a controversial meeting over whether or not the Ogoni should participate in the 12 June Presidential elections in Nigeria, the matter was put to vote. The majority vote was for boycotting the elections, championed by radicals who felt that participating in the elections would amount to legitimizing an election conducted by an illegal military government. Thus, Dr Garrick Leton and Chief Edward Kobani, President and Vice President, resigned from the MOSOP Executive. Ken Saro-Wiwa was elected the new President of MOSOP, with Ledum Mitee as his deputy. With their emergence as the leaders of MOSOP the movement became more radicalized even as state repression was intensified.

In January 1994 the Rivers State Internal Security Task Force (RSIST) was ostensibly formed to contain communal conflict in Rivers state, but in reality its aim was to neutralize Ogoni resistance. Lieutenant Colonel Paul Okutimo (and later Major Obi Umahi) headed the RSIST. It unleashed a reign of terror in Ogoniland in a security operation that was clearly targeted at destroying MOSOP and its popular base in the Ogoni people. Through raids, arbitrary arrests, torture, extortion and intimidation a siege was laid against the Ogoni to break their spirit of resistance and force them to accept the authority of the state-oil alliance over the resources found in Ogoniland (Human Rights Watch, 1995; Robinson, 1996; Rowell, 1996; Obi, 2001a).

It was against the background of the split in MOSOP, repression, and resistance that four Ogoni elite linked to the Garrick Leton faction of MOSOP were murdered by a mob in Gokana, Ogoniland, on 21 May 1994. The next day Saro-Wiwa and his deputy were arrested. In November 1994 they were arraigned before a military tribunal for inciting the murder the four Ogoni elite. After a trial described widely as flawed, in which the defence counsel for Saro-Wiwa and four others withdrew from the case citing lack of access to their clients and the bias of the Tribunal, nine of the accused were found guilty (except Ledum Mitee), and sentenced to death by hanging on 31 October 1994. In spite of worldwide appeals for their lives to be spared Saro-Wiwa and eight other Ogoni activists were hanged on 10 November 1995 (Birnbaum, 1995a, 1995b; CLO, 1996). The hangings sent shock waves around the world. Nigeria was suspended from the Commonwealth, whose summit had been going on at the time, and some of whose leaders had appealed to General Sanni Abacha, then Nigeria's military Head of State not to execute the 'Ogoni Nine'. While the trial of the Ogoni Nine was on, Shell had put in a watching brief. After the sentences were passed some pressure was placed on Shell to use its leverage with the Nigerian state to spare the lives of the Ogoni Nine. But Shell had insisted that it would not intervene in politics. Saro-Wiwa's brother however alleged that based on a meeting he had with the Chairman and Managing Director of Shell Nigeria, Brian Anderson, that the company refused to intervene because Saro-Wiwa and MOSOP had refused to stop the 'international campaign that was hurting Shell' (Wiwa (1995). Whatever the case may be, the company kept to 'its business' of producing oil behind a military shield all through the crisis in the Niger Delta. It was (now late) Claude Ake, Nigeria's foremost political scientist and National Merit Award Winner, who put Shell's 'rejection of blame' in clear perspective: 'Shell Petroleum Development Company of Nigeria shows no sign of remorse for causing the strife in Ogoniland which has thrown Nigeria into one of the deepest crises of its history. It insists defiantly that it will not change its ways and denies any part whatsoever in the environmental degradation of the Niger Delta, which it blames on indigenes conniving at oil spills to collect compensation' (Ake (1995). Thus, within the politics of Big Oil, Shell was more intent on salvaging its image, but not at the cost of loosening its grip on the oil reserves in the Niger Delta.

Following the 'beheading' of MOSOP with the hanging of the Ogoni Nine, even more violence was unleashed against the Ogoni who tried to continue with the struggle. Many Ogoni suspected of being MOSOP sympathizers were targeted, arrested and detained, or they went underground, or fled the country. Most of them ended up in the United Nations High Commission for Refugees camps (UNHCR) in Benin Republic, a neighbouring country. Others went to other neighbouring countries such as Togo, Ghana, or even farther afield. Living under poor conditions, the Ogoni refugees in Benin, numbering thousands, were constantly in fear of being abducted by Nigerian security operatives who hovered around the camps (Project Underground nd; Robinson, 1996; Snow, 1997). There were also allegations that Shell had located its office in Benin just behind the Come camp further heightening the anxiety of the Ogoni refugees. It was from these camps that the odyssey of the Ogoni into exile and migration in the 1990s began.

Ogoni Migration in the 1990s

Ogoni migration in the 1990s was tied to refugeeism. Labelled as 'environmental' or 'corporate' refugees, many Ogoni fled from repression at home. There are no exact figures of the number of Ogoni that fled, but it is estimated that they were in the thousands. A few were able to flee to the West without transiting through the camps. It has also been difficult to state exactly how many Ogoni made it to the West but there was ample evidence of the presence of Ogoni exiles in the major cities in North America, Europe and Australia from where they coordinated the MOSOP resistance abroad, and kept the memory of Ken Saro-Wiwa alive. For some of the refugees, their journey to Europe, America and Canada was facilitated by the UNHCR based on MOSOP appeals to the UN, international organisations and the various governments. Such appeals arose from the poor conditions in the camps, coupled with the threat posed by Nigerian security agents who crossed the borders with ease. A lot of the refugees in the camps felt unsafe, and lived in the fear of abduction by these agents (Project Underground nd; Robinson, 1996; Snow, 1997).

Some Ogoni refugees thus made the transition to migrant status. The MOSOP arm in diaspora continued the international campaign to isolate the Nigerian military regime, expose Shell as a violator of human rights, and demand the release of 20 Ogoni youth who had been detained, and were being tried for the same offences for which the Ogoni Nine were tried and hanged. The MOSOP in exile has since undergone some transformation and assumed a low(er) profile. This observation is inferable from the noticeable inactive states of MOSOP's websites in Canada, US and the UK, and the reality that other sites that carried news on the Ogoni struggle are now mostly dated. However, this must not be taken to mean that these global MOSOP branches are no longer active (Idemyor, 2004). Also of note is a story on the lives of Ogoni refugees in the US carried on the website of the PBS. Focusing on two Ogoni families in the Chicago area (Israel and Ngozi Nwidor and Barine Wiwa-Lawani), it is pointed out that most Ogoni refugees 'are hopeful about their new lives in America'. However, upon arrival in the US, they are shocked and confused that they have to struggle with low-paying jobs, and also suffer from discrimination. In the case of Barine Wiwa-Lawani, sister of the late Ken Saro-Wiwa, it is reported that she had to juggle three part-time jobs (www.pbs.org). However, it must be pointed out that some highly qualified Ogoni professionals such as Dr Idemyor, who is the Director of Pharmaceutical Services at Advocate Bethany Hospital, is making recognized contributions in the area of the treatment of HIV/AIDS in the US, as well as the Niger Delta.

Three things are clear from the foregoing. First is that the Ogoni migrants had high expectations about life in the US, but they found out that they met a different struggle there. Second, in spite of their initial problems these families have decided to remain in the US, even after the death of General Sanni Abacha, the end of military rule, and the inauguration of a democratic government in Nigeria in May 1999. It would appear that the Ogoni migrants have elected to remain permanently in their new home(s) abroad, while maintaining links with their original homes. They have also been focused on the issue of acquiring new skills and surviving in their new homes. The reasons are not difficult to fathom. The Nigerian state-Shell partnership is still alive and strong, even though Shell has not returned to Ogoniland after leaving in 1993. Also the Niger Delta remains highly militarized, with security forces on the alert to put down any threat to the oil companies and oil installations. In this regard, there have been some incidents in Ogoniland since 1998 in which protests have been put down by security forces. Third, and perhaps most fundamentally, is that the MOSOP in exile is in eclipse, partly the result of schisms in the movement. At the heart of the division is the issue of the strategy that MOSOP should adopt. This broadly reflects the differences between those that seek accommodation with Shell and the government and those that insist Shell must remain 'persona non grata' in Ogoniland until it agrees to respect the rights of the people as laid down in the OBR. This fractionalization that became noticeable in 1999, has weakened the organization, and undermined the international support for the MOSOP agenda. It appears that the globalized struggle for Ogoni resistance has in the process fallen between the cracks of fractionalization and dwindling global support.

Although the Ogoni struggle has been kept alive, and the name of Ken Saro-Wiwa remains the symbol of Ogoni resistance both locally and globally, it may be safe to argue that the struggle is in a 'low intensity' phase, having been severely traumatized by military repression, global power, fractionalization and personality differences within the Ogoni elite and individuals. In this regard, the evidence suggests that the linkages between Ogoni migrants and the resistance movement at home have become largely uncoordinated, individualized and programmatic.

Conclusion: From Homeland to Hopeland?

There is no doubt that the contradictions spawned by economic globalization were the driving force(s) behind Ogoni migration in the 1990s. But just as globalization propelled migration, and its core countries gestured to the Ogoni refugees fleeing their homeland as a safe haven and a land of hope, so also some its discourses empower local claims and resistance. Globalization is thus for the Ogoni a complex reality, with its economic face as a potent danger, but its liberationist and rights discourses acting as a source of empowerment linking local to global struggles.

Although, it could be argued that the cold facts do show that these global discourses could not save the Ogoni Nine from the gallows, or stop thousands of Ogoni from fleeing their homeland and becoming migrants in the West, the reality today is that the Ogoni have become a trans-global community, having two homes – the one they left behind, and the one they presently live in – which are separated by thousands of kilometres and the Atlantic. With time a new generation of Ogoni that did not experience the MOSOP revolution will emerge in the diaspora, and perhaps they too will be joined by new waves of Ogoni migrants as the contradictions spawned by corporate oil globalization continue to dig deeper into the land and swamps of the Niger Delta.

It is, however instructive that after its huge public relations offensive to contain the damage inflicted on its image by the international campaign waged by MOSOP, and the repression of the Ogoni, Shell appears to be recanting in recent times. According to the BBC news report of 11 June 2004: 'oil giant, Shell has admitted it inadvertently fed corruption, poverty and conflict through its oil activities in Nigeria' (BBC, 2004). Coupled with this, are the widely publicized Shell Annual Reports that showcase the huge amounts spent by Shell on community development projects in the Niger Delta, but which have been described by critics as inadequate or PR stunts (Friends of the Earth, 2003). But this hardly means much given the relations of power between the company and the oil communities. More so since the statement did not make any commitments to correcting past wrongs, nor did it make any new concrete promises to the people of the Niger Delta. What it does show is that a major actor of corporate globalization has confirmed what was already known to the people of the local oil rich communities and the human rights community within and outside Nigeria. More important perhaps is that the militarization of the Niger Delta continues unabated, while the oil multinationals are locating to new sites of oil exploration and production off-shore to avoid the complications of having to deal with protesting oil communities.

In the light of the foregoing, it is pertinent to raise the following question: have the Ogoni migrants reached the land of hope, or does hope lie in their return to their original homes? Although Shell has not returned to Ogoniland since 1993, many Ogoni lost their homes and earthly possessions in the waves of repression that swept their land in the 1990s. Beyond this the state-oil alliance remains a formidable force of occupation. Under the circumstances it is understandable that the Ogoni migrants have decided to settle as transnational communities around the world – their new homes where they have come to stay. They have moved their place of refuge and survival from the local to the global. The conditions that drove them out of the Niger Delta have fundamentally remained the same – poverty, environmental degradation and a military presence, and will remain so as long as the oil continues to flow and spew extreme inequities and pollution. For the Ogoni, hope continues to inhere in survival and the dream that someday, the Ogoni shall be free.

References

Aina, T., Chachage, S. and Annan-Yao, E., eds. (2002), *Globalisation and Social Policy in Africa* (Dakar: Codesria).

Aina, T.A. and Chachage S.L. Chacage and E. Annan Yao eds. (2000). *Globalization and Social Policy in Africa* (Dakar: Codesria).

Ake, C. (1995), Letter of resignation from the Niger Delta Environmental Survey, 15 November 1995.

Ake, C. (1996), 'Shelling Nigeria Ablaze', *TELL,* 29 January 1996.

Akokpari, J. (1999), 'The Political Economy of Migration in Sub-Saharan Africa', *African Sociological Review,* **2,** 1.

Assefa, T., Rugumamu, S. and Ahmed, A. (2001), 'Introduction' in *Globalisation, Democracy and Development in Africa: Challenges and Prospects* (Addis Ababa: Organisation for Social Science Research in Eastern and Southern Africa).

BBC News (2004), 'Shell Admits Fuelling Corruption'. http://www.news.bbc.co.uk/hi/business; (11 June 2004).

Birnbaum, M. (1995a), 'A Travesty of Law and Justice: An Analysis of the Judgement in the Case of Ken Saro-Wiwa and Others', Article 19, December 1995.

Birnbaum, M. (1995b), 'Nigeria, Fundamental Rights Denied: Report of the Trial of Ken Saro-Wiwa and Others', Article 19.

Boele, R. (1995), *Ogoni: Report of the UNPO Mission to Investigate the Situation of the Ogoni in Nigeria* (The Hague: Unrepresented Nations and Peoples Organisation (UNPO)).

Civil Liberties Organisation (1996), *Ogoni: Trials and Travails* (Lagos: Civil Liberties Organisation (CLO)).

Doyle, J. (2002), *Riding the Dragon: Royal Dutch Shell and Fossil Fire* (Boston: Environmental Health Fund).

Duodu, C. (28 January 1996), 'Shell Admits Importing Arms for Nigerian Police', *The Observer.*

Esparza, L. and Wilson, M., 'Oil for Nothing: Multinational Corporations, Environmental Destruction, Death and Impunity in the Niger Delta', a US Non-Governmental Delegation Trip Report, 6–20 September.

Friends of the Earth (2002), *Failing the Challenge: The Other Shell Report 2002* (London: Friends of the Earth).

Friends of the Earth (2003), *Behind the Shine: The Other Shell Report 2003* (London: Friends of the Earth).

Ghazi, P. and Duodu, C. (11 February 1994), 'How Shell Tried to Buy Berretas for Nigerians', *The Observer.*

Global Policy Forum (May 2000), 'Facing the Challenges of Globalization: Equity, Justice and Diversity', (Peoples Summit). Available at www.globalpolicy.org/ngos/role/globalact/challenge.htm.

Human Rights Watch (July 1995), 'NIGERIA, the Ogoni Crisis: A Case Study of Military Repression in South-Eastern Nigeria' in Report 17. 5. Human Rights Watch (ed.).

Human Rights Watch (October 2002), 'THE NIGER DELTA: No Democracy Dividend' in *Report. 14. 7 (A).* Human Rights Watch (ed.).

Idemyor, V., 'President MOSOP-USA' (November 2004), Interview with Author.
.Lock, C. (2000), 'Ken Saro Wiwa, or "The Pacification of the Primitive Tribes of the Lower Niger"' in *Ken Saro-Wiwa: Writer and Political Activist.* McLuckie, C.

and McPhail, A. (eds.) (Boulder, Col.: Lynne Rienner).

Morse, E. (fall 1999), 'A New Political Economy of Oil', *Journal of International Affairs* 53.

Naanen, Ben (March 1995). 'Oil-Producing Minorities and the Restructuring of Nigerian Federalism: The Case of the Ogoni People'. *Journal of Commonwealth and Comparative Politics* 33:1.

Obi, C. (1997), 'Globalisation versus Local Resistance: The Case of the Ogoni versus Shell', *New Political Economy*, **2**, 1.

Obi, C. (2001a), 'The Changing Forms of Identity Politics in Nigeria under Economic Adjustment: The Case of the Oil Minorities Movement of the Niger Delta', *Research Report*, **119**, (Uppsala: Nordic Africa Institute).

Obi, C. (2001b), 'Global, State and Local Intersections: Power, Authority and Conflict in the Niger Delta Oil Communities' in *Intervention and Transnationalism in Africa: Global-Local Networks of Power*. Callaghy, T., Kassimir, R. and Latham, R. (eds.) (Cambridge: Cambridge University Press).

Obi, C. (2003), 'Green Partnership? Oil Multinational Response to Environmental Activism in Nigeria's Niger Delta', paper presented at conference on Africa: *Partnership as Imperialism*, organised by the Centre for West African Studies (CWAS), University of Birmingham, UK. 3-7 September 2003.

Obi, C. (2004a), *The Oil Paradox: Reflections on the Violent Dynamics of Petro-Politics and (Mis)Governance in Nigeria's Niger Delta*, (Pretoria: Africa Institute Occasional Paper 73).

Obi, C. (2004b), 'Globalisation and Nigeria's Oil Industry: Implications for Local Politics' in *Nigeria's Struggle for Democracy and Good Governance: Festschrift in Honour of Oyeleye Oyediran*. Diamond, L., Agbaje, A. and Onwudiwe, E. (eds.) (Ibadan: Ibadan University Press).

Ogoni Bill of Rights (1990), 'Presented to the Government and People of Nigeria'. www.waado.org/NigerDelta/RightsDeclaration/Ogoni.html.

Okome, M. (1 September 2003), 'The Antinomies of Globalisation: Some Consequences of Contemporary African Immigration to the United States of America', *Irinkerido: A Journal of African Migration*.

Okome, O. (2000), *Before I am Hanged, Ken Saro-Wiwa: Literature, Politics and Dissent* (Trenton and Asmara: Africa World Press).

Olukoshi, A. (2003), 'Globalisation, Equity and Development: Some Reflections on the African Experience', paper presented at the GDN annual conference, Cairo. 19–21 January 2003.

Project Underground, *Shell-shocked*, www.moles.org.

Robinson, D. (1996), *Ogoni: The Struggle Continues* (Geneva and Nairobi: World Council of Churches) and all African Council of Churches).

Rowell, A. (1996), *Green Backlash: Global Subversion of the Environmental Movement* (London and New York: Routledge).

Saro-Wiwa, K. (1989), *On a Darkling Plain* (Port Harcourt: Saros International).

Saro-Wiwa, K. (1992), *Genocide in Nigeria: The Ogoni Tragedy* (Lagos: Saros International).

Saro-Wiwa, K. (1995), *A Month and a Day: A Detention Diary* (London: Penguin).

Snow, K. (1997), 'No Safe Haven', Published as Zak Harmon, *Toward Freedom* 46: 6 November 1997. www.pbs.org/independentlens/newamericans/newamericans/

ogoni_intro.html.

Watts, M. (1999), 'PETRO-violence: Some Thoughts on Community, Extraction and Political Ecology', *Berkeley Workshop on Environmental Politics Working Paper INP* 99–1.

Wiwa, O. (1995), 'A Testimony', prepared by Greenpeace on behalf of MOSOP. http://archive.greenpeace.org/comms/ken/owens.txt.

Wiwa, O. (2001), 'The Paradox of Poverty and Corporate Globalisation'. www. globalisationdebate.be/2001/conferencetracks/speeches/wiwaspeech.pdf.

Wiwa, O. (2004), Former Volunteer Executive Director, MOSOP-Canada, Interview with author, November 2004.

Chapter 11

Migrancy and Thabo Mbeki's African Renaissance

David Johnson

Faculty of Arts, Open University, UK

'The Paintings of Malangatane of Mozambique'

From the late 1990s, South Africa's official post-apartheid ideology of 'the rainbow nation' has gradually been supplemented by an ideology of 'the African Renaissance'. Official endorsement of the African Renaissance has gained momentum since Thabo Mbeki assumed the presidency, as Mbeki has argued in a number of speeches that an African Renaissance should inspire the cultural, political and economic re-generation of the African continent, with South Africa leading the way.[1] The content, as well as the rhetorical power of Mbeki's promotion of the African Renaissance, is best conveyed by extended quotation:

> To perpetuate their imperial domination over the peoples of Africa, the colonisers sought to enslave the African mind and to destroy the African soul. They sought to oblige us to accept that as Africans we had contributed nothing to human civilisation except as beasts of burden in much the same way as those who are opposed to the emancipation of women seek to convince them that they have a place in human society, but only as beasts of burden and bearers of children. In the end, they wanted us to despise ourselves, convinced that if we were subhuman we were, at least, not equal to the colonial master and mistress and were incapable of original thought and the African creativity which has endowed the world with an extraordinary treasure of masterpieces in architecture and the fine arts. The beginning of the rebirth of our continent must be our own rediscovery of our soul, captured and made permanently available in the great works of creativity represented by the pyramids and sphinxes of Egypt, the stone buildings of Axum and the ruins of Carthage and Zimbabwe, the rock paintings of the San, the Benin bronzes and the African masks, the carvings of Makonde and the stone sculptures of the Shona .... In that journey of self-discovery and the restoration of our own self-esteem, without which

---

1   There have been many responses to Mbeki's 'African Renaissance'. For sympathetic engagements, see Mbigi (1995), Makgoba (1999) and Mulemfo (2000). For more critical discussions, see Griggs (2000), Magubane and Klopper (2000), Moloka and Le Roux (2000), Comaroff and Comaroff (2001), Herwitz (2003) and Lazarus (2004). Note that the term 'African Renaissance' has also been used by African scholars more widely to refer to the post Cold War efforts to re-generate post-colonial African societies by drawing on indigenous cultural and material resources. For a sample of this work, see Cheru (2001), Okum (2002), and Abdulai (2001).

we would never become combatants for the African renaissance, we just retune our ears to the music of Zao and Franco of the Congo and the poetry of Mazisi Kunene of South Africa, and refocus our eyes to behold the paintings of Malangatane[2] of Mozambique and the sculpture of the Dumile Fine of South Africa (Mbeki, 1998, p. 299).

Mbeki's argument is hardly original, in that it draws upon, adapts and fuses the ideas of any number of major anti-colonial and Pan-African writers and philosophers, with traces of inter alia Frantz Fanon, Steve Biko, Léopold Senghor, and Julius Nyerere marking his prose. However, Mbeki's elevation of the African Renaissance to an official ideology of Southern Africa's regional super-power is original, and as such raises fresh questions and expectations about South Africa's relationship with its relatively impoverished neighbours.[3] In particular, has Mbeki's African Renaissance reversed, or at least ameliorated, the subordination of sub-Equatorial Africa to the needs of the apartheid state?

Migrancy in Southern Africa: A Brief History

Significant cross-border migration into South Africa can be dated back to the nineteenth century, when large numbers of workers from present-day Mozambique, Malawi, Lesotho and Zimbabwe came to work on white-owned farms and particularly the sugarcane plantations of Natal from about 1850 onwards, and on the diamond mines of Kimberley from 1870 onwards.[4] With the discovery of gold on the Witwatersrand a decade later, the demand for cheap labour increased further, and the numbers of migrants working on South African mines rose sharply.[5] During the period 1890–1920, a formalized contract labour system was introduced to regulate the supply of cheap migrant workers for the South African mines.[6] The mining companies negotiated agreements with the governments of neighbouring colonies so that migrants without their families could travel to work on the mines for fixed periods and then return home afterwards. Recruiting stations were established throughout the region and transport routes were built to deliver migrants to the mines. From the migrant workers' point of view, as their livelihoods in the neighbouring

---

2   Mbeki is presumably referring to Malangatana Valente Ngwenya, the most acclaimed Mozambican artist of the 1960s. That Mbeki (or his speech-writer) spells his name incorrectly is unfortunate. See Navarro (2003) for a substantial recent study of Malangatana.

3   For a collection of poetry, testimony, art and photography that exposes rainbow nation xenophobia, and sympathetically encourages all African cultures, see Adams (2001). For further refugee and migrant testimony, see Johnston and Simbine (1998) and Gunn and Tal (2003).

4   For the history of migrant labour on the Kimberley diamond fields, see Worger (1987), and on the movement of Mozambicans to South Africa more generally in this period, Harries (1994).

5   For the histories of the role of migrant labour in the gold-mining industry, see Crush and Yudelman (1991), James (1992), Crush and James (1995), Paton (1995) and Moodie (1994).

6   The legislation passed to regulate migrant workers in this period is described in Jeeves (1985).

colonies were being threatened by colonial land grabs, taxation and the destruction of peasant agriculture, mining wages however minimal provided cash for consumer goods, for guns to defend against further colonial encroachment, for agricultural equipment to use on surviving subsistence farms, and also for *lobola* (dowry) for marriage. The migrant labour system established at the end of the nineteenth century enabled the white Randlords and their acolytes to acquire spectacular wealth, and at the same time consigned millions of black southern Africans and their dependents to economic exploitation and racial oppression.[7]

During this period, in addition to mine workers on fixed-term contracts, there were other significant groups of migrant workers. Indeed, the arduous nature of mine work meant that when alternative work was available, migrants would often try to leave the mines, and in the process precipitate labour shortages. The second major source of employment was on white-owned farms, and farmers in the north and east of South Africa in particular benefited from this abundance of cheap labour, and organized recruiting companies to intercept and sign on migrants at the borders.[8] These migrant workers outside the mine contract system had to pay for their own transport or travel on foot, and often worked en route to their final destination. Once in South Africa, they were subject to pass laws and police harassment, and many were arrested and sentenced to farm work under the prison labour system. Also of importance were migrant women workers, who found employment in domestic service in white households, as well as in informal trading, liquor production and sex work. Like their South African counterparts, they were always marginalized in local labour markets, and their work was frequently criminalized.[9] South African employers, colonial governments and chiefs in 'supplier' regions had a shared interest in keeping women in rural areas, but despite their efforts women continued migrating to South African cities throughout the twentieth century, initially with spouses and later as young, single women.[10]

There have been shifts and fluctuations in both the numbers and in the regional origins of the migrant workers travelling to South Africa's mines. The most rapid phase of expansion was between 1920 and 1940, when the numbers doubled from 100,000 to 200,000. The major supplier for long periods was Malawi (peaking at 120,000 workers in 1973), followed by Mozambique, Lesotho, Botswana and Swaziland. In the interwar years, there were also migrants from Zambia, Tanzania and Angola, with only Zimbabwe (with its own mines and commercial farms) not sending significant numbers of migrants to South Africa. Few rural areas in Southern Africa were unaffected by the labour imperatives of South Africa's mines, and the

---

7 Of the many useful historical studies that convey the texture of migrant miners' lives, see Packard (1989) on the mining industry's indifference to issues of workers' health, and Coplan (1994) on forms of cultural resistance developed by Basotho mine-workers.

8 For the history of the movement of migrant workers from neighbouring colonies to South African white-owned farms, see Jeeves and Crush (1997).

9 Bozzoli (1991) details the negative attitudes to the presence of rural women in South African cities.

10 Cockerton (1996) uncovers the hitherto unacknowledged extent of migration by women from Bechuanaland to South Africa from 1850 to 1930. See Dobson (1998 and 2001) for more recent developments in the migration of women.

economies of Lesotho and southern Mozambique were especially integrated. One constant throughout these fluctuations and shifts has been the South African mining industry's pursuit of its right to choose what it considered to be the best labour from the entire region. This pressure has manifested itself in a number of ways. First, the efficient movement of workers to the mines was guaranteed by ensuring that travelling passes initially and later identity documents and passports were relatively easy to obtain, and there were no border posts. Secondly, migrant workers deemed unsuitable were excluded, notably in the case of the Tropical Labour Ban, which operated between 1913 and 1930, and excluded miners from north of the 22 degrees south latitude (Zimbabwe, Angola, Tanzania and Malawi) from entering South Africa because of their susceptibility to pneumonia and other lung diseases. Thirdly, under the apartheid regime (through its successive departments of Native Affairs, Bantu Affairs and Home Affairs) there were efforts by the state to restrict foreign labour, but these were so successfully resisted by the mining industry that in the early 1970s 80 per cent of the 400,000 mine workers in South Africa were from the neighbouring states. Fourthly, when the newly independent states of Tanzania, Zambia, Angola and Zimbabwe withdrew their citizens from working in South African mines as an anti-apartheid measure, the shortfall in labour was met largely from alternative frontline states rather than from South Africa itself. Finally, the principal piece of legislation regulating migration, the 1937 Control Aliens Act, cohered entirely with the needs of the mining industry: it ruled that migrant workers would never become South African citizens by laying down the requirement that prospective citizens must 'be readily assimilable by the white inhabitants [and not threaten] the language, culture, religion of any white ethnic group'[11]. The mining industry's recruitment and retention of this cheap migrant labour is perhaps best understood by noting that had South Africa's low-grade minerals been discovered in Canada, Australia or the United States, labour costs in these countries would have been too high to make any mining profitable.[12]

As African colonies won independence in the 1960s, the attitude of the apartheid regime towards migrants from the north hardened – border posts were erected, passport requirements were tightened, and foreign women in South Africa in particular were targeted and expelled by police. Many migrants returned home during this period, never to return to South Africa, and the number of foreign women in South African townships fell markedly. Acquiring South African citizenship through naturalization remained impossible, as the requirement that applicants be assimilable by the white inhabitants remained on the statute book until 1991. The apartheid government's hostility towards black immigrants contrasted with its attitude towards white immigrants. As successive colonial regimes fell – Kenya in 1963, Zambia and Malawi in 1964, Mozambique in 1974, Angola in 1975, and Zimbabwe in 1980 – so their white minorities moved south, and were welcomed into South Africa with open arms.

---

11 Besides its explicit intention to exclude black immigrants, the 1937 Aliens Control Act also sought to prevent German Jews fleeing Nazi Germany entering South Africa.

12 See Crush and Yudelman (1991), 1.

Another development in the final quarter of the twentieth century was the movement for the first time of significant numbers of refugees (as opposed to economic migrants) within Southern Africa. From the time of Sharpeville massacre in 1960, and again following the Soweto Uprising in 1976, political refugees had fled South Africa for the frontline states, where they were generously received and supported.[13] Moving in the opposite direction, in the 1980s there was an influx of approximately 350,000 refugees from Mozambique to South Africa escaping the civil war between the FRELIMO (Frente de Libertação de Moçambique) government and the apartheid-backed RENAMO (Resistência Nacional Moçambicana) forces.[14] Bordering countries such as Malawi, Zimbabwe and Swaziland took in refugees, while South Africa tried to keep them out, electrifying border fences and deporting as many refugees as it could. As South Africa had never signed international protocols protecting refugees, the state's resources were unapologetically allocated to policing and expelling, rather than protecting and supporting, the fleeing Mozambicans.

Post-apartheid Continuities

Migration policy in South Africa remained substantially the same in the years immediately following the end of formal apartheid, with the continuation of what has been termed the 'two gate' system – one system for mine workers, regulated by bilateral agreements between mining companies and supplier governments, and a second system for all other migrants, regulated by the Aliens Control Act. It is useful to treat each of these 'gates' in turn.

First, as regards mine workers, there were major changes in the mining industry from the late 1980s to early 1990s, which included the expulsion in 1986 of Malawian mine-workers from South Africa following a dispute over AIDS testing on the mines,[15] and the large-scale retrenchment of both South African and foreign miners, with the former proportionally more heavily affected (from 1983 to 1994, the number of South African gold- and coal-miners dropped from 495,000 to 321,500, while during the same period the number of non-South African miners dropped from 183,000 to 147,000).[16] This trend continued, with the loss of over 100,000 South African jobs between 1990 and 2000, and migrant workers too being retrenched, though at a slower rate. One complicating development has been a change in the make up of foreign workers, with the number Mozambicans employed on the mines actually increasing in the 1990s (from 45,000 to 57,000, a percentage increase from 12 per cent to 25 per cent of all miners), while the number of workers from Lesotho

---

13 The scale of the sacrifices made by frontline states in the anti-apartheid struggle are detailed in UNECA (1989).

14 For political and economic accounts of this fraught period of Mozambique's history, see Hanlon (1986, pp. 131–150, and 1991) and Finnegan (1992).

15 See Chirwa (1997) for the details of the Malawian expulsion.

16 The statistics in this summary below are drawn from two sources: the Canadian-based Southern African Migration Project (SAMP) publications located at http://www.queensu. ca/samp/ and a recent report by the International Labour Office (ILO) Southern Africa Multidisciplinary Advisory Team (1998).

has continued to drop (100,000–58,000). By 2000, the ratio of South African to non-South African miners had stabilized at 50 per cent. The wage gap between South African and foreign miners has remained substantial: studies by the South African National Union of Mineworkers, the Central Bank of Lesotho and the Southern African Migration Project concur that foreign miners are paid on average up to 40 per cent less than their South African counterparts. One of the few progressive moves on migrancy since the end of apartheid was the new South African cabinet granting in 1995 of a 'miners' amnesty', which gave long-serving foreign miners who had voted in the 1994 elections the right to apply for permanent residence in South Africa, a right that was exercised by 52,000 miners.[17] This concession, however, has proved to be an aberration, and subsequent legislation governing workers from neighbouring states has continued to serve the interests of the mining industry. Most tellingly, despite vocal ANC commitments to protect South African worker interests against those of foreign workers, the 2002 South African Immigration Act entrenches the status quo with regard to the contract labour system, allowing the migration of men without families to the mines and farms of South Africa to continue as before.[18]

The second 'gate', the Aliens Control Act, continued to regulate migrants in South Africa outside the contract labour system.[19] The Act was amended in 1991 to delete the explicit racial exclusions of the original 1937 Act, but its key requirement remained in place – that to employ foreign workers, South African employers had to convince the Department of Home Affairs that no South Africans were available for the relevant job. With the Department of Home Affairs headed by the Inkatha Freedom Party leader Gatsha Buthelezi after 1994, the requirement was interpreted as denying employment in South Africa to all immigrants in unskilled or semi-skilled categories. This informal policy was confirmed in the 1996 Amendment Act, which explicitly excluded the issuing of work or immigration permits to foreign workers seeking employment in occupations where there are sufficient South Africans. The effect of this policy has been to criminalize migrant workers entering South Africa without the requisite permits. They are protected to some extent from prosecution by their South African employers, who are eager not to relinquish their cheap, vulnerable and non-unionized labour. Employers are helped in particular by Section 41 of the Act, which allows them at the discretion of the Minister to register post hoc their undocumented migrant labour force. The low pay, unregulated working conditions, short terms of employment, and harassment from police and Internal Tracing Units (ITUs) have prompted one commentator to liken migrant farm workers to slaves:

---

17 In 1996, a second amnesty was extended to citizens from neighbouring states who had resided in South Africa before 1991 and met certain further stringent criteria. The Department of Home Affairs received just less than 200,000 applications under this amnesty.

18 Detailed statistical data and analysis on the movement of migrants into South Africa has been published by The Southern African Migration Project. Especially relevant in relation to Mozambican migrants are the publications by de Vletter (1998), McDonald et al. (1998) and Dobson (1998). For a general overview of post-apartheid migration, see Crush (1998). On how migrants have been and continue to be treated in the South African legal system, see Murray (1986), Klaarens (1996) and la Hunt (1997).

19 See Crush (1999) for a succinct summary of the Aliens Control Act and its impact in the 1990s.

The rampant exploitation of Mozambican refugees by employers in the 1980s has continued since .... Press exposés in 1990 indicated that some farmers were paying refugees only R30-R40 [£3-£4] per month. Professional labour touts were also reported to be dragooning labour from Mozambique and bringing it over to the farmers at a fee of R100-R150 [£10-£15] per head. These workers, virtual 'slaves', were reported to the police if they refused to work, who then arrested and deported them (Crush (1999, p. 8).

Vulnerable both to prosecution by the Department of Home Affairs and to exploitation by South Africa's white commercial farmers, ever greater numbers of agricultural migrant workers have suffered these hardships since 1990. The one significant piece of legislation to ameliorate the Alien Control Act has been the 1998 Refugee Act. However, the ambit of the Refugee Act is limited, as it offers minimal support and lays down strict requirements for refugees to qualify for asylum in South Africa (by 2003, 63,000 applicants for asylum had been received, and 13,000 had been successful).

The resilience of the 'two gates' approach in post-apartheid South Africa ultimately rests upon a fundamental continuity from the apartheid to the post-apartheid eras in the hostility of South African policy-makers towards migrants from other African countries. This hostility assumes many forms, from negative stereotyping in the press to more direct and extreme forms of anti-migrant violence. Indeed, recent comparative research suggests that South Africans are the most xenophobic citizens in the world, and further, that Southern Africans more broadly express a growing 'regional xenophobia' directed against Africans from north of the frontline states.[20] Hein Marais has noted that migrants are blamed for the country's ills:

... its high unemployment rate, rising crime, the proliferation of hard drugs on city streets, the spread of HIV/AIDS and even the low wages paid by small firms. No longer able to blame the apartheid government for their hardships, South Africa's poor have turned black foreigners into a convenient target for their frustrations. Indeed, xenophobia functions morbidly as another bonding agent among the poor. It also means that blame is deflected away from business and government – other Africans serve as scapegoats for travails in which they have no hand. By and large, government has chosen not to challenge those sensibilities. In some instances, on the contrary, it promotes them (Marais, 2001, p. 252).

These kinds of attitudes towards migrants are not confined to sensationalist newspapers and South Africa's ill-informed poor; they enjoy support in academic publications sponsored by the Department of Home Affairs, and it is to these arguments I now turn.

A number of publications engaging sympathetically with the ANC government's 'problem with illegal immigration' have been published.[21] Hussein Solomon's *Of Myths and Migration. Illegal Immigration into South Africa* (2003) is the most recent

---

20 See McDonald et al. (1998) for details of SAMP research on South African attitudes to migrants.

21 The main publications promoting the view of migration in Southern Africa as a problem of control, security and policing national borders are: Minnaar and Hough (1996), Majodina (2001) and Solomon (2003).

effort in this tradition. For Solomon, migrants must be understood principally in the context of national security. He does not contest the argument that illegal immigrants are exploited and that they are the targets of criminals, but nonetheless insists that 'the traditional view of illegal immigrants is largely correct: they hold severe socio-economic and political costs for the Republic of South Africa' (Solomon, 2003, p. 99). Rejecting research that characterizes the immigrant population on South Africa as relatively highly educated, Solomon argues that 'a survey of 6,348 illegal Mozambican households ... found that most do not have more than three years of formal education and no work skills outside those of subsistence agriculture' (Solomon, 2003, p. 102). From this Solomon deduces that 'illegal immigrants would be competing with low-skilled South Africans in the job market' (Solomon, 2003, p. 102), and that given high unemployment rates in South Africa, 'the negative impact of illegal aliens on the job market cannot be underestimated' (Solomon, 2003, p. 104). Moving on to the issue of crime, Solomon cites a recent National Operation Police policy document that declares 'illegal immigrants [to be] "South Africa's Number One Public Enemy"', and quotes the statistic that 'illegal immigrants contributed to 14 per cent of all crime in South Africa and that these crimes included diamond smuggling, small arms proliferation, narcotic trafficking, car hijacking, taxi violence, burglaries, stock theft and involvement in political massacres by hiring themselves out as assassins' (Solomon, 2003, p. 105). In addition to their negative impact on unemployment and crime, Solomon alleges thirdly that migrants overburden South Africa's social services, by making demands on the state's 'provision of adequate education, health, housing and pensions' (Solomon, 2003, p. 106). Acknowledging the difficulty of measuring in financial terms the impact of migrants on South Africa's economy, Solomon nonetheless goes on to quote sympathetically Colonel Brian Van Niekerk, National Coordinator of Border Control and Policing in the South African Police Services, who argued that in 1994 'illegal immigrants cost the South African taxpayer R1985 million' (Solomon, 2003, p. 108). Solomon argues that deportation costs (R200 million in 1997) should be added to Van Niekerk's total. Solomon concludes his case against migrants in South Africa by arguing that they can contribute to domestic political instability, and they can also frustrate the ANC's foreign policy initiatives. As an example of the former, he cites the formation of organizations like the Crisis Committee and National Immigrant Workers' Association and their links with South African political parties (other than the ANC), and as an example of the latter, he cites the example of the Nigerian Wole Soyinka National Liberation Coalition, which set up an anti-Abacha radio station in South Africa and broadcast messages at odds with the ANC's policy of diplomatic engagement with the Nigerian regime. In both cases, Solomon believes the integrity of South Africa's internal political processes were compromised.

Malangatana's Subjects?

There is a dissonance between Mbeki's inclusive rhetoric of an African Renaissance and the state's policies in relation to migrants since the end of apartheid. Part of the explanation for this contradiction lies in the fact that fierce political debates are still being fought out over the issue within the ANC government. Most obviously, the uncompromising implementation of anti-migrant policy by Buthelezi's Department of Home Affairs certainly offends the views of more sympathetic (but less influential) elements within the ANC. But it is a contradiction that goes beyond personal differences and political factions within the ANC, as it is deeply embedded within government discourse. For example, in a speech published in 2001, Lindiwe Sisulu, then deputy minister of Home Affairs, moved briskly from arguing in favour of detaining migrants in reception centres 'as the best means to de-link the institution of asylum from economic migration in order to curtail corruption and crime and to end the abuse of the asylum institution' (Majodina, 2001, p. 9), to a resounding affirmation of Mbeki's African Renaissance:

> ... the attainment of democracy in South Africa must be seen as part of a broader process of democratisation in Africa: a robust democratisation process underpinned by the principles and practices of mass participation, transparency and accountability. For us, the African Renaissance is both a strategic objective and a call to action. As President Mbeki has emphasised many times, the key is the economic regeneration of the continent. It is a regeneration of which economic development; popular participation and respect for human rights are seen as part and parcel of the same process (Majodina, 2001, p. 10).

Much like Solomon, Sisulu does not see the strict policing of economic migrants as in any way compromising the African Renaissance, democratisation, or human rights.

The contradiction between the inclusive gestures of the African Renaissance and the exclusive workings of South Africa's migration policies is more than a question of a muddled political discourse. There is also a crucial economic dimension to the plight of migrants in the new South Africa. The economic policies Mbeki has pursued in conjunction with the ideology of African renaissance suggest an asymmetry between the desire to rejuvenate the cultural ethos of anti-imperialist struggles and pre-colonial Africa on the one hand, and the individualistic and competitive nature of the neo-liberal economic policies Mbeki and the ANC have chosen to follow on the other hand.[22] The economist John Saul makes this argument as follows:

> [Mbeki's ideas of African Renaissance] have come to be attached precisely to the rather narrower definition of 'black empowerment' .... In a speech to a meeting of black managers ... the emphasis was on the need to strive to create and strengthen a black capitalist class, a black bourgeoisie. Since ours is a capitalist society, Mbeki continued,

---

22 That the ANC's economic policies and the ideals of the African Renaissance are in fact consistent is assumed rather than argued by Mulemfo (2000, pp. 88–90) and Vil-Nkomo and Myburgh (1999, pp. 266–279). Vil-Nkomo and Myburgh note the damaging effects of structural adjustment programmes on the economies of Sub-Saharan African countries, conceding that their 'economies did not emerge from this experience as stronger economies capable of eliminating or alleviating the poverty of their people and reducing inequalities in their own societies' (1999:271). However, in a remarkable display of intellectual evasiveness, they fail utterly in the balance of their chapter to address the fact that Mbeki's own economic policies are substantially identical to the structural adjustment programmes so unsuccessful in the rest of Sub-Saharan Africa.

the objective of the de-racialization of the ownership of productive property is key to the struggle against racism in our country …. One fears that as the celebrated African renaissance comes to be more and more about the 'embourgeoisment' of the favoured few it becomes a very tawdry thing indeed (Saul, 2001, p. 17).

Saul's point is that under Mbeki's zealous promotion of the free market model of economic growth – through self-imposed structural adjustment policies that include privatisation, cutting public spending on education and health, elimination of trade barriers, promotion of free trade, and export-led production – the differences between rich and poor in South Africa have widened significantly in the last ten years.[23] As a result, invoking a return to the cultural resources of the African Renaissance represents little material comfort both to South Africa's poor, and more especially to poor migrants from the rest of Africa seeking a livelihood in South Africa.

Two economic pressures have been of particular importance since the 1990s in defining relations between South Africa and its neighbours, and by extension in determining the lives of economic migrants. The first was the adoption by Southern African countries of structural adjustment programmes under pressure from the World Bank and International Monetary Fund. Always controversial, even former supporters of structural adjustment now acknowledge the damaging effects these policies have had on Southern African in particular. The International Labour Office review 'Labour Migration to South Africa in the 1990s' (1998), for example, concludes that '[i]n the 1990s, southward migration trends were accentuated by structural adjustment programmes in several Southern African Development Community countries. In many cases, these reform programmes helped accelerate rates of economic decline' (International Labour Office, 1998, p. 19.) This rapid economic decline precipitated high unemployment, and the southward movement of workers in search of work. The second economic pressure undermining the economies of South Africa's neighbours and thus triggering southward migration was the differential terms of trade negotiated in the 1990s. The same ILO review notes that in this period 'South African goods, supported by South African export incentive policies, gained easier access to neighbouring national markets. The expiry of long-standing trade pacts led to higher tariffs for trading partners in the region, with devastating consequences' (ILO, 1998, 21). At the same time, '[w]ithin South Africa, a strong lobby argued for the preservation of the defensive tariff and non-tariff barriers which limited SADC countries' access to South Africa's domestic markets' (ILO, 1998, p. 21.) This precise combination of arguments from powerful trading nations – for free trade with respect to their own exports reaching the markets of poorer nations, and for protectionism with respect to poorer nations gaining access to their internal markets – has been put forward from the British Empire in the 18th century to the American Empire in the

---

23   Economic arguments against Mbeki's policies like those of Saul have gathered growing support in recent years. For example, see Bond (2000), Marais (2001) and Hart (2002) for critical discussions of ANC economic policy, and Lodge (2002) for a more sympathetic account. Murobe (2000, pp. 43–67) criticizes Mbeki's neo-liberal economic policies, and argues that instead of a Pan-African Renaissance ideology, the African philosophy of *ubuntu* with its emphasis on community should be nurtured. For a critical discussion of the range of meanings of *ubuntu*, see Johnson and Du Plessis (2001, pp. 206–210).

20th century.[24] South Africa as a developing country complains of protectionism as it struggles to gain access to the markets of the European Community and the United States, but as a regional super power utilises the same kinds of trade policies against its neighbours to protect its own economy.

What I have highlighted in this chapter is the distance between the inclusive rhetoric of Mbeki's African Renaissance and the hardships experienced by migrants in post-apartheid South Africa as a direct result of exclusionary state policies. Perhaps this distance is best conveyed in conclusion by noting the contrast between Mbeki's embrace of Malangatana's paintings in his African Renaissance appeal, and the systemic marginalization of the subjects of Malangatana's paintings – Mozambique's poor – in the economic and social policies of the ANC government.

References

Abdulai, D. (2001), *African Renaissance: challenges, solutions and the road ahead* (London: Asean Press).

Adams, K., ed. (2001), *We Came for Mandela: the cultural life of the refugee community in South Africa* (Rondebosch: Footprints).

Bond, P. (2000), *Elite Transition. From Apartheid to Neoliberalism in South Africa* (London: Pluto).

Bozzoli, B. (1991), *Women of Phokeng: Consciousness, Life Strategy and Migrancy in South Africa, 1900-1983* (Portsmouth, N.H.: Heinemann).

Cheru, F. (2001), *African Renaissance: roadmaps to the challenge to globalization* (London: Zed Books).

Chirwa, W. (1997), '"No TEBA .... Forget TEBA": The Plight of Malawian Ex-Migrant Workers to South Africa, 1988-1994', *International Migration Review*, **31**(3), 628–654. [PubMed 12292956] [DOI: 10.2307/2547289]

Cockerton, C. (1996), 'Less a barrier, more a line: the migration of Bechuanaland women to South Africa, 1850-1930', *Journal of Historical Geography*, **22**(3), 291–307. [DOI: 10.1006/jhge.1996.0018]

Comaroff, J. and Comaroff, J. (2001), 'Naturing the Nation: Aliens, the Apocalypse and the Postcolonial State', *Journal of Southern African Studies*, **27**(3), 627–651. [DOI: 10.1080/13632430120074626]

Coplan, D. (1994), *The Time of the Cannibals: The Word Music of South Africa's Basotho Migrants* (Chicago: University of Chicago Press).

Crush, J. (1999), 'Fortress South Africa and the Deconstruction of Apartheid's Migration Regime', *Geoforum*, **30**(1), 1–13. [PubMed 12322615] [DOI: 10.1016/S0016-7185%2898%2900029-3]

Crush, J. and James, W. (1995), *Crossing Boundaries: Mine Migrancy in a Democratic South Africa* (Cape Town: Idasa/IDRC).

Crush, J., ed. (1998), *Beyond Control. Immigration and Human Rights in a Democratic South Africa* (Cape Town: IDASA).

---

24 See Semmel (1993) for an intellectual history of these long-running arguments.

Crush, J., Jeeves, A. and Yudelman, D. (1991), *South Africa's Labour Empire. A History of Black Migrancy to the Gold Mines* (Boulder: Westview) Press and Cape Town: David Philip).

de la Hunt, L.A. (1997), *Refugees and the Law in South Africa,* ' (Cape Town: Centre for African Studies), unpublished seminar paper).

De Vletter, F. (1998), *Sons of Mozambican Miners and Post-Apartheid South Africa* (Cape Town: IDASA).

Dobson, B. (1998), *Women on the Move: Gender and Cross-Border Migration to South Africa* (Cape Town: IDASA).

Dobson, B. (2001), *Gender Concerns in South African Migration Policy, Migration Policy Brief No. 4*, (Queen's University Canada): Southern African Migration Project.

Finnegan, W. (1992), *A Complicated War. The Harrowing of Mozambique* (Berkeley: University of California Press).

Griggs, R.A. (2000), *Boundaries, Borders and Peace-Building in Southern Africa: the spatial implications of the South African renaissance* (Durham: University of Durham International Boundaries Research Unit).

Gunn, S. and Tal, M.-M., eds. (2003), *Torn Apart. Thirteen Refugees Tell their Stories* (Cape Town: Human Rights Mediate Watch).

Hanlon, J. (1986), *Beggar Your Neighbours. Apartheid Power in South Africa* (London: James Curry).

Hanlon, J. (1991), *Mozambique. Who Calls the Shots?* (London: James Curry).

Harries, P. (1994), *Work, Culture and Identity: Migrant Labourers in Mozambique and South Africa, c. 1860-1910* (Portsmouth, N.H.: Heinemann).

Hart, G. (2002), *Disabling Globalization. Places of Power in Post-apartheid South Africa* (Berkeley, Calif.: University of California Press).

Herwitz, D. (2003), *Race and Reconciliation: Essays from the New South Africa* (Minneapolis: University of Minnesota Press).

International Labour Office Southern (Africa Multidisciplinary Advisory Team), (1998) (1998), 'Labour Migration to South Africa in the 1990s, Policy Paper Series No. 4', (Harare: ILO).

International Labour Organization (2005). http://www.ilo.org/.

International Organization for Migration (2005). http://www.iom.ch/.

James, W. (1992), *Our Precious Metal: African Labour in South Africa's Gold Industry, 1970-1990* (Cape Town: David Philip Publishers).

Jeeves, A. (1985), Migrant Labour in South Africa's Mining Economy: The Struggle for the Gold Mines' Labour Supply, 1890-1920', (Montreal and Kingston, Ontario: McGill-Queen's University Press).

Jeeves, A. and Crush, J., eds. (1997), *White Farms, Black Labour: The State and Agrarian Change in Southern Africa, 1910-1950* (Portsmouth, N.H.: Heinemann).

Johnson, D., Pete, S. and Du Plessis, M. (2001), *Jurisprudence. A South African Perspective* (Durban: Butterworths).

Johnston, N. and Simbine, C. (1998), 'The Usual Victims: The Aliens Control Act and the Voices of Mozambicans' in Crush (ed.), 160–180.

Klaarens, J. (1996), 'So Far Not So Good: An Analysis of Immigration Decisions under the Interim Constitution', *South African Journal on Human Rights*, **12**, 605–616.

Lazarus, N. (2004), 'The South African Ideology: The Myth of Exceptionalism, the Idea of Renaissance', *South Atlantic Quarterly*, **103**(4), 605–626. [DOI: 10.1215/00382876-103-4-607]

Lodge, T. (2002), *Politics in South Africa: From Mandela to Mbeki* (Cape Town: David Philip).

Magubane, P. and Klopper, S. (2000), *African Renaissance* (London: Struik).

Majodina, Z., ed. (2001), *The Challenge of Forced Migration in South Africa* (Pretoria: Africa Institute of South Africa).

Makgoba, M W. (1999), *African Renaissance: The New Struggle* (Cape Town: Mafube/Tafelberg).

Marais, H. (2001), *South Africa. Limits to Change*, 2nd edn (London: Zed Books).

Mbeki, T. (1998), *Africa. The Time has Come* (Cape Town: Tafelberg).

Mbigi, L. (1995) *Search of the African Business Renaissance: An African Cultural Perspective* (Randburg: Knowledge Resources).

McDonald, D. et al. (1998), *Challenging Xenophobia: Myths and Realities about Cross-Border Migration in South Africa* (Cape Town: IDASA).

Minnaar, A. and Hough, M. (1996), *Who Goes There? Perspectives on Migration and Illegal Aliens in Southern Africa* (Pretoria: HSRC).

Moloka, E. and Le Roux, E., eds. (2000), *Problematising the African renaissance* (Pretoria: Africa Institute of South Africa).

Moodie, T.D. (1994), *Going for Gold: Men, Mines and Migration* (Berkeley: University of California Press).

Mulemfo, M.M. (2000), *Thabo Mbeki and the African Renaissance: the Emergence of a New African Leadership* (Pretoria: Actua Press).

Murobe, M. (2000), 'Globalisation and African Renaissance: An Ethical Reflection' in Moloka (ed.) and and Le Roux, 43–67.

Murray, C. (1986), 'Mozambican Refugees: South Africa's Responsibility', *South African Journal on Human Rights*, **2**, 154–163.

Navarro, J., ed. (2003), *Malangatana Valente Ngwenya*. McGuire, H.C., Nunes, Z.C. and Rougle, W.P. (trans.) (Dar es Salaam: Mkuki na Nyota).

Okumu, W.A.J. (2002), *The African Renaissance: history, significance and strategy*, (Trenton, N.J.: Africa World).

Packard, R. (1989), *White Plague, Black Labour: Tuberculosis and the Political Economy of Health and Disease in South Africa* (Berkeley: University of California Press).

Paton, B. (1995), *Labour Export Policy in the Development of Southern Africa* (Basingstoke: Macmillan).

Saul, J. (2001), 'Cry the Beloved Country: the Post-Apartheid Denouement', *Monthly Review*, **52**(8), 1–51.

Semmel, B. (1993), *The Liberal Ideal and the Demons of Empire. Theories of Imperialism from Adam Smith to Lenin* (Baltimore: Johns Hopkins Press).

Solomon, H. (2003), *Of Myths and Migration. Illegal Immigration into South Africa* (Pretoria: University of South Africa Press).

Southern African Migration Project, http://www.queensu.ca/samp/.

UNECA (1989), *South Africa's Destabilization: The Economic Cost of Frontline Resistance to Apartheid* (New York: United Nations).

Vil-Nkomo, S. and Myburgh, J. (1999), 'The Political Economy of an African Renaissance: Understanding the Structural Conditions and Forms' in Makgoba (ed.), 266–279.

Worger, W. (1987), *South Africa's City of Diamonds: Mine Workers and Monopoly Capitalism in Kimberley, 1867-1895* (New Haven, Conn.: Yale University Press).

PART III

ASIA

PART III

ASIA

Chapter 12

Emigration and Sociocultural Change in Iran

Taghi Azadarmaki

Sociology Department, University of Tehran, Iran

Mehri Bahar

Cultural Studies, Communication Department, University of Tehran, Iran

Preamble

The two categories – immigrant and asylum-seeker/refugee – are often mistakenly conflated. This leads to misapprehensions about the condition of people who have emigrated from their countries, and the degree of their contact with and influence in their home countries. In considering the differences between the connotations of immigration and asylum-seeking it is important to take into account the role that immigrants and asylum-seekers continue to have in their homeland from social, economic and cultural points of view. My main objective in this chapter is to describe the role and influence of Iranian emigrants on the homeland.

Asylum-seekers/refugees are those migrants whose departure is a consequence of their incommensurable objections to the prevailing ideological situation in the homeland. Asylum-seekers leave their homeland because they find it impossible to remain there, irrespective of personal and domestic attachments – a situation that is usually expressed in the sentiment: 'I had no future in my own country' (Farmanfaryan, 1997, p. 99). In other words, asylum-seekers define their status in terms of ideological (and thereby social and cultural) isolation, which provides the ground for the individual to cut off ties with his or her society. Departure under such circumstance is usually indefinite. Contrary to the concept of asylum-seeking, immigration (that is emigration from the homeland) is characterized by economic motives and a continuous and vital link to the homeland. Though, according to Saroukhani, 'immigration is the intentional movement of people to a geographical location and entails a permanent or long term change in place of residence' (Saroukhani, 1992, p. 450), there exists for the immigrant an ongoing attachment to the homeland and the possibility of voluntary return. Immigration is primarily motivated by economic reasons, and occurs when immigrants seek permanent, seasonal or temporary employment in a country other than their homeland.

Immigrants are different from asylum-seekers/refugees in that they do not cut off ties with their homeland and have, in different ways, a continuous influence therein. Usually, immigrants undertake migration from their homeland because they wish to support and benefit their families. That naturally entails an ongoing set of interchanges and exchanges between immigrants in their locations and their families in the homeland. The main aim of Iranian immigrants is to provide for and support their families, which, from a wider perspective, is a contribution to social stability. Thus, after emigration, immigrants generally have a positive and constructive role in their homeland from a social point of view. The notion of an eventual return to the homeland is implicit in this effort. Asylum-seekers/refugees, in contrast, by undertaking an indefinite departure are unlikely to have a positive role in the construction of their homeland.

Assumptions and Background

Following from the above, this discussion of the social impact of migrants from Iran within Iran is based on a number of assumptions. One, a strict distinction needs to be made between asylum-seekers/refugees and immigrants, since they have different kinds of impact on their homelands and on their recipient lands. Two, immigrants have observable positive and negative impacts on their homeland and the recipient lands. Three, immigrants are innovative, floating, and fluid entities between the two main societies.

Iran both accepts immigrants and exports immigrants to other countries. Those entering Iran are mainly refugees. According to a 1995 United Nations survey, there are about 15 million refugees throughout the world. Of these only 1 million have been living in developed countries while the rest have been living in developing countries (UNHCR, 1995). According to the same survey Iran, with more than 2 million refugees, was (despite the fact that about 1.5 million of Afghans had returned to their homeland (see Jamshidiaha and Babai, 2002) and continues to be top of the list of countries that accept refugees. Leaving Iran are significant numbers of immigrants to European and American countries. The background of emigration from Iran dates back to the nineteenth century, after Iran's acquaintance with the West. Before the start of the Second World War the rate of immigration was very low. From the beginning of the regime of Mohammad Reza Shah Pahlavi, and with gradual increase in rate of literacy, expansion of relationship with the West, and greater acquaintance with life in other countries, emigration from Iran has increased. According to the Deputy Consular of the Iranian Ministry of Foreign Affairs, the number of Iranians living abroad is about 3 million: 'The first country in which a considerable number of Iranians live is the USA and in the second place is Canada and then comes European countries such as Britain, France, Germany, Sweden and Australia' (Hadi, 2003). Surveys published by the International Monetary Fund show that Iran's brain drain is the highest among 61 developing countries; it is estimated that the overall proportion of brain drain from Iran is about 15 per cent whereas from other main Asian countries it is less than 9 per cent (Carrington and Detragiache, 1999).

Theoretical Approach

In this chapter I do not address the causes of and factors leading to emigration from Iran and as a result I do not need to evoke the usual theoretical frameworks – such as functionalist theories or theories of change and development – that are called upon to explain immigration and asylum-seeking. Most of these theories are not particularly useful for examining the effect of emigration on the home country. For the latter, it seems to me that Samir Amin's 'theory of dependency', adapted for this purpose, is likely to be the most productive. Amin has developed his ideas in a consistent and linked fashion since the 1970s (see particularly Amin, 1974; Amin, 1977; Amin, 1990; Amin, 1997) – instead of a detailed exposition it is best here to touch upon some key notions. As regards immigration, he maintains that: 'one can not differentiate the causes of immigration from its effects. On the one hand immigration is the result of unequal development and on the other hand causes its expansion' (Amin, 1997, p. 120). Immigration is thus both a symptom and a product of a larger problem: that of unequal development which holds developed and developing contexts in a constant relationship of mutual dependency. Following Amin's cue, my main concern in studying immigration in the context of Iran is to effectively uncover the unequal relations that exist between different societies.

The most important idea that is mentioned in Amin's dependency theory is the relationship of 'centre-periphery', which leads to the greater dependency of periphery to centre. This has to do with the nature of capitalist expansion. According to Amin, at a certain stage of development the capitalist system expands outwards from the centres of capital circulation, and structures the relationships that characterize the surrounding world. This leads to the dominance of a developed centre over and at the expense of the periphery which consequently remains underdeveloped. This process enables countries at the centre with capitalist structures to coexist with pre-capitalist structures which prevail in peripheral countries.

Two points emerge from Amin's ideas that are particularly relevant here: 1) it is in the nature of the capitalist system that the centre dictates policy to the periphery; and 2) the tendency toward dependency is concretized through the immigration of individuals and the transfer of capital from periphery to centre. These two points, drawn from Amin's ideas, suggest that only a one-way relationship can exist between centre and periphery.

Interestingly however empirical observation shows something contrary to this. This contrary indication is, it seems to me, of great interest and forms the main thrust of this chapter. It appears that one of the principle factors in adjusting the centre-periphery relationship is that of immigration, which can be understood as a floating phenomenon between periphery and centre. The immigrant, as I have observed above, is someone who floats between homeland and recipient land, and is someone who belongs to both. The immigrant has a fluid relationship with both. The fluidity of the immigrant causes the expansion of his or her social world to comprise a mix of the past and present. And this fluidity disturbs the neat one-way passage between, and static relationship of, centre-periphery which Amin postulates.

This is clearly seen with regard to Iranian immigrants. The main reason why Iranian immigrants enter into this fluid in-between space is, as I have suggested above, because of the importance and role of the family (see also Azadarmaki, 1992, p. 30). The Iranian immigrant rarely tries to immigrate without his or her family and attendant social traditions, or without maintaining a continuous relationship with the family in the homeland. In other words, it is the social structure of the family that supports immigration at times of poverty or other crises. The immigrant who reaches a better economic position in the new country is expected to and usually undertakes to support his family back home. This allegiance ensures that Iranian emigration does not lead to a simple transfer of capital and manpower from periphery to centre. On the contrary, an interactive relationship between immigrant in the recipient country and the home country develops, structured through the family, which leads to cultural, economic and social reconstruction on both fronts – and particularly in the home country. In other words, the interaction that takes place between recipient country and home country through Iranian emigrants abroad attempts to create an Iranian social world which is much advanced than the Iranian social world of yesterday. Indeed, Iran needs no longer be referred to as a confined geopolitical territory, but as a cultural domain (of which the territory of Iran is the major part). In this cultural domain of Iran American Iranians, European Iranians, Australian Iranians and many other Iranians all have a coherent place.

The phenomenon of Iranian immigration abroad, or of Iranian emigration, could be thought of as consisting of two stages. In the first stage emigration is considered as the factor that disturbs the static state of the surrounding home society, by the establishment of a critical environment and by the transfer of manpower and capital abroad. In the second stage immigration is considered in terms of settlement and consolidation in a recipient country, with subsequent returns to the homeland. The positive impact of migration on the home society is discerned in this stage. In the latter, through the transfer of experience, new knowledge, capital and new interests to their own home society migration becomes an important factor in cultural, economic and social changes therein. The impact of emigrants on the homeland can be seen in the modification of political structures, formation of new social forces, transfer of new values, reconceptualization of Iranian and contemporary worlds, and so on. The following figure conveys concisely the situation that I have delineated above.

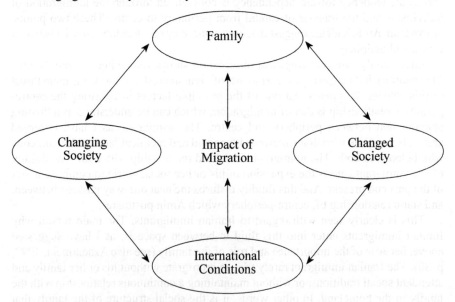

Figure 12.1   The impact of migration

In the remainder of this chapter I examine the role of Iranian immigrants as a floating entity between home country and recipient country and their impact on Iran.

The Increase in Emigration Trends in Iran

Emigration from Iran has a long history. The following table indicates relative rates of emigration and types of emigrants according to historical period:

Table 12.1   Emigration according to historical period

Era of emigration	Amount of emigration	Range of emigration
Qajar (till 1925)	Minimum	Limited: students, politicians
Pahlavi (1925-1979)	Maximum	Varied: students, professors, physicians and politicians
Islamic Republic (1979 onwards)	Maximum	Wide: students, professors, physicians, politicians, investors, skilled and ordinary people

1st − Qajar Era:
This era saw the lowest rate of emigration from Iran. Only a small number of students were dispatched to Europe, and some of politicians, opponent of the regime, migrated to Europe.

2nd − Pahlavi Regime:
Emigration started from the beginning of the Pahlavi regime and occurred in several stages. The first serious emigration period began after the Second World War, which led to the occupation of Iran and the fall of Reza Shah. Students and politicians departed in significant numbers. During the Mohammad Reza Shah era and until the Islamic Revolution emigration maintained its ascending trend. The majority were students who were sent abroad for studies, many of whom did not return to Iran upon completion of their studies. UNESCO surveys in 1976 showed that between 1969 and 1973 the number of immigrant students studying in foreign countries throughout the world had increased from 297,575 to 400,686. Most students resided in the USA. According to statistics of the US Department for Examining Applications for Residency in 1973 nearly 17 per cent of Iranian students applied for permanent residence in the USA upon arrival. Most Iranian immigrants had higher education qualifications. Between 1970 and 1975 about 28.1 per cent of migrant

Iranians were professionals and specialists, with the largest group among them consisting of physicians and surgeons. In 1971, nearly 30 per cent of physicians who graduated from Iranian universities emigrated from Iran and entered the labour market of other countries, including the USA (Dehghan, 1980/1368, pp. 192–3). West Germany, Britain and France were among countries that also attracted many Iranian immigrants. In subsequent years, however, the share of the USA of these individuals was higher than that of other Western countries. In the academic year 1977–1978 nearly 100,000 Iranian students were studying abroad, of whom 36,220 students were accepted by USA higher education institutions (Hosany-Nejad, 1980/1368, pp. 190–1), and the rest were located in Britain, West Germany and France as well as in Australia and Italy.

3rd – Islamic Republic of Iran:
Before the Islamic revolution a considerable number of Iranian students were studying or living abroad. An extensive wave of asylum-seeking immigrants from Iran appeared abroad from the early 1980s. During 1982–1983 particularly Turkey and some European countries faced the dilemma of dealing with significant flows of Iranian immigration and asylum-seeking. The majority of these immigrants crossed the borders of Turkey and Pakistan illegally. Most were men. Figures published by the United Nations Higher Commission of Refugees (UNHCR) indicated that only 3 per cent of all refugees (not just Iranian) who entered Turkey in 1982–1983 were single women (Farmanfarayan, 1997/1375, p. 94). According to a report published by Bozorgmehr and Sabbagh (1998), based on the USA census of 1980, about 23 per cent of Iranian immigrants held a Master's or Doctorate degree – which is a considerable figure compared to the of 12.5 per cent of other immigrants and 7.5 per cent of the total population. The immigration of educated people from Iran to foreign countries continues to show an ascending trend (Dehghan, 1980/1368, p. 223).

Typology of Iranian Immigrants

Different types of Iranian immigrants in the world can be discerned based on age group, assets and ownership at the time of immigration, chronology, type of immigration, time of and reason for immigration, and so on. Of these ownership is, it seems to me, the main index for categorizing Iranian immigrants and assessing their impact on the home country and in their recipient countries. This is because the possession of a house, land or an institute or organization can provide substantial explanatory grounds for understanding the impact of immigration/emigration. From this perspective three different types of Iranian immigrants can be discerned:

1   Immigrants with no ownership whatsoever in Iran, who emigrate in order to improve living conditions and acquire ownership status. Poor people, skilled workers seeking better jobs, and younger people are examples of this group. Those in this group often cross the border to Turkey, Central Asian countries and Arabic countries to seek work, before moving toward their final destinations. Iranian workers in Kuwait before the Persian Gulf War and Iranian immigrants in Turkey during the War are examples of this group.

2   Immigrants with a moderately good economic (ownership) position in Iran, who decide to emigrate in order to improve living conditions further.
3   Immigrants with a sound or affluent economic (ownership) position in Iran, who were forced to emigrate because of political conditions.

The following table summarizes further details of these three categories, some of which are expanded in following subsections:

Table 12.2   Ownership by immigrants

	Without ownership	Moderate ownership	Good Ownership
Social force	Workers, students, specialists	Intellectuals and educated people	Businessmen and others
Job prior to emigration	Unemployed or low income jobs	Specialists and professionals	Bazar, government and business partners
Activity affecting homeland after emigration	To purchase property and create possibility for return	To form social, political, cultural and academic gatherings for reinforcing the homeland.	Investment in export and import of goods
Location	Arabic countries and countries in region as well as European countries	North American countries and European countries	European and North American countries
The possibility to return	High	Medium	Very low
Degree of influence	Low	High	High

With this typology of Iranian migrants, and the above observations on the character of Iranian migration, in mind it is now possible to assess the impact of Iranian immigrants on their recipient countries and of Iranian emigrants on their home country.

Factors behind Impact of Iranian Emigration

In examining the influence of emigrants on the homeland, and concordantly of immigrants in their recipient countries, it is necessary to bear in mind certain factors. These are: the nature of their connection with the homeland, the location of immigration, and the reason for emigration.

The Connection with Homeland

The reason why Iranian emigrants have some influence on Iranian society is their close ties with their homeland. At an average in each family category in every Iranian city there is at least one person per family living abroad. The range of influence that emigrants have on their homeland is therefore considerable. On the other side, Iranians living abroad are permitted to retain their Iranian passports. In recent years, many refugees have received Iranian passports too. Mr Hadi, the Deputy Consular of the Ministry of Foreign Affairs, has declared in 2004 that: 'According to the comparative statistics of 80 countries, in 1998 the people visiting our consular departments have increased by 40 per cent. We have given passports to 20,000 refugees' (Hadi (2004).

Location of Immigration

The impact that emigrants have on Iran also depends on the location that they have chosen for immigration. If immigrants enter recipient countries that have a positive and transparent policy toward immigration Iranian immigrants find the opportunity to support their families in the homeland. If however immigrants enter a country that offers limited prospects to them then their influence on the homeland is diminished. This relationship is shown in the following table:

Table 12.3   Influence of location on immigrants

Location	Type of influence	Rate	Range
Countries in region	Economic	Limited	Local, family
European countries	Cultural and political	Medium	Press and universities
USA	Political and economic	High	Market and politics

Table 12.4   Reason and results of emigration

Reason for emigration	The result of emigration
1- Political	Criticism of the current situation in Iran
2- Economic, to improve living conditions	Investment in Iran
3- To gain skills and knowledge	To increase the knowledge and know-how as well as transfer of technology
4-Entertainment	Emphasis on life and welfare

The Reason for Emigration

The reason for emigration determines the rate and type of influence that emigrants might have on their homeland. If an emigrant left the country because of political reasons and remains critical of the social and political order, his or her influence from a cultural and economic point of view is likely to be limited. The emigrant who leaves Iran for educational purposes has the possibility of importing new ideas and technology to Iran, and consequently has a higher level of influence. The different kinds of influence are summarized in Table 12.4.

The Impact of Iranian Immigration on Recipient Societies

Since immigrants come from different cultural and social backgrounds from those in the recipient countries they naturally face some difficulties on arrival and in establishing themselves therein. These difficulties are, however, usually surmounted by the contribution of their skills and abilities, their willingness to take higher risks, by their energy and investments, and by the fact that they are generally young and adaptable – these feed into immigrants creating a new society in the recipient countries.

Difficulties Due To Negative Attitudes

Iranian immigrants in their new living environments face various difficulties. The first problem is the negative attitude of the recipient country toward immigrants. Iranian people also have a negative attitude toward immigrants from other countries, such as Afghanistan, Iraq and northern countries before and after the collapse of the Soviet Union. Khajehpour Khouie has concluded from the results of his research on Afghan immigrants that:

> The first and most clear conclusion that one would reach in this research is that majority of Tehran citizens have a negative look at the presence of Afghans refugees in Iran. In fact only 8.9 per cent of the interviewees have considered their presence as positive while 66.7 per cent of the people being interviewed have considered their presence as negative and 25.4 per cent have considered their presence as having no effect whatsoever. We find out the low level of accepting immigrants among Tehran citizens when 88.4 per cent of the interviewees were refused to have a business partnership with Afghan refugees and 69.1 per cent did not want to even live in neighborhood of a refugee. About 70 per cent of Tehran citizens believed that the immigration of Afghans had a negative impact on Iran economy (Khajehpour Khouie, 1997/1375, pp. 33).

A trend of growing negative attitudes toward Afghan immigrants in Iran both among the public and in policy has been noted by several researchers (Turton and Marsden, 2002; Strand, Suhrke and Harpviken, 2004; Stigter, 2005). As the introduction to this book observes, judging from recent research such negative attitudes toward immigrants are widespread in countries which receive significant numbers of immigrants. Though little specific data on the reception of Iranian immigrants in

America or Europe is available there is circumstantial evidence that this is consistent with the general trend. Iranian immigrants face similar difficulties on arrival and in settling down as other groups of immigrants in recipient countries.

Creating a New Society

Since most Iranian immigrants are solvent and are highly educated they make a significant contribution to the recipient country. For example, about 165,000 Iranian specialists holding a university degree are working for scientific centres as well as for industries in the USA, 57 per cent of them have Bachelor's degrees or higher degrees. In fact, from an academic point of view, Iranian immigrants are in third place after Indian and Chinese immigrants in terms of educational qualifications in the USA in 1990 about half of Iranian immigrants working in the USA were active at managerial and specialized levels (Bayat, 1997/1375, p. 12).

The Impact of Iranian Emigration on the Home Society

There are various kinds of impact that emigrants have on Iran. These include: creating a nostalgia culture, representing the attractions of a floating life, raising emphasis on literacy and wealth, reinforcing the role international organizations, putting pressure for more democracy, developing international economic links, contributing to urban development, encouraging awareness of globalization. In this section I discuss these in terms of their positive and negative nature.

Negative Impacts

The emigration of nearly 3 million people from Iran has had damaging cultural, social and economic effects in recent years. The departure of many intellectuals and their families resulted in a considerable loss of financial and cultural capital. It resulted in the loss of the investment made by Iran for their education and training, as well as of the contribution they could have made to Iranian society and Iran's economic growth. The emigration of skilled workers from Iran also creates problems. When skilled and specialized people leave the country the ones who are not so skilled replace them and a cycle of non-development or impeded development sets in.

Positive Impacts

The positive impact of emigrants on Iran can be perceived from political, economic, cultural and social points of view. Brief observations on each of these are given here.

a) Social and Cultural Impact

Migrants occupy, I have observed, an in-between and fluid presence between two worlds, that of their homeland and of the recipient society. They cannot wholly adapt themselves to either, and need to be cognizant of both and negotiate between both.

Sometimes they try to return to the values of the home society to define their place in the new situation. This results in their making a new kind of social and cultural impact on their homeland.

In general, immigrants suffer from nostalgia about their former homeland and culture (see also Ivanov, this volume). Nostalgia entails not only idealization of the past, but also a dislocation of the sense of present reality and time. The past exists in the present and the present constructs the past. Nostalgia also creates a desire for return at the same time as generating anxieties about return. This is often expressed in Iranian immigrants' attempts to create an Iranian world in exile, with the notion of an immediate and temporary retreat or return involved, and hiding an ultimate desire for return to the homeland. But such microcosmic creations of Iranian cultural spaces abroad is a product of the immigrant condition, and not based on social and cultural realities.

However, since immigrants often entertain a constant desire to return to their homeland, they try to recover their social traditions and culture. In this way they create an atmosphere which enable critical reflection on and examinations of social and cultural issues pertinent to their homeland. Thus, Nafisi observes:

> Traditions set the ground for making a population knowledgeable about their borders, and through this people reinforce and confirm individual and collective identity. In this way, traditions are an important tool for experiencing the feeling of belonging to a group. That is why events such as wedding celebrations, birthday parties and new years have a special place in the cultural complex of immigrants' lives. In this way immigrants draw up their collective borders and reinforce them (Nafisi, 1960, p. 59).

Such understanding of Iranian cultural and historical background as exists abroad is largely due to the work of intellectual immigrants. They have been responsible for rejuvenating the study of Iranian music, literature, history of thoughts and minds, and for examining and discussing such internationally important Iranian events such as the Constitutional revolution, Petroleum national movement, Islamic revolution and collapse of monarchy. Much academic collaboration and scholarship is due to the efforts of Iranian immigrants, which has had a salutary effect both on self-understanding in Iran and on understanding of Iran abroad.

Iranian emigrants have also had a substantial role to play in negotiating between individual rights and the nation-state in Iran, which is an important aspect of the naturalization of the nation-state. Iranian immigrants abroad have exercised the advantage of their simultaneous removal from and connection to the homeland to offer new meanings of individualism and naturalization of nation-state. These individuals are often therefore defenders of individual rights, civil society and new social values in Iran.

In art and music too Iranian emigrants have played an important role in Iran. They have contributed to the introduction of pop music and in emphasizing the importance of both old singers and new groups (such as Arian). The cultivation of performance arts and creative thinking is encouraged by the creation of various television and radio channels dedicated to Iranian culture abroad (Bahar, 2001/1380, p. 93). There are now 20 such television and radio channels in the USA These channels do not necessarily broadcast programmes against the Islamic Republic of Iran; while providing critical debate about the social traditions and religious rule in Iran they provide their own cultural views. They introduce to many Iranians what living in a foreign country is like, raise awareness of historical figures, advertise new and old goods, and so on.

b) Economic Impact

Despite the break in political ties between Iran and the USA the USA continues to be one of the main foreign business partners of Iran. The relations between the countries at political as well as economic levels are substantially mediated by Iranian immigrants there.

There is a United Nations programme aimed at effecting transfer of knowledge through immigrants so as to compensate for the brain drain in developing countries. This program enables volunteer skilled immigrants to travel to their homelands and participate in short training courses of 3–12 weeks. Through such training courses they help the government, universities and private and public sectors in their homeland. In this scheme the air ticket and accommodation expenses of volunteers are paid. Many Iranian immigrants have used this opportunity to revitalize and reorganize the educational atmosphere in Iran. On the business front, a number of Iranian immigrants are directly involved in the sale and purchase of US dollars, and the export of carpets and pistachios. The trade in foreign currency abroad has created a powerful network of Iranian and foreign business men. This network not only exchanges dollars to rials and vice-versa, but also has entered into property development abroad and inside Iran. International companies managed by such Iranian immigrants have now entered in businesses such as transportation of passengers, visa and migration services, Internet resources. The export of carpets is also under the control of immigrants in the USA and Europe. By establishing companies in partnership with people inside Iran and non-Iranians they have tried to import goods that otherwise would not have been possible to import by the government.

c) Political Impact

The great interest among Iranian immigrant intellectuals in Iranian history, and in particular in events that took place during the Pahlavi regime, have led to some kind of revival of interest in royalist thought in Iran. The introduction of topics such as homeland's king and nationalism by people such as Seyed Javad Tabatabaie and Daryoush Shayegan and others have acquired a more definite meaning than heretofore. One of the consequences of this research is the growing interest in the role of influential families such as of Farmanfarmaian and Lajvardi families in the modern Iran.

Iranian immigrants and asylum seekers abroad do often try to generate a pessimistic view of Iran's society and of the government in their interactions with foreigners. It seems to me that this is primarily an attempt to justify their departure from Iran. Even immigrants who have not been successful in their recipient countries occasionally try to pretend that their condition is ideal. In studies carried out on Iranian immigrants and refugees in England in 2001 (Nateghpour, 2004/1383, pp. 10–12) this was found to be the case. Here 33.3 per cent of the immigrants surveyed considered living in Iran before the immigration as living in hell, and 23.2 per cent considered living in Iran as hard. And 82.3 per cent expressed satisfaction at leaving their country, the rest are not satisfied. If the proper conditions arise about 29.3 per cent of these immigrants said they would like to return to Iran, and the rest said that they will never return to Iran.

In 2004, the deputy consular of the Ministry of Foreign Affairs announced that they are considering the possibility of political participation of Iranians living abroad in the parliament. It would become possible for Iranians living abroad to be represented by three seats in the Iran parliament.

The observations of this section are summarized in the following table.

Table 12.5   Kinds of impact of emigration

Different Impacts	Areas
1 – Social Impacts:	1 The emergence of the Immigrant Group
	2 Pro-Social development
	3 Pro-new social relations
	4 Pro-nuclear Family
	5 Pro-open relationship among boys and girls
	6 Sensitive towards women's, prisoners', and minority groups' rights
	7 New social forces in making public spheres.
2 – Cultural Impacts:	1 Pro-Pop Music
	2 Criticizing social traditions
	3 Supporting the previous regime
	4 Presenting new definition of Iranian identity
	5 Making a sub-culture and producing nostalgic literature.
3 – Political Impacts:	1 Criticizing the new government
	2 Pro-Human Rights
	3 Pro–open and free relationship with the world
	4 Pro-political democracy
4 – Economical Impacts:	1 Investment in rug industry, housing, properties, and luxuries
	2 Balance between foreign currency and Iranian money
	3 Importing consumer products
	4 Exporting rugs, tiles, handicraft, and pistachio

Conclusion

I have argued in this chapter that Iranian immigrants abroad have a close tie with their homeland during the migration and after settlement, and substantially impact the affairs of their homeland from economic, political, cultural and social perspectives.

The factor that creates the setting for such influence to be exerted is the family of the immigrant in the homeland. This involves encouraging family members to learn, travel and understand the wider world, following the world issues, investing in Iran by purchasing house and property, paying to support and care for parents and family. Educated Iranian immigrants are involved in transfer of technology to the homeland and translation of books or publication of books about issues in Iran. Most scholarly books about political and social developments of the new era have been prepared by the intellectuals living abroad.

References

Amin, S. (1974), *Accumulation on a World Scale*, (Trans. Brian Pearce. London: Monthly Review Press).

Amin, S. (1977), *Imperialism and Unequal Development* (Hassocks: Harvester).

Amin, S. (1990), *Delinking: Toward a Polycentric World*. Wolfers, M. (translated by) (London: Zed).

Amin, S. (1997), *Capitalism in the Age of Globalization: The Management of Contemporary Society* (London: Zed).

Azadarmaki, T. (1992), *Socio-Cultural Changes in the Iranian Family* (Tehran: University of Tehran).

Bahar, M. (Winter 2001/1380), 'Social-Cultural Changes and Institutional Changes in Iran: The Case of Bazar', *Human Science Journal* (Tehran: Mazanderan University) 3, 77–102.

Bayat, K. (Spring 1997)/1375), 'Soviet Union's Refuge in Iran', *Ghoftegho* [Discourse] 11, 7–25.

Bozorgmehr, M. and Sabbagh, G. (1998), 'High Status Immigrants: A Statistical Profile of Iranians in the United States', *Iranian Studies*, **21**, 3–4, 5–36.

Carrington, W.J. and Detragiache, E. (June 1999), 'How Extensive is the Brain Drain?', *Finance and Development*, **36**, 2.

Dehghan, M. 1980) 'Brain Drain: Unknown Phenomenon', '*Ettelaat Siyasi-Eghtesadi*' [Political and Economic Journal], 190-191, 220–234.

Farmanfaryan, A. (1997/1375), 'Phnahandeghi: Ghosaste Phavandenha', *Ghoftegho*, **11**, 89–104.

Hadi, M.A. (2003), 'Korsie Namayandeghi Majles barayeh Iraniane Mohazer', *Shargh*, **211**.

Hadi, M.A. (2003/1381), 'Korsiye Majles baraye Iraniane Kharej az Keshvar' ('Parliament for Iranians Abroad'), *Shargh*, **211**, 11 Khordad, 24 May.

Hadi, M.A. (2004), 'Iraniane Kharez az Kheshvar dar liste siyah nistand', *Shargh*, **18** Khordad.

Hadi, M.A. (2004/1383), 'Iraniane Kharej az Keshvar dar Liste Siyah Nistand' (Iranians Abroad are not in the Black List), Shargh 18 Kordad, 1 July, 12.

Hosany-Nejad, S. (1980)/1368), 'The Dimensions of Brain Drain', *Ettelaat Siyasi-Eghtesadi* 192-3, 23–98.

Jamshidiaha, G. and Babai, Y. (2002/1381), 'Factors on Returning Afghani Immigrants', *Nameh Olume Ejtemai* [Social Science Journal] 20, 71–90.

Khajehpour Khouie, B. (1997/1375), 'Refuge and Citizenship', *Ghoftego*, **11**, 25–33.

Nafisi, A.A. (1960/1343), *Farhanghe Nafisi [Nafisi's Encyclopedia] 5th vol* (Tehran: Khayam Publications).

Nateghpour, Z. (2004/1383), *Iranian Emigrants in United Kingdom* (Tehran: Social Science Faculty, The University of Tehran).

Saroukhani, B. (1992/1370), *Daramadi bar daeratoal Olume Ejtemaeih [Introduction to Encyclopedia of Social Science]* (Tehran: Kayhan).

Stigter, E. (2005), *Transnational Networks and Migration from Herat to Iran* (Kabul: Afghanistan Research and Evaluation Unit).

Strand, A., Suhrke, A. and Harpviken, K.B. (July 2004), 'Afghan Refugees in Iran', *Policy Brief, CMI/PRIO*.

Turton, D. and Marsden, P. (2002), *Taking Refugees for a Ride?*, *The Politics of Refugee Return to Afghanistan* (Kabul: Afghanistan Research and Evaluation Unit).

UNHCR (1995), 'The State of the World's Refugees' in *Search of Solutions* (Oxford: Oxford University Press).

Chapter 13

Imaginary Migrations in Contemporary Chinese Public Culture

Yue Daiyun

Chinese and Comparative Literature, Peking University, Beijing, China

A Different Inflection on Economic Migration

Economic migration is usually understood in terms of the physical movement of peoples from one location to another, both within a country and across countries, for the sake of earning a livelihood or to improve material conditions. From the Chinese point of view there have been, in recent years, two kinds of significant physical migrations which have been the subject of much research and contemplation. An overview of both the expanding flow of rural to urban migration within China, and the significant flow of Chinese migrants to overseas destinations is available in Huang Ping and Frank Pieke's report *China Migration: Country Study* (2003). The cultural, political and economic implications of rural-urban migrations have received attention separately too (see Davin, 1999; Solinger, 1999; Cai, 2000; Murphy, 2002), as has the manner in which Chinese immigrants are received abroad (Chin and Lin, 1999; Benton and Pieke eds. 1998; Wang, G., 2000). In this chapter it is not my intention to provide a survey of or attempt to contribute to this valuable research. In fact, for this chapter a rather different inflection is given to the idea of economic migration: not one that has a sociologically or economically determined focus on the causes and effects of physical migration, but one that attempts to see migration as an abstract cultural process *inside* China that is attached to the economic logic of market liberalization. This chapter is therefore not a contribution to research on economic migration along conventional lines. It provides instead an impressionistic account of contemporary Chinese society, wherein imaginary migrations and migratory cultural impacts become a continuous social experience, in which migrational desires and anxieties become an immediate internal reality are conceptualized as a metaphor. Within the urban Chinese location and from the Chinese cultural studies perspective this chapter assumes, this sense of internal migrations bound by an economic logic seems to me more immediately relevant than the physical experience of Chinese migration. Also, this mode of thinking about economic migration appears to me to enable a deconstruction of the more rigorously but narrowly defined sociological understanding of that phrase.

Instead of quoting facts and figures then, in this chapter I present some observations on changes in the cultural environment of urban China. The prevailing cultural environment is best discerned in what I think of as the public cultural productions of contemporary China. How internal imaginary migrations are becoming bound up with the subsuming logic of commercialization and commodification is demonstrated by describing such cultural productions. What is occurring in China now, I argue, is a dislocation of public culture from Chinese heritage and history, and the installation of a post-modern neuterness where the Chinese are caught up in a constant flux of imaginary migrations held together by a tight economic logic. Behind this lies the disappearance of a promising and distinctively Chinese public culture that seemed to be emerging in the 1980s – in the final section I turn briefly to the songs of rock star Cui Jian as an instance of that failed promise.

Public Culture in China

Public culture (mass culture, popular culture) in the contemporary period emanates from large industrial processes, involving cultural production for repetitive mass consumption. The production and consumption of popular audio-visual and print commodities – such as commercial movies, teleplays, spectacle sports, advertisements, pop songs, news stories, sensational features, cartoons – are at the heart of contemporary public culture. These commodities acquire concrete and marketable forms through different (but linked in complex ways) mass media: television, radio, cheap paperbacks, newspapers, magazines, videos, DVDs, CDs, cinema shows, theatre performances, the Internet. Such cultural productions depend on creating and expanding cultural markets, planning corporate strategy and scale of enterprise to maximize profits. The cultural value of the product is realized through effective marketing and distributing. Public culture is overtly and unabashedly commercialized. Since the Second World War, through processes which were anticipated in Walter Benjamin's 1932 essay 'Work of Art in the Age of Mechanical Reproduction' (Benjamin, 1973), and which have been examined by Marcuse (1964), Adorno (1991), Baudrillard (1999) and many others, commercialization has subsumed the cultural domain, reconstructing it according to its own image.

The recent and rapid development of the market economy in China has led to an extraordinary transformation of society, particularly of the cultural landscape. Since the 1980s commercialized mass cultural production has reached all areas of Chinese society, and has become especially deeply embedded in urban social life. Public culture, as understood here, now provides the primary structure and impetus in constructing the ideology of the present. An important shift is involved here: because public culture developed substantially during the process of China's transformation from a planned economy to a market economy, it is inextricably connected to – indeed embodies – the transformation of Chinese values and ideology.

As observed above, the critique of public culture as it is expressed here has already been substantially undertaken by theorists and intellectuals in the capitalist West in the course of the twentieth century. That critique has unravelled and been debated over a prolonged period. In the context of contemporary China that critique acquires a particular and renewed relevance, and is worth reiterating, because of the extraordinarily intensive and rapid transformations in China. The sheer power of commercialization and the seismic changes in public culture take us back to something like the anxieties of, for instance, the Frankfurt School because the contrasts are so very sharp, and have been effected within a couple of decades.

Public Culture and Changes in Class Structure

In the 1950s Chinese society was divided into three classes: workers, peasants and intellectuals. The use of this kind of classification to describe contemporary society, however, is obviously inadequate. A new configuration of classes has emerged through the 1990s, which could be delineated as follows.

The top class now is the 'new rich'. These successful people are no longer the 'millionaires' of the early 1980s – the solitary traders who just happened to get rich, and who have since disappeared. The 'new rich' have capital holdings in billions; their assets are equal to half or even more of the GNP, though they constitute only 1 per cent of the population. Most of the 'new rich' possess social resources that allow them to form symbiotic relationships with those who have power, both economic and political. Among the 'new rich' are some who become rich through their technological know-how and innovations, but these are relatively few. Most consolidate their positions by protecting their own and furthering each other's class interests. The 'new rich' are the élite of today's society, and their taste for luxury consumption goods must be catered to.

The next class is that of the 'white collar worker': a wide spectrum of office-workers and professionals who earn moderate to comfortable livings. This class includes middle-level managers and bureaucrats, technicians and engineers, doctors, teachers, small traders and company personnel – roughly the equivalent of what is thought of as the middle-class in the West. This class is now widely regarded as being the key to the market, the fastest-growing section of consumers with enormous spending power. The electronics, textiles, food and real estate industries are largely geared toward the demands of this class. So-called 'high-taste' literature, music, plays and art are also tailored to their tastes.

The third class is that of the 'unskilled labourer', those without technical skills. Most of these come from the rural areas without registered permanent residence in the cities. Their numbers are huge, and in the metropolis of Shanghai alone there are two million of these. They often watch videos and movies, and they are the main readers of romantic novels and low-priced popular travel books. Their cultural tastes exert an increasing influence on the production of best-sellers, movies, teleplays and popular songs. Publishing companies and popular magazines cannot ignore this big market, and it is they who usually dictate print and broadcast cultural production targeted at metropolitan suburbs and even the rural areas.

Finally, there's the class consisting of the unemployed, the retired, and those who are 'ready-to-work', that is officers, workers, and people who live on meagre salaries. Those in this class sometimes depend on support from traditional family networks. In every family there may be one or two members belonging to the three classes mentioned above, and they will feel that they are responsible for supporting their parents and their brothers and sisters whose living conditions are not so good. The members of this class are still protected by the socialist economic system: despite low salaries, they are able to enjoy free medical treatment, education, low-priced housing. They are everyday consumers and cultural consumers.

In a society configured along the above class lines, public cultural norms are naturally set by perceptions of the first class stratum – the 'new rich' – which has become the focus of aspirations. *Success* is the cultural code of the 'new rich'. *Success* easily translates into wealth, but wealth also translates into images of lifestyle and elegant consumption – signified by top-brand cars, five-star hotels, golf, tennis, membership of clubs and gymnasiums, designer clothes and top-brand equipment. To be of the 'new rich', to succeed, is to conform to images replete with these significations; to wish to be 'new rich', to want to succeed, is to aspire to such conformity or to define one's desires by such images. Public cultural productions through all media endlessly reproduce, reiterate and normativize images of the 'new rich' lifestyle, with its significations of consumables. Here is how the writer Wang Xiaoming sees the image of the 'new rich' and its perpetuations:

> It is usually a man, middle-aged, little fat belly, and fine clothes. He is very rich. He drives his new BMW to work. He might have studied abroad, so he has Western habits. Before leaving for work with the contracts in hands, he will not forget to kiss his beautiful wife goodbye. He pays attention to lifestyle, playing golf at the weekend and going to concerts in the evening ... in the past five or six years, he has become the most glamorous identity. When entrepreneurs build a block of apartments, their advertisements and street banners will say that they are 'ideal homes' especially for him (Wang, X., 2000, p. 11).

Hotels, restaurants, clubs and all sorts of places welcome him, and hope that he will frequent them. Newspapers and magazines try their best to guess his tastes, changing the format, paper and even the contents, for the sole purpose so that they will be put into his living room. Novelists and authors of teleplays and movies, inspired by him, write complicated stories about him and his women ....

Wang Xiaoming argues that the desires and dreams aroused by these 'successful people' reassure people: everyone will have cars, houses and a lot of money, and the remote 'communist society' of the future is replaced by the concrete desire of enjoying the present. This is a 'reality' in which, with money in the pocket, there is freedom because there is nothing that cannot be bought. It is 'style' and 'dignity' when the 'successful people' spend extravagantly and watch others doing their bidding. It is 'beauty' when they wear expensive and the most fashionable clothes. The 'successful people' ideology exerts a strong force on the horizons and desires of people today, with the result that society is crass, utilitarian and pursues only sensual gratification.

The new kind of class configuration appears to mark a convergence of Chinese society towards the capitalist societies of the West. Similar kinds of class inequality, unevenness of distribution of wealth, differentiations of cultural expressions are becoming manifest. But that, in this context, is not so much of interest as the observation that the normativized lifestyle of the 'new rich', which is perpetuated and disseminated through the dispersal of public culture, and which defines the aspirations of the classes arraigned beneath, mark a dislocation which is not experienced in the West. These images mark a departure from the many previous perceptions of the good life, or concepts of pleasure and cultural value, in China, and seem to describe a placeless capitalist world that has been apprehended in China only recently. The images of the 'new rich' seem to describe a land in itself, a pastiche of many places and unreal everywhere, toward which the Chinese people are imaginatively migrating.

Changing Spaces and the Imaginary Migrations

Let me reflect on Hengshan Road in Shanghai to elucidate the meaning of imaginary migrations. This 2.3 km stretch provides a concretization of the manner in which the contemporary social imagination of time and space impinges on the local scene. Hengshan Road was first built by the French as a 'fly place' (a region rented by the Chinese Government to a foreign country), and named Beidang Road in 1922. French phoenix trees line the street and there are many green strips; the buildings are in various styles. Since 1998, it has been revamped by the district government and changed from an uptown to a downtown street. The government has invested six million USD into this project. The resulting 'Oriental Champs Elysées' has become a paradise for high-class consumers. According to recent statistics (Bao, 2000, p. 119), in January 2000 there were 175 businesses in this street, 116 of which were bars and restaurants. Located here also is the Hengshan Road Gallery with its collection of European classical and imagist paintings. Wang Hongtu (Wang, H., 2000) describes the establishment Sasha's on Hengshan Road in the following words:

> Everything has an artificial edge: the grey bricks in the wall, the round lantern hanging from the ceiling, the candle burning in an old oil lantern on the street. What is important is that it seems as if you are in Europe or somewhere in the West: you have been placed in a country with a culture totally different from your own. But this is not in fact so. This is Shanghai, in China. The waiters with yellow skins keep interrupting your hallucination. With the flavour of cappuccino on your lips, you step out of this 'fly place' embedded with Chinese characteristics. After crossing the street, if you turn back, you will see Sasha's standing in the shade, and it becomes more illusory and unreal. You can destroy it with just a snap of the finger (Quoted in Bao 2000, p. 123).

Nearby is O'Malley's, an Irish pub. It is a 'yesterday again' pub, modelled after the old days in Shanghai. Lily and the Red Tomato are music restaurants, the Bourbon Street Bar can provide you with the dynamic experience of being in New Orleans, and at the Xi's Garden you can taste very good traditional Chinese food.

In fact, the act of consumption is not just passive acceptance of material satisfaction; it incorporates active construction of pleasure and different worlds. For the nostalgic, by being in a 'yesterday again' bar the 'old' becomes actually 'new' again, and nostalgia becomes a new kind of feeling to be nurtured and fed. The only thing that remains unchanged is the desire. The act of consumption is not only the relationship between person and commodity, but also the relationship between person and society, person and universe. For some writers born in the 1970s the content of life is mainly in the bars, and the bars located on Hengshan Road are the epitome of Shanghai. Unsurprisingly, Wei Hui's major works, such as *Shanghai*

Baby (2001), describe Shanghai as a huge 'secret garden' which narrates a special ideology, a knowledge system that those who share this ideology can appreciate.

The bars in Shanghai mean different things to different people. For the ordinary people, the bars are a specific entity. For the capitalist, they are paradises of the leisure industry. For the media, they are resources for stories. For the state authorities, they are new landscapes representing a prosperous culture. For the consumers, they are an exotic 'fly place' where they can relax. For the x-generation, they are life itself. For modern writers, they are stages for the performance of desire. For the intellectual, they are illusive cultural images. In short, they are unclear public areas with traces of a spreading capitalism that continuously produce ambiguous meaningful spaces and complex dialogues.

Advertisements Fashioning People

Since 1992 some expensive leisure magazines have appeared which keep pace with overseas trends. The most popular are *ELLI – World Fashionable Clothes* and *Fashion-Cosmopolitan*, and their prices are 10 times more than the common magazines. These are cultural products especially created for the 'successful people', aimed at teaching them how to raise the level of their awareness in high-price material consumption. It focuses mainly on food, housing, travel, shopping, and leisure. These have replaced the former political lectures and ideologically-led reflections on life by pure material consumption. At the same time they construct people's imaginations. The things they advocate have nothing to do with most people, but they excite their desires and imaginations, and thereby extend the culture of consumption and the market for consumables.

Generally speaking, the commodity does not carry an ideology, because it is a kind of embodiment of ideology in itself. The importance of the brand name is not so much the assurance of the quality, as the association of lifestyle. This has been argued cogently by Williamson (1978), Williams (1980) and others – more recently the politics and scope of branding practices have been perceptively examined by Klein (1999). Consider, for example, an advertisement for Parker pens in *Fashion-Cosmopolitan* entitled: 'Transcend time and space and keep pace with the great men'. It reads: 'The value of a century-old pen is not just as a writing tool. When you are holding a pen which many famous people have held, you can fully imagine that you are facing important things just like them'. Depicted are world leaders such as Yeltsin, Bush, Reagan, Gorbachev, Eisenhower and Nixon using a Parker pen at historic events. So having a Parker pen is not only holding a good pen but also holding success and nobility. Here we can see that advertisements not only sell commodities but also identities, feelings, characteristics and also the sense of honour that the commodities have been associated with. In China advertisements are both constructing, and available as manifest symptoms of, a new consumerist ideology. Arguably people are becoming standardized into a single and commercialized cultural form, gradually diminishing in complexity as human beings. While it stimulates the desire of people to pursue material things, it also conceals their real needs.

Advertising has become a profitable new trade in China. As a matter-of-fact the amount of business transacted in advertising in China at 1981 was only RMB 118 million (not including Hong Kong, Macao, Taiwan); in 1995, it had increased to 3,539 million, and 1999 it went to 6,220.5 million (see Tian, 2000).

In an advertisement of the real estate company, Singaporean Beautiful Trees Gallery, are catchphrases like the following: 'This luxury building in the centre of the city can't be matched anywhere'; 'gold-plated Shanxi South Road No. 888'; 'DESLAND – Singaporean multi-national brand'; 'Singaporean Beautiful Trees Gallery, an upper-class place, home of elites and CEOs'. In this advertisement, all kinds of cultural signifiers are mixed together: 1. The multi-national dream – Singapore, DESLAND, emphasis on multi-cultural brands; 2. The superstitious symbolism of 888 or 'rich, rich, rich' (in Cantonese phonology the number 'eight' sounds close to 'be rich and prosper'); 3. The idea of the new class – it is the upper class that can afford luxury; 4. The notion of high culture – 'art gallery'. Several days later, the advertisement added something new that explains its connotative meanings. 'When wealth cannot represent your nobility, and art is the real reflection of your achievements and temperament, the European classical gate will fully reveal your splendid nobility and temperament! We warmly thank the elites, the noble people, and the outstanding people ... who honour us'. And further: 'There are many ways to relax. In the leisure hub of the elites in the Beautiful Tree Gallery, you can find a swimming pool with warm water all the year, a gymnasium, a room for eurythmics, a sauna, a Turkish bath ... and the golf practice site in Guoling'. Evidently, this advertisement targets the 'new rich', who are wealthy but lack confidence. Their identity as upper class has not yet been fully affirmed. They are eager to decorate and become patrons of culture and art. It is interesting that this advertisement was published in the *Xinmin Evening News*, belonging for a long time to common townspeople, whose readers definitely could not buy these apartments. The aim of this advertisement is not sales itself but to add some high social status to these apartments. Those who live in these apartments will be regarded as upper class *among* the common people. Therefore, these advertisements add non-material elements to the material apartments – a 'noble community' is formed.

The Other Side of Cultural Fashion

Contemporary popular culture in China is the result of the market economy; it reflects the central system of the market economy. In the early phase of China's transition toward market economy popular cultural productions had been undertaken, in popular musical forms associated with the West for instance, that were in fact rooted in the Chinese context of economic and political realities. Sadly, those salutary efforts have not been developed. Instead, as seen above, those promising productions have been replaced by various popular cultural productions that reflect internal migrations away from political and economic realities toward an imaginary landscape of 'success' and 'new rich lifestyles', which is configured and held together by a pervasive economic logic of commodification and consumerism. To move toward a conclusion for this chapter, I would like to recall the work of Cui Jian, Chinese king of rock and roll, as an example of popular cultural production rooted in the economic and political realities of China.

Cui Jian was born in Beijing in 1961 to a Korean family (Chinese minority). He had learnt to play the trumpet under his father's tutelage since 1975, and was a trumpet player in the Beijing Symphony Orchestra in 1981. His first successful performance was at a concert with nearly a hundred other singers for national peace in May 1986, where he sang one of his most famous songs, *I Have Nothing*. He took part in the charity performance in 1987 for the Asian Games. From 1987 to 1989 he performed in many of the colleges and universities in Beijing and was enormously popular with students. In March 1989, he received an award for the 'Best Songs for the Past Ten Years', and went to London to take part in the Asian pop songs contest; then in April, he went to France to participate in the International Rock and Roll Festival. In February 1990, he held a solo concert entitled *Start at the Beginning* in Beijing Worker's Gymnasium. In March, the concert was prohibited, but it was still performed secretly in big cities both at home and abroad. In fact, the 'underground' performances were more popular than the normal ones. At one 'underground' performance, the audience became so excited that Cui had to shout out: 'Order! Keep order! To keep order is to protect Rock and Roll in China' (Zhou, 1992, p. 27). As the 'Father of Chinese Rock and Roll', Cui has been remembered by history, not only as a great performer but also as a brilliant writer of lyrics. Many of his songs – like *I Have Nothing*, *Space Here* and others – have been collected in *Classical Literary Works in China During the Past One Hundred Years* (Xie Mian ed. 1996). Some of his works are regarded as 'required reading' for courses on 'literary phenomena at the end of 20th century'. Cui has become canonized and recognized in cultural and literary history.

His lyrics, deeply connected to the Chinese context and sensibilities as they were, speak for themselves. In his first successful performance, at a concert for national peace in May 1986, he sang *I Have Nothing* and became an overnight sensation (author's translation follows):

> I ask you repeatedly to come with me,
> But you laugh at me – you have nothing.
> I offer you my dream and freedom,
> But you laugh at me – you have nothing.
> The land slides beneath me and water flows alongside,
> You laugh at me – you have nothing.
> Why do you always laugh, why do you always follow,
> Is it perpetually true that I have nothing?
> I confront you and say, I have waited long, for the last time:
> Let me take your hands, come with me.
> Your hands tremble, your tears flow.
> Do you mean you love me though I have nothing?

A journalist who attended the concert wrote of the first reception of this song: 'During those few minutes, the audience seemed to have experienced a century. Their hearts were full of mud and they were totally at a loss. Then suddenly there was a flash of lightning. Their blood boiled, and their hearts missed a beat. They had vague desires but they wanted to catch something. Although they could not really do this, they felt there was something to pursue. So at that moment, cheering, the sound of stamping feet, clapping and the clinking of the chairs mingled together' ('Cui Jian, the Best', 1999). Such was the outpouring of emotions, confusion, and anger of that generation. Singing and dancing together had replaced oppression, awakening had replaced blindness, and music had crushed ideology. Other songs by Cui had a similar impact – notably, *A Piece of Red Cloth* (author's translation follows):

> You covered my eyes and the sky
> with a piece of red cloth.
> You asked me what I could see;
> I see happiness, I replied.
> The feeling is comforting
> For I forget I am homeless.
> You asked me what I wanted;
> To go with you, I replied.
> I couldn't see you or the road
> But you held my hand.
> You asked me what I was thinking;
> That I am in your hands, I replied.

When performing this song on the stage Cui wore a green service uniform, with a piece of red cloth covering his eyes. This image became a potent cultural symbol throughout the 1980s and 1990s. One of those in audience said that everyone was profoundly moved by this symbolism. 'You were first moved by Cui's songs, then by other fans, and lastly by yourselves' (Zhou, 1992, p. 16). At a performance in Zhengzhou the audience sang, clapped and danced. The cheering lasted so long that a local official exclaimed: 'What's wrong with them all?' (Zhou, 1992, p. 30.) He could not understand why those obedient people had suddenly become so wild. But it was not just the losses and desires that his generation experienced which Cui expressed in his songs, he also engaged with the unfolding social realities – for instance in *An Egg Laid by the Red Flag* (author's translation follows):

> The sudden opening to the outside is not sudden at all.
> Do you know what's to be done when the opportunity arrives?
> The red flag still wavers uncertainly, the revolution continues.
> Old men are rejuvenated, there's money flying in the sky.
> Despite the bracing breeze we entertain no ideals.
> We cannot see far ahead though the opportunity is here.
> We lack courage, as if bound foetal from
> An egg laid by the red flag.

Here we can see the familiar irony, but this is clearly a response to an immediate social reality. It responds to the commercial trend brokered at the end of 1993, which cut off the relationship between the 1980s and 1990s.

Cui was successful because he invoked and extended the lingering memory of the Cultural Revolution, framed through a discourse of love that resonated with the younger generation of the 1980s. The disillusionment with the recent past is expressed in his words: 'I have nothing!' His concerts unleashed the anxieties and bitterness felt by members of the generation which remembered the painful experiences of the Cultural Revolution and, at the same time, released the joy of blaspheming and rejecting in total what the Cultural Revolution represented. This established a bond between the narrative of reality and history and the enchantment of rock music with its tension and convulsions.

Cui's rock and roll is a combination of subversive political jokes and narcissistic youth from beginning to end. Words once regarded as sacred were now toyed with, such as 'the egg of the red flag', and this set a trend which can be traced, for instance, in Wang Shuo's works (for example Wang, S., 1992). Cui's music is rich in imagination and forcefulness but also contains the pain and disillusionment of knowledge. It not only fights against those times but also bears witness to those times, and pushes cultural perceptions forward. His performance in rock and roll style of the famous revolutionary folk song *Nanniwan*, to cite an example, broke entirely with the conventional rendering in people's minds. He gave it a modern spirit. The familiarity of the song reminded people of past history, while the rock tunes represented modern times. Thus, the 1990s vogue for singing revolutionary songs in pop style came about, albeit in a soft and ethereal rather than rock style. These shifts were themselves evidence of the growing commercialization and popularization of ideology.

The birth of Chinese rock and roll represented by Cui Jian is national and belongs to that time. It is not based on the introduction of Western music. For example, *I Have Nothing* borrows the tune of *Xin Tian You* from north-west China. Cui sang it as a 'Qin tune' but it was accepted by his audiences. His national style represented the new visage of the China of that time to face the world. The prohibition of rock and roll has since been lifted. Popular rock and roll singers are now recommended by the DJs, and are often interviewed by newspaper and television journalists. In the mid-1990s, rock and roll, through co-operating with the new mainstream – the commercial market – became a new god that needs not to be worshipped any longer but can be consumed to the fullest. However, for the new generation, the charm of Cui has gone forever.

Conclusion

Since Deng Xiaoping's 1992 visit to the south, the commercial trend has spread all over China and has changed the country. Chen Pingyuan maintains that

> In the past century Chinese intellectuals have suffered an unprecedented 'cultural defeat', and the crushing oppression from money today has left them with deep feelings of humiliation. Their pain and their feelings of devotion to China are nothing in the changed situation in which commercial values reign supreme. So the modern Don Quixotes of China will be abandoned by the market because of their ideals, expectations and enthusiasm, rather than punished because of their deviation from the canon and rules (Chen, 1993, p. 53).

Subsequently, various popular cultures have appeared to pave the way for a vigorous cultural market. This advertisement-based culture, one of luxury fashion magazines, weekend leisure newspapers, travel agencies, fans, Karaoke, family cinema, brand-name commodities and fashion clothes, Macdonald's and Pizza Hut, dumps Western phenomena, culture, value and ideology. While profits are made by exploiting the huge popular cultural market, it in turn is provided with models that can be copied and 'localized'.

Popular culture needs neither the 'permission' of the authorities nor the 'guidance' of intellectuals. The cultural market repeats itself endlessly and covers the whole country. In fact, this is a form of co-operation between the authorities and the public. Commercialization and the development of a market economy, important components of reform and opening to the outside and the building of socialism with Chinese characteristics, represent the mainstream authority. This can be seen in the dictums 'let some people become rich first', 'work for a comfortable life', 'walk on the road to common wealth', and the call for and finally the development of a middle class.

References

Adorno, T. (1991), *The Culture Industry*, (ed.) J.M. Bernstein, (London: Routledge).

Bao, Y.M. (2000), 'Shanghai jiu ba' ['Bars in Shanghai'], *Jian zai xin yishi xingtai de longzhao xia (Under the Vesture of New Ideology)* (Nanjin: Jiang Su People Press).

Baudrillard, J. (1999), [first published 1970], *The Consumer Society* (London: Sage).

Benjamin, W. (1973), 'The Work of Art in the Age of Mechanical Reproduction', '(1937)' in *Illuminations*, trans. Harry Zohn (Glasgow: Fontana).

Benton, G. and Pieke, F.N., eds. (1998), *The Chinese in Europe* (Basingstoke: Macmillan).

Cai, F. (2000), *Zhongguo liudong renkuo (The Problem of China's Floating Population)* (Wugang: Zhengzhou) Renmin Chubanshe).

Chen, P. (June 1993), 'Jin bai nian jingying wenhua de shiluo' ('Loss of Elite Culture Over the Past Hundred Years'), *Ershiyi shiji (Twenty First Century)*, Vol. 17 (Hong Kong; University Press).

Chin, K. (1999), *Smuggled Chinese* (Philadelphia: Temple University Press).

'Cui jian, zhi zun' ['Cui Jian, The Best'] (1999), 9 October, *Nanfang nongcun bao [South Countryside News Paper]*.

Davin, D. (1999), *Internal Migration in Contemporary China* (Basingstoke: Macmillan).

Huang, P. and Pieke, F.N. (2003), 'China Migration: Country Study', Paper presented at the conference on *Migration, Development and Pro-Poor Policy Choices in Asia*, organised by the Migratory Movements Research Unit, Bangladesh and Department of International Development, UK. Can be downloaded at: http://www.livelihoods.org (March 2005).

Klein, N. (1999), *No Logo* (London: Flamingo).

Marcuse, H. (1964), *One-Dimensional Man* (London: Routledge and Kegan Paul).

Murphy, R. (2002), *How Migrant Labour is Changing Rural China* (Cambridge: Cambridge University Press).

Solinger, D.J. (1999), *Contesting Citizenship in Urban China* (Berkeley: University of California State).

Tian, M.H. (2000), 'Dui dangqian zhongguo guanggao chanye de jidian renshi', '['A Few Clarifications of China's Advertisement Production']', *Xiandai guanggao (Modern Advertisement)* 6.

Wang, G. (2000), *The Chinese Overseas* (Cambridge, Mass.: Harvard University Press).

Wang, H. (2000), 'Sasha's: xiuzhen feidi', '['Shasha's: mini fly place'], *Shanghai wenhua*, [*Shanghai Culture*] 1.

Wang, S. (1992), *Wo shi ni baba [I am Your Papa]* (Beijing: People Literature Press).

Wang, X. (2000), *Ban bian lian de shenhua [The Myth of the Half Face]* (Guangzhou: South Daily Press).

Wei, H. (2001), *Shanghai Baby*. Humes, B. (translated by) (London: Robinson Healthcare).

Williams, R. (1980), 'Advertising – The Magic System' in *Problems of Materialism and Culture* (London: Verso).

Williamson, J. (1978), *Decoding Advertisements* (London: Boyars).

Xie, M., ed. (1996), *Classical Literary Works in China During the Past One Hundred Years*, Vol. 7 (Beijing: Peking University Press).

Zhao, J. (1992), *Cui jian zai yiwusuoyou* zhong *naihan – zhongguo yaogun beiwanglu*', [*Battle Cry of Cui Jian in his 'I Have Nothing' – Memorandum for Chinese Rock'n Roll*], (Beijing: Beijing Normal University Press).

Chapter 14

Media Representations in India of the Indian Diaspora in the UK and US

Subarno Chattarji

English Department, University of Delhi, India

Introduction

The so-called Non-Resident Indians (NRIs) and People of Indian Origin (PIO)[1] have always exerted an ambivalent and powerful force in popular culture representations, particularly in Hindi films. Some of that ambivalence remains, especially in discourses that stress 'traditional Indian values', and present NRIs as 'corrupted' by the morally licentious West. With the liberalization of the Indian economy and the push and pull factors of globalization the moral rhetoric has been jettisoned in favour of assiduous wooing and reportage on the achievements and stature of NRIs and PIOs. India as a nation now basks in the reflected glory of people who emigrated from its lands most often to seek better economic opportunities and quality of life. The welcome home message is perhaps best articulated in the *Pravasi Bharatiya Divas* (Overseas Indian Day) initiated by the former coalition government led by the Bharatiya Janata Party (BJP). The BJP's advocacy and celebration of NRI-PIO causes are representative of a resurgent nationalism coalescing with economic pragmatism; it is both a call for return to roots and for NRI investments in India. This chapter examines representations of diasporic Indians in the UK and US in the Indian print media, focusing on two mainstream English language publications, *The Times of India* and *India Today*, which encapsulate the aspirations of the fabled Indian middle class and its projection of a globalized existence.

---

1 NRI is a term formalized retrospectively by the Indian government to designate Indian immigrants abroad and to tap their economic potential. In the 1970s and 1980s the term referred almost exclusively to immigrants in the US, Canada, and UK. In informal and popular culture discourse particularly Hindi films, the NRI was a source of fascination and criticism from the 1950s. In both these domains, the NRIs in the Gulf States – the foremen, truck drivers, and nurses – were ignored. PIO is a term of more recent provenance – the 1990s – formalized and used by the Indian government and available in media language. PIO includes, by definition, people who have some connection to India which is not necessarily that of being born in the country, such as descendants of indentured labourers in Fiji and the West Indies. While this casts a wider net it limits membership to the entity of India post-1947, ignoring the subcontinental nature of forced or voluntary migration before the creation of Pakistan and Bangladesh. Within this ambit the Government of India now has a minister for NRI/PIO affairs and will grant dual citizenship to NRIs and PIOs in designated countries.

Benedict Anderson's conception of the newspaper as a cultural product can be extended to include the newsmagazine *India Today*. Newspapers/magazines create imagined linkages between anonymous readers, and the act of reading could be perceived as a mass ceremony creating this 'community' and furthering its sense of confident existence (Anderson, 1991, p. 33). Part of that confidence is based on the idea that Indian products and cultures are now gaining currency in the metropolitan centres, and that the nature of cultural globalization is different from that of economic globalization. This encapsulates the commonplace idea that while 'economic globalization has undoubtedly travelled from the (stronger) West to the (weak) East [...] cultural globalization has not necessarily followed this line. Excellent cultural products do not necessarily grow on the materially rich soil, whereas they might well grow on the comparatively poor soil where there is usually a long and splendid cultural heritage and rich literary practice' (Ning, 2001, p. 211). Wang Ning's argument is unexceptionable and true in some cases the cultural products being purveyed as 'Indian' in the West vary from Indian classical music to the cinema of Satyajit Ray, from Bollywood to henna tattoos. It is the latter category that is aggressively marketed and projected as 'Indian' by and for the diasporic communities. In the media reportage that I analyse, there is a filtering back as it were of Indian pride at the presence of Indian communities and products at the cosmopolitan centre. The reportage creates a trans-national bond between the diasporic 'other' and the Indian readers physically located in India. I examine various articles over a period of 1 year, beginning April 2003. For the sake of convenience I divide my analysis into five sections: film and entertainment, politics, the brain drain syndrome, *Pravasi Bharatiya Divas*, and seamier aspects of the Indian immigrant community. These articles reveal contradictions between the surge towards a globalized economy in India on the one hand, and a land of poverty, illiteracy, and communal violence on the other. They tell us as much about contemporary India as they do about contemporary Indians in the UK and US.

Film and Entertainment

Although Aishwarya Rai is not an immigrant Indian it is appropriate to begin with her because articles on her set off the contours of debates ranging around the global Indian in the world of film and entertainment. Designated by Julia Roberts as the most beautiful woman, voted the most attractive woman of 2003 in a hellomagazine. com poll, and featured on *The Late Show with David Letterman* on CBS television in the US in February 2005, Rai was the subject of an editorial in *India Today*, 'Bond with the Best: England quivers with excitement at the thought of another Virgin Queen'. The editorial was in response to an article in *The Daily Mail* 'about the former Miss World becoming the first virgin Bond girl' (*Today*, 28 April 2003, p. 4). Quivering with indignation, *India Today* stoutly defended one of India's more recent exports, the beauty pageant industry that has rolled out numerous Miss Worlds and Universes over the past decade.

> Living as it does in the protected environment of suburban homes with lace curtains that
> flutter in the afternoon sun, it does not believe the natives have evolved enough to have

a sex life. It has also, quite clearly, not heard of cultural stereotyping. [...] weren't they also the country where the Virgin Queen ruled for 45 years? Our royals have been known to be more robust (*Today*, 28 April 2003, p. 4).

In its attempt to defend Rai and critique cultural stereotyping, the editorial practices some delicious reverse profiling of British and Indian royalty. There's an element of the surreal and the comic in which the editorial trumpets a competitive sexual prowess amongst Indians and will not allow Rai to be slighted on account of her virginity. Why *India Today* thought it fit to editorially defend Rai is a mystery. There is a curious insecurity and assertiveness at work here and Rai is merely a site for the expression of native pride, reverse racism, and insistence on global belonging.

In a film review section Rai is restored to her rightful place as Lalitha in Gurinder Chadha's *Bride and Prejudice*, a diasporic take on Austen's *Pride and Prejudice*. 'Speaking about her lead cast, Chadha says, "Ash will be the perfect Lizzy Bennett. She is headstrong and says what she thinks"' (*Today*, 28 July 2003, p. 21). The slurs of virginity and Indian timidity are laid to rest as the Bennetts become Bakshis, and Gurinder Chadha, an icon of British-Asian success, recognizes Rai's worth. In a feature on Gurinder Chadha and Mira Nair, the value of Indo-British and Indo-American filmmakers is extolled. Both Chadha and Nair were shooting in 'London, the capital of multicultural cool'. Chadha calls her film a 'truly global' one, 'It has an international perspective because Indians have it' (*Today*, 6 October 2003, p. 102). What is interesting is the way in which Chadha is appropriated by the Indian media and she plays to it by highlighting their 'international perspective'. The article displays a level of self-reflexivity by referring to the possibility of an Oscar for both women. 'Chadha knows of the hopes of several million Indians who have decided to embrace her – they are happy to forget that she was born in Kenya and would dearly love her to knock off the British in her hyphenated identity. She knows she has a winner on her hands' (*Today*, 6 October 2003, p. 103). The celebration of Chadha's and Nair's achievement within the matrix of 'multicultural cool' coexists with the desire to see 'Indianness' and Indian achievement in the works of expatriate filmmakers. In a very different context much the same has happened to V.S. Naipaul, who is now embraced as a writer of Indian origin even though his Caribbean roots are vital to most of his works. While Chadha's work is nuanced in her awareness of the fissures in multicultural Britain, media representation in India makes her an icon of an unproblematic 'multicultural cool'. It highlights the interface between Bollywood and world cinema and the currency that Bollywood occupies within the Asian community in Britain.

The compliment was returned by Channel 4 television's 'Bollywood Star', 'the western world's very first search for a Hindi film star from within the 22-million strong diaspora' (Ahmed, 18 January 2004). The six who qualified were taken to Mumbai to act in a Mahesh Bhatt film and embody 'the hyphenated videshi [foreigner] trying to reclaim his popular heritage, for example Bollywood'. According to Richard McKerrow, Bollywood Star's executive producer, the journey back to India was to be one of 'self discovery'. The return to roots saga was mediated through the agency of television and film and mass entertainment, conferring a type of 'authenticity' on those who participated in this programme. Films and filmmaking are thus mentioned here in terms of markets, not in terms of exploration of troubled relations between the immigrant and her 'home' country, or the immigrant within alienating cultures. A culture of pastiche and kitsch is celebrated as the arrival of Indian culture on a global scale. Although this particular article is somewhat tongue in cheek, it participates in a wider need to generate success stories that validate the 'home' country through its valorization of the diasporic 'other'.

Politics

Print media representations of politics and the Indian community ranges from stories on appointments – Karan K. Bhatia's elevation to the post of Assistant Secretary of Transportation for Aviation and International Affairs in the Bush administration – to 'Clinton's India Connection'. The latter profiles people who form a part of Clinton's charmed circle. Clinton's high profile visit to India during his presidency and his continuing engagement with India (the deal on low cost AIDS drugs, for instance) lend him a Midas quality that transforms and elevates the people of Indian origin in the US who are associated with him. In the UK, Rashmee Z. Ahmed profiled Uma Fernandes 'waiting to make history as the Conservative Party's first woman MP of Indian origin and Hindu birth'. The article concentrates on the Hindu identity of the politician, asserting that 'sections of Brent East are miffed with Tony Blair's incumbent party because it refused to field a Hindu for parliament. In theory, the Hindu anger could make history' (Ahmed, 17 September 2003). In actuality 'Hindu anger' did not translate into victory in the parliamentary by-election for Uma Fernandes and what is obviously significant is the idea that it would or should have done so. The article creates an affinity between 'Hindu anger' in India and that in Brent East, which is historically false and politically unsustainable. The discourse of 'Hindu anger', so prevalent in political discourse in India over the past decade, is pasted on to Brent East without analysis. Uma Fernandes featured in just this one article in the print media in India and dropped out of the news because she lost. Yet this piece points to more dangerous liaisons and desires whereby the Indian diaspora is appropriated by the media to create the sense of a pan Indian and global Hindu identity, a project ably furthered by the Vishwa Hindu Parishad (VHP, the World Hindu Council) and the BJP.

Someone who did stay in the news during his campaign for governor of Louisiana was Bobby Jindal. There was a flurry of articles, an editorial, and a feature on the Indian-American's strong bid for political office. A feature in the *Sunday Times of India*, 26 October 2003, indicated that he had 'dropped his first name Piyush at the age of four in favour of Bobby after a character on the popular TV show *The Brady Bunch*.' He converted to Catholicism and 'while filing his papers for the governor's election, Jindal left the column for race blank'. This apparent race blindness is what *India Today* defined as 'cultural osmosis at its best' (Padmanabhan, 20 October 2003, p. 102). The problematic and seemingly effortless jettisoning of race was further complicated by the fact that 'Jindal [...] forged ahead not on the basis of minority support but on a hard, right, white, conservative platform that includes opposing gun control and abortion' (Rajghatta, 1 October 2003). In a state that last elected a black governor in the 1870s and once had David Duke of the Ku Klux Klan as gubernatorial front runner, Jindal's embracing of the Republican agenda and his valorization in the Indian media has interesting spin offs. According to Padmanabhan: 'Many conservatives believe that Jindal's political ascendancy could be a boost to Bush's South Asia policy. Especially in improving relations with India, a country they see as a critical ally in the fight against Islamic fundamentalism'. While this analysis ignores the contradictions in Jindal's own statements and positioning as a mainstream American, it gets to the nub of the matter in its championing of a conservative grand alliance between the US and India against 'Islamic fundamentalism'. The Catholic convert immigrant from Delhi is metonymically transformed into the right wing soldier who will fight the forces of 'Islamic fundamentalism'. This would partly explain the Indian media's fascination with the Jindal campaign, for it fed into a dominant political discourse of a state besieged from within and without by the forces of reactionary Islam. In passing, one may note the extent to which immigrant Indians in the US and UK fund and support right wing organizations in India, particularly in Gujarat.

In an editorial, 'American Desi: The Indian media's hype over Bobby Jindal is misplaced', *The Times of India* attempted to place the media coverage in perspective. It noted that 'Bobby Jindal has captured our imagination because he seems so much an integral part of a collective narrative – of our pride and imagination: The story of the great Indian diaspora conquering the world' (*Times*, 16 October 2003). It went on to state that 'Mr Jindal is the equivalent of a born-again immigrant who is brown in nothing but his skin colour' and asked the question that I have raised, 'Why then are we so keen to corral him as an "Indian" and dub his achievements as a great Indian success story?' In attempting to answer this question the editorial veered into an essentialist and conveniently evasive niche with references to A.O. Hume, Annie Besant, and Mother Teresa, reflecting on what it called an 'old innocence, where identity was a state of mind rather than a fact of biology or geography'. At one level it is remarkable that the *Times of India* editorially raised some uncomfortable questions about the lionizing of Jindal in the Indian media. At another level, the constructed nostalgia of an apolitical, universal identity – where all who are associated with India become Indians by some magic of 'cultural osmosis' – relates precisely to the 'collective narrative' of immigrant Indians as global players and their glory reflecting the resurgence of a shining India. Jindal's defeat in the election was widely covered in print and on television with some dark mutterings about racial prejudice that allowed his rival Kathleen Blanco to triumph. In the reportage of the defeat Jindal's own disavowal of racial identity was forgotten. Identity as a 'state of mind' was replaced in defeat by crude generalizations about race and racism in American politics. It was as if another opportunity for bolstering Indo-US conservative alliances and the fight against demonic Islam had been inexplicably defeated.

The Brain Drain Syndrome

While extolling the achievements and presence of immigrant Indians in the US and UK, the reportage that I have considered thus far ignores an underlying cause of that immigration: economic betterment. Whether it was Indian doctors joining the National Health Service in the UK or cab drivers in New York or techies in Silicon Valley, the flight from India was largely predicated on the desire for a better quality of life in the west. In the pre-liberalization era this migration was berated and bemoaned in terms of a 'brain drain'; in the age of the global Indian this phenomenon is co-opted into a larger narrative of a resurgent India. In fact the IT revolution and India's eminent position within that world is attributed precisely to those Indian Institute of Technology (IIT) graduates who fled the mother country. Occasionally, however, as in Shobha John's article '20 percent IIT-ians still leave India ... And we thought brain drain was over' (*Times*, 3 August 2003) we return to the theme of qualified but dispirited Indians leaving for better opportunities abroad. The article details the fact that 15–20 per cent of IIT graduates leave India for the US which is more attractive because of higher salaries. A BTech in the US earns \$40–60,000 per annum, a PhD in finance \$130,000 per annum, an engineering PhD from IIT \$70,000 per annum. In contrast, a BTech in India fetches Rs. 20,000 per annum, an MBA with engineering degree Rs. 40–80,000 per annum. While the salary differential is substantial it is not absolute for it does not take into account differences within the Indian context where millions are either unemployed or live on less than a dollar a day. The latter do not exist in the imagination and lexicon of media reportage except when they crop up inconveniently in news items of dead or deported migrants. Their desire to belong to the global community is occasionally reflected in immigration scams attributed to the likes of Daler Mehendi and Mallika Sarabhai. In the latter case it is interesting to note the ways in which nativism (the Gujarati *asmita* [pride] insulted by Sarabhai's outspokenness on the Gujarat riots) is combined with a vestigial suspicion of immigration which is then used as a convenient ploy to nail the activist. Simultaneously Gujarat's Chief Minister woos the diasporic Gujarati with dreams of an investment haven. These connections and patterns are not mentioned in the media.

John writes that a better work environment in the US also lures the IIT graduate and quotes several immigrants. 'You are given credit for what you do. Facilities are excellent.' In India 'the environment – corruption, inefficiency, *bijli pani* [electricity and water] issues – drains one out.' 'There is less pay here, politics, company promises which are not adhered to, no work culture, and lack of transparency' (John, 3 August 2003). The contrast between a hopelessly backward India and an efficiently utopic US may be exaggerated, but it gives the lie to the projection of a continually progressive India. Despite this damning indictment the article ends on a note of hope that the 'brain drain' will be reversed. John quotes one Abhijit Choudhury – Indian Institute of Technology - Kharagpur (IIT-KGP), 1972 – currently teaching business strategy and technology at Bryant College, Rhode Island: 'Reverse brain drain is bound to happen. As the economy grows, the number of Indians going back to India would increase. India would get back its best and brightest, but only after suitable exposure to the West' (John, 3 August 2003). In Choudhury's formulation immigration is a type of rite of passage, a staging point after which India's sons will return to the motherland. In that return lies the hope for the future of India, a hope cultivated by the *Pravasi Bharatiya Divas*. Why this reversal will happen is neither explained nor analysed in this article, it is seen as an inevitability that will wish away the corruption and inefficiency, the lack of work culture and transparency that led to the migration.

Two Sundays later Shobha John dwelt on the reasons why Indian immigrants were returning without addressing the issues raised in her earlier piece. 'What brings them back? A dream.' Dr Parag Bhargava articulates one such dream: 'My friends and I wanted to apply our ideas to root out illiteracy from India. It materialized with the birth of Prabudha Bharat, a group running an education-cum-library-cum-activity centre for poor children near IIT' (John, 17 August 2003). Despite lack of detail this dream is at least cognizant of poverty and illiteracy in India. For Jayant Sinha, formerly of IIT Delhi and Harvard and a partner in McKinsey, India 'is an exciting place to be in. We are now entering a new phase of nation-building. Technology, IT services and telecom are all growing rapidly in India' (John, 17 August 2003). Sinha's dream is perhaps the more dominant one, eyeing the huge market potential inherent in the country, and 'nation-building' can comfortably co-exist with profit making. Despite the fact that India has 2 per cent of the world market share in IT services, it is a myth of economic prowess that sits easily with the idea of India as a global presence. Another reason for the return of immigrants is the constant fear of losing jobs and the desire to refocus on family ties. This is particularly true post-9/11 and in the context of the economic recession in the US. 'The US always seemed alien' says one returnee. The sense of alienation is related to homesickness and an emphasis on cultural rootedness. Dr Bhargava says he 'found a certain shallowness abroad'. This relates to earlier representations of the NRI as deracinated and desirous of the 'substance' offered by home, a myth of 'depth' in India that can be recovered and is enabling for the returnee. A further link is available in the desire to raise children in an Indian milieu so that they are not deprived of their cultural capital. What is left unsaid here, and only briefly dwelt upon in a slew of articles on the returning immigrant, are realities of race and colour prejudice. As John Oliver Perry points out, 'despite their relatively high economic position, Diasporan Indians are soon made aware that multiculturality in America does not mean either social equality for different ethnic groups nor absence of racism, sexism, and prejudice based on ethnic stereotypes' (Perry, 2002, p. 98). Thus, while the global Indian is valorized for his deeds abroad, those deeds are fraught with contradictions and tensions. Media reportage largely ignores these fissures and creates a dominant narrative of achievement which is paradoxically revealed when the immigrant returns to his roots, thereby validating not only his worth but also the intrinsic value of the country of origin.

Anil Padmanabhan celebrates the phenomenon of reverse 'brain drain': 'the expatriates are coming back. The epiphany that had lured them to the US has been transferred to their native land – complete with a robust economy, infinite opportunities and improved lifestyles – and it is drawing them back to their own country' (Padmanabhan, 11 August 2003, p. 93). The quality of life has certainly improved for the NRI ensconced in Gurgaon or Noida (suburbs of Delhi) with their shopping malls and apartment blocks named Hamilton Court, Richmond, Carlton, and Beverley Park. The nomenclature and mall culture represents a desire for the *desi* (native) as well as a return 'home' for the NRI. It is crucial that 'home' for the NRI is a spatial construction that approximates to the lifestyle that he and his kids enjoyed in the US. The social and cultural aspect of 'home' can include more 'Indian' aspects such as tradition and ceremony. The pride in globalization, however, barely conceals the underbelly of that process. India's 8 per cent GDP growth is seldom contextualized in terms of illiteracy, poverty, or the *bijli-pani* problems that beset the exclusive enclaves of the nostalgic NRI. The dominant rhetoric is one of celebration whereby the 'two-way mobility' of the global Indian creates its own momentum of growth and development, never mind the irritants that litter ones existence.

The concentration is on the nostalgia of return, whether in actuality or through television dramas such as *Second Generation*. This drama presents three of the lead characters returning to India. 'Two of them – a Bengali Hindu-Muslim pairing – are beer-swilling, bhangra-rapping, British-born-and-bred. [...] But, for the first time ever on British TV, the British-Indian second generation is shown to reject the bright lights of London for the alien-but-dimly-remembered chaos and camaraderie of Kolkata' (Ahmed, 13 September 2003). Director Jon Sen, quoted in a pre-release interview, declared that his television show was a 'bench mark production because it took the British Asian narrative on, even as it started from a position of Indian pride, wealth and success' (Ahmed, 13 September 2003). Various kinds of nostalgia related to place (Kolkata), politics (the Hinmdu–Muslim pairing), and possibility (the seamless interweaving between the metropolitan centre and the dimly remembered margin) coalesce with the 'position of Indian pride, wealth and success'. Ultimately it is the latter that matters the most both in terms of diasporic movement, cultural exchange (if one may define *Second Generation* in such terms) and the idea of a booming, successful community abroad.

In 'Karisma of a "brown" Mela', Karisma Kapoor's jetting into London to inaugurate a 3-day mela is precisely the type of 'Indian pride, wealth and success' that is celebrated. 'Asian-ness is not just fashion but big business, with the two million strong Asian community's collective spending power now estimated at an impressive 10 billion pounds' (Ahmed, 10 October 2003). The mela is not just about curry and henna tattoos but about Ford and British Telecom spending huge sums to make their presence felt. It's about a makeover in the image of British Asians who are newly being categorised as a fast-growing, acquisitive, label conscious, status-seeking niche market. 'It's a sign we're integrating but not assimilating', says Anjna Raheja who authored a report for the advertising industry in Britain on the untapped potential of the 'brown pound'. Pride in economic visibility is perhaps justified and it is seen as a signifier of integration without giving up on one's roots. This is the ideal situation where tradition or their variants (henna tattoos) are in perfect sync with the consumerist instinct. Label consciousness adds to racial profile (the 'brown pound') and simultaneously erases racial difference, with the market as a great equalizer. Such reportage ignores the nuances of race identity, the anxieties and travails of immigrant existence explored in films by diasporic filmmakers such as Gurinder Chadha. The fantasy of integration and rootedness is perhaps best indicated by the presence of Bollywood at the inaugural. This desired imaginary space is dealt with in Bollywood films which cater effectively to conservative constituencies in India and further the nostalgic bond of the Indian abroad to his mother country. It is this bond which the BJP led coalition hoped to cash in on through its *Pravasi Bharatiya Divas*, which is emblematic of a diasporic triumphalism seamlessly connected to conservative agendas.

Pravasi Bharatiya Divas

The return of the prodigy and the prodigal was, over the last few years, carefully orchestrated by the former National Democratic Alliance (NDA) government and its founding of the *Pravasi Bharatiya Divas*. The Congress led United Progressive Alliance (UPA) government has continued with the *Divas*. The first *Divas* with V.S. Naipaul as chief guest was held in the aftermath of the Gujarat riots, an event that reverberated during the deliberations. The unwelcome intrusion highlights the cusp within which the jamboree functions: that of economic desire and political conservatism. The *Divas* held in January 2004 was attended by 2,000 NRIs and PIOs from 60 countries. Arun Kumar Das celebrated the economic fall out of the event in terms of hotel occupancy. This, however, is not the only highpoint of the 3-day event. 'A highlight of the event is the cultural evenings, during which 5,000 years of Indian *shringar parampara* [heritage of adornment and dress] will be showcased through a unique blend of the spiritual and the sensual. Officially speaking, the focus of the conference is on the Gen Next of *pravasis* [migrants]. "We want this generation to know about the country of their origin, its culture and people," says [Vivek] Bharti (adviser to FICCI [Federation of Indian Chambers of Commerce and Industry] and coordinator of the summit). "This will go a long way in strengthening bonds between NRIs, PIOs and India." After all, irrespective of wherever an Indian might be on the globe, *phir bhi dil hai Hindustani*' ['the heart is still Indian' – taken from a popular Hindi film song] (*Das,* 8 January 2004). The blend of the spiritual and the sensual along with the emphasis on an unshakeable *Hindustani dil* hark back to media and film representations of NRI/Indian identity in the 1950s and '60s as ineluctably fixed no matter what the actual political and cultural location might be. In this, Indian media representations were/are unwittingly similar to dominant western media discourses about the mysterious and unruly 'other' even if that 'other' has IT specialists and call centres. That this is a powerful myth is evident in the ways in which the *Divas* constructs Indian *parampara* and reconstitutes identity in a majoritarian discourse. In fact, the *Divas* provides a meeting ground for conservative immigrant ideations of Indianness and a political dispensation that is happy to cater to nostalgic and mythic fantasies.

Rashmee Z Ahmed, however, pointed out that the economic hoopla surrounding the summit was unjustified. In a rare critical article Ahmed writes, 'The great diasporic Diwali is on and India we are told "is shining". There is no connection. These are two, almost-but-not-quite mutually exclusive phenomena. Where, for instance, on that list of privilege yellow-carded foreign delegates to the *Pravasi Bharatiya Divas*, were the following: Lakshmi Mittal; Arun Sarin; Gulu Lalvani?' (Ahmed, 11 January 2004). The three corporate giants of Indian origin are based in the UK and have no wish to do business in India. As Lalvani puts it, 'I'm already there [India], doing charity work and so on, it's just in business that I don't have the patience to wait for licenses, etc.' Ahmed concludes, 'The *dil-hai Hindustani* routine may still go down well in Mumbai's multiplexes but it has the glossy factory finish of the ultimate theatrical flight of fancy. Ask the big boys of business. They know'. That NRIs and PIOs are still wary of putting money where their nostalgia is, is an uncomfortable fact that the article highlights. Many immigrants in the Gulf region (the nurses, foremen, cooks) who are not as upwardly mobile and represent the basic economic impulse behind immigration do not figure in the *pravasi* discourse at all. Ahmed's cautionary tale of three NRIs who wish to have no stake in the Indian pie is a stunning counterpoint to the hype surrounding the *Divas* and indicates the ways in which the very wealthy and the down-at-heel NRIs share a common scepticism of their home country.

The story of the *pravasi* does not, however, end in gloom as one of the trio decides to finally invest in India. 'Nearly 30 years after he left Kolkata to build a 13-nation steel empire, Lakshmi N Mittal plans to come home. "India is at the take-off stage, and we want to have our footprint there"' (Ahmed, 14 February 2004). Mittal is clear that it is 'profit, not patriotism, that drives him towards India. He argues for globalization of mindset, commerce without passports', but his return is touted in terms of the return of a native son. 'The significance of Mittal's interest in the land of his birth can hardly be overstated. Until last year, he firmly kept India out of his business plans, saying "conditions were not right because India did not have the right infrastructure, such as good ports or railway facilities, and the necessary electricity supply"' (Ahmed, 14 February 2004). The turnaround specialist preferred to invest in former communist states such as Romania, the Czech Republic, and Poland which was 'an insult' to free, democratic, and desperately globalizing India. The insult can now be forgotten since 'this particular government opened up the whole country for investment'. The implications of that opening up are entirely positive; it is enough that Mittal has spoken and added substance to the *Pravasi Divas* from which he was absent.

Seamier Aspects of the Diaspora: Crime and Terrorism

While the dominant media representations of the global Indian are positive, feel-good stories, there are occasional lapses which indicate that the NRI/PIO may be involved in crime and terrorism abroad. I could not find any such article in *The Times of India* but *The Hindustan Times* had a front page piece by S. Rajagopalan and Vijay Dutt, 'Indians abroad in big time fraud' (11 September 2003). 'From Los Angeles to London Indian white-collar criminals have been leaving a trail of fraud – and setting some dubious records in the process.' The article provides a rogues gallery ranging from 55-year-old Surinder Singh Panshi, an Indian American doctor sentenced to 16 years in jail for Medicare fraud amounting to $20 million, to 26-year-old Sunil Mahtani sentenced to 9 years in the UK as Britain's biggest credit card fraudster. Mahtani also pleaded guilty to child pornography charges. 'According to Mahtani's defence counsel, he embarked on the crime course in order to keep up with his high-flying financier girlfriend Elizabeth Ryan, who as a merchant banker took home much more than him' (Rajagopalan and Dutt, 2003). This is a rare article on the flip side of immigrant success stories, although it was a stand-alone piece with no follow-up. Mahtani's defence touches upon some of the pressures, economic and social, which immigrants (among others) might face and which are never mentioned in mainstream media in India.

India Today carried a cover story, 'Hemant Lakhani: Trading in Terror' by Anil Padmanabhan and Sandeep Unnithan, which details an FBI and international sting operation whereby Hemant Lakhani, a former rice and garments trader, was caught trying to sell shoulder-fired missiles for possible use by terrorists. Originally from Ghatkopar in Bombay and based in Britain he is probably a small fry in the illegal arms trade, but the article links him to Dawood Ibrahim and Al Qaida. In conclusion the article blames Lakhani's greed rather than terrorist outlook or ideology. This is a curious article that shares the paranoia about terror networks and terrorism prevalent in post-9/11 US and UK, links India to that paranoia, and takes pride in exposing a small component of much larger networks. There can be little doubt about Lakhani's dubious business ethics and functioning, but his role in terrorist networks seems hyped. Once again this is a story that was not followed up. At an obvious level this is not a positive story. However, in exposing this bad egg and tying up with global concerns regards terrorism, the article reinforces India's position as a staunch ally in the war against terror, as a country that is a victim of terrorism and desires restitution. The exposé of Lakhani's deals serves to reintegrate India within the global fraternity. It also contributes to the sense of 'truth', 'objectivity', and 'balance' in reportage whereby *India Today* is not afraid to deal with traitors within and without its borders.

My analysis is by no means exhaustive but it indicates that there is a clear bias toward feel-good stories regarding the diasporic community. As stated earlier, they tell us as much about India as they do about the immigrants themselves. In its 19 January 2004 issue *India Today* attempted to reposition Indians abroad by defining them as Overseas Born Indians (OBIs), and through that redefinition to characterize second generation Indians. Inevitably, however, that characterization can only take place by reference to the mother country. Kaveree Bamzai in her essay 'AB But No Longer CD' writes: 'Their growing numbers have given them confidence, as has the global emergence of the nation their parents still call home and the warmth with which it envelops them. With men and women running around in tights, no longer is yoga a cruel ethnic joke. As Indian movies acquire iconic status, what was an embarrassment has become a proud anthem' (Bamzai (2004, p. 99). We have here familiar tropes of the welcoming *bharat mata* (mother India) which is now a global player and the reference to yoga indicates the ways in which ethnic chic has been successfully marketed. One is not sure for whom Indian movies have 'acquire [d] iconic status' apart from the diasporic community, since Bollywood's offerings to the Oscar altar are embarrassing in content and in their regular rejection in the foreign film category. The articles in the issue go over familiar ground enumerating the achievements and role of well-known OBIs such as Bobby Jindal, Manoj N. Shyamalan, Parminder Nagra, Rhona Mitra, and Bobby Friction. 'Immigrants,' write Anil Padmanabhan and Ishara Bhasi, 'value success, and that has brought acceptance for their children. Success has happened when the second generation has assimilated the best, when it has broken through the glasshouse of ethnicity' (Padmanabhan and Bhasi 19 January 2004, p. 100). One wonders what that breakthrough means and whether it is predicated solely on 'success'. Undoubtedly, second generation migrants are better adjusted to their diasporic status, but whether they can live in a post-ethnic community or imagination is open to question. In any case, dominant media discourses in India are more interested in how these American/Brit *desis* relate to India, and in that focus we see a nation straddling two worlds. On the one hand are the mantras of globalization (India as IT giant and BPO powerhouse), economic growth (8 per cent GDP, booming stock markets, and the India Shining campaign), and political leverage (India as deserving of a permanent seat at the UNSC, staunch ally in the war on terror). On the other hand, are the problems that are seldom mentioned, but ones that will not go away: poverty, illiteracy, communal violence and identity politics (Gujarat), the defanging of trade unions, and the increasing inequities within the nation. By focusing on the achievements of the NRI/PIO/OBI and their interaction with the land of their birth, dominant media representations bolster the sense of a nation on the move. At the same time it is a nation that remains rooted in its ethos and culture, whatever that might mean and however conservative it may be. As Saira Mohan, an OBI model for Chanel and Calvin Klein puts it, 'India is the most virtuous country in the world'. Amen.

References

Ahmed, R.Z. (10 October 2003), 'Karisma of a Brown Mela', *The Times of India*.

Ahmed, R.Z. (11 January 2004), 'The great diasporic Diwali is not a highlight for India', *Sunday Times of India*.

Ahmed, R.Z. (13 September 2003), '*Passage to India* II: Children of diaspora return via tube', *The Times of India*.

Ahmed, R.Z. (14 February 2004), 'LN Mittal heads home, wants footprint in India', *The Times of India*.

Ahmed, R.Z. (17 September 2003), 'Will Brent East Make History?', *Sunday Times of India*.

Ahmed, R.Z. (18 January 2004), 'Hyphenated videshi emerges as Bollywood Star', *The Times of India*.

Anderson, B. (1991), Imagined Communities: Reflections on the Origin and Spread of Nationalism, (Verso).

'Austen Powers' (28 July 2003), *India Today*.

Bamzai, K. (19 January 2004), 'AB But No Longer CD', *India Today*.

Das, A.K. (8 January 2004), 'Delhi's a stage for pravasis worldwide', *Delhi Times*.

'Editorial' (16 October 2003), 'American Desi: The Indian media's hype over Bobby Jindal is misplaced', *The Times of India*.

'Editorial' (28 April 2003), 'Bond with the Best: England quivers with excitement at the thought of another Virgin Queen', *India Today*.

John, S. (17 August 2003), 'The brains are coming back after the drain', *Sunday Times of India*.

John, S. (3 August 2003), '20 percent IIT-ians still leave India … And we thought brain drain was over', *Sunday Times of India* Special.

Ning, W. (2001), 'Seeking a National Identity and Constructing Chinese Critical Discourse in the Age of Globalization', *Conference Proceedings: International Conference on Subjectivity/Cultural Identity in an Age of Globalization* (Taipei: Shih Shin University Press).

Padmanabhan, A. (11 August 2003), 'Return Flight', *India Today*.

Padmanabhan, A. (20 October 2003), 'What Makes Bobby Tick?', *India Today*.

Padmanabhan, A. and Bhasi, I. (19 January 2004), 'At Home in the World', *India Today*.

Padmanabhan, A. and Unnithan, S. (1 September 2003), 'Hemant Lakhani: Trading in Terror', *India Today*.

Perry, J.O. (2002), 'A Dialysis of Diasporan Difficulties', *Journal of Contemporary Thought*, (Special Number: Identities Local and Global).

Rajagopal, S. and V. Dutt (11 September 2003). 'Indians abroad in big time fraud' *The Times of India*.

Rajghatta, C. (1 October 2003), 'Jindal rises to the top', *The Times of India*.

Chapter 15

Globalizing Hinduism, Hinduizing India: The Paradoxical Purposes of the Vishwa Hindu Parishad

Tapan Basu

English Department, Hindu College, University of Delhi, India

Introduction

This chapter focuses on the politics of the production and projection of 'heritage' in the context of the Hindu nationalist movement in India, especially in its contemporary phase. In recent years, it has been assiduously attempting to obtain for itself a global reach beyond its Indian roots. The climax of this phase of the so-called Hindutva (which may be translated as 'Hinduness') enterprise was arrived at 9 months after the Vishwa Hindu Parishad (VHP), roughly translating as the World Hindu Council, had successfully realized its mission of demolishing the Babri Masjid (Mosque) in Ayodhya, constructed, according to the VHP, on the birth-spot of the Hindu god Lord Ram. In September 1993 the VHP of America set up a conference entitled *Global Vision 2000* in Washington DC. The conference was ostensibly organized to commemorate the centenary of Swami Vivekananda's address to the World Parliament of Religions in Chicago in 1893. In convening this meet, the VHP, by now nationally notorious (and indeed banned for 2 years by the Indian state) as an anti-democratic communal organization, was not only flaunting its formidable international following, but also establishing for itself a hundred-year-old lineage.

This chapter examines the somewhat contradictory trajectories of the so-called Hindutva enterprise that emerge out of this self-fashioned VHP lineage, that is, the ambivalent discourses and dichotomous agendas associated with Hindutva as it ventures to operate as a worldwide movement.

The Hindutva 'Heritage'

I begin my examination of Hindutva 'heritage' on ground laid down by the Hindutva ideologues themselves, beginning with Vivekananda's (1863–1902) attempt to endow Hinduism with the status of a transnational religion. As even the ideologues of Hindutva acknowledge, there was neither an international Hindu constituency nor a national Hindu consolidation at the moment of Swami Vivekananda's epic journey from the East to the West as a pioneering Hindu missionary.[1] His was essentially an individual initiative at propagating Hinduism among 'sisters and brothers of America', as his famous Chicago addresses attest (2002, pp. 1–18).

A desire to instruct Christians of the West about Hinduism of the East, and thus contest colonial condescension towards Hindus, was clearly the dominant note in the lectures that Vivekananda delivered. Nonetheless, his defence of Hinduism was marked by recognition of the essential sameness of all religions:

> To the Hindu, then, the whole world of religions is only a travelling, a coming up, of different men and women, through various conditions and circumstances, to the same goal. Every religion is only an evolving of God out of the material man, and the same God is the inspirer of all of them. Why, then, are there so many contradictions? ... The contradictions come from the same truth adopting itself to the varying circumstances of different natures (2002, p. 13).

Unlike latter-day ideologues of Hindutva, Vivekananda believed in the possibility of a universal religion:

> ... one which will have no location in place or time; which will be infinite, like the God it will preach, and whose sun will shine upon the followers of Krishna and of Christ, on saints and sinners alike; which will not be Brahmanic or Buddhistic, Christian or Mahommedan, but the sum total of all these, and still have infinite scope for development ... (2002, p. 14).

In Vivekananda's addresses to the Chicago Parliament there was no assertion of Hindu superiority over other religions or the threat posed by other religions to Hinduism, motifs flaunted by latter-day Hindutva ideologues. Instead, he expressed himself forcefully in favour of the principle of peaceful co-existence of all religions:

> Much has been said of the common ground of religious unity. But if any one here hopes that this unity will come by the triumph of any one of the religions and the destruction of the others, to him I say: "Brother, yours is an impossible hope." Do I wish that the Christian would become Hindu? God forbid. Do I wish that the Hindu would become Christian? God forbid.
>
> [...] The Christian is not to become a Hindu or a Buddhist, nor a Hindu or a Buddhist to become a Christian. But each must assimilate the spirit of the others and yet persevere with his individuality and grow according to his own law of growth (2002, pp. 17–18).

In the post-Chicago phase Vivekananda began to represent more and more a type of Hindu patriotism in his utterances. In a speech delivered by him in Madras on his return, he extolled this land of the Hindus as his *maatribhumi* (motherland) and his *punyabhumi* (Holy Land), terms which anticipated the influential thesis on Hindutva by V.D. Savarkar published in 1923. He spoke of the need to rejuvenate India by

---

1   The significance of Swami Vivekananda's 1893 visit to the United States and especially of his addresses to the World Parliament of Religions in Chicago, from the Hindutva point of view, has been recorded through detailed analyses of the event on Global Hindu Electronic Network: Swami Vivekananda Study Center (http://hindunet.org/vivekananda/).

rejuvenating Hinduism. Hinduism, according to him, 'is the life of our race, and ... must be strengthened'. He therefore exhorted Hindus with the following words:

> You have withstood the shocks of centuries simply because you took great care of [your religion], because, you sacrificed everything for it. Your forefathers underwent everything boldly, even death itself, but preserved their religion. Temple after temple was broken by the foreign conqueror, and no sooner had the wave passed than the spire of the temple rose up again. Some of these old temples of Southern India, some like Somnath of Gujarat, will teach you volumes of wisdom, will give you a keener insight into the history of the race than any number of books. Mark how this temple of Somnath bears the marks of a hundred attacks and a hundred regenerations, continually destroyed and continually springing up out of the ruins as strong as ever. That is the national mind, that is the national life current. Follow it, and it leads to glory (1922, pp. 237–238).

However, even in this Hindu patriotic phase, Vivekananda remained keenly alive to the fault-lines within Hinduism's practices and precepts. He was a trenchant critic of caste and class divisions within the Hindu community, as well as of its tendency to turn superstitious and obscurantist. And, in the ultimate analysis, he refused to accept that the Hindus had sole claim over the land which had historically given them their name:

> The word Hindu, by which it is the fashion now-a-day [sic] to style ourselves, has lost all its meaning, for this word merely means those who lived on the other side of the river Indus. This name, Sanskrit Sindhu, was murdered into Hindu by the ancient Persians, and all people living on the other side of the River Sindhu were called by them Hindus [...] There may not be any harm in using the word, of course, but, as I have said, it has lost all its significance, for all the people who live on this side of the Indus, you may mark, in modern times, do not follow the same religion as they did in ancient times. The word, therefore, covers not only Hindus proper, but Mohammedans, Christians, Jains and all the others who live in India. I, therefore, would not use the word Hindu (1922, p. 17).

Despite persistent efforts on the part of the VHP, a conglomeration of Hindu religious leaders, and its parent organization the non-religious Rashtriya Swayamsevak Sangh (RSS), to set up Vivekananda as a founding father of a worldwide Hindutva movement, Vivekananda continues to be, at best, a problematic prophet for Hindutva (Sharma, 2003, pp. 70–123).

Hindutva, as a self-styled movement, took off only as late as the 1920s, and significantly did not requisition the patronage of the Hindu religious leadership of that era. Nor did any Hindu religious leader of that era attempt to mobilize support for Hindutva beyond the shores of India. In 1920, following in the footsteps of Swami Vivekananda, Paramhansa Yogananda (1893-1952) sailed to the United States of America to participate in a religious congress, the International Congress of Religious Liberals, convened in Boston that year. Like Vivekananda, Yogananda had travelled abroad to propagate the Hindu religion. And, like Vivekananda, Yogananda was open to dialogue with other religions and interacted with religious leaders of different persuasions. Yogananda's definition of the Hindu too, like that of Vivekananda's, precluded an easy conflation of the religious identity and the national identity of the Indian people:

The term Hindu is used often in a misleading sense. Its proper meaning would include only the religious adherents of Hinduism. But it is commonly used in a national sense, and I myself have been guilty of so using it […]. The right word to use in national sense, when designating the different people of India would be "Indians". Thus all Mohammedans, Hindus, Parsis, and other peoples that live in India are Indians, while only those professing Hinduism are Hindus (Yogananda, 1926, pp. 30–34).

Ironically, it was in the 1920s that another definition of the Hindu began to gain currency, one that premised a Hindu religious identity upon a Hindu national identity. This definition of the Hindu, in other words, held that Hindu as a national denomination determined Hindu as a religious denomination. The first to propound this 'secular' construction of Hinduism was V.D. Savarkar in his monograph, *Hindutva! Who is a Hindu?* (1923). Modern Hindutva really comes into its own with Savarkar's description of the Hindu as, 'one who looks upon the land that extends from Sindu to Sindu – from Indus to the Seas – as the land of his forefathers – his Fatherland (pitribhu) … and who, above all, addresses this land, this Sindhusthan, as his Holyland (punyabhu)' (1989, pp. 115–116) The implications of the *punyabhum-pitribhumi* equation were extremely emotive, especially in the context of an emergent nationalist consciousness within India. While effectively evoking nationalist sentiment for Bharatvarsha (India), however, Savarkar's rhetoric rendered the nationalism of the Indian Muslims and the Indian Christians suspect, since, with their Holy Lands in Arabia and Palestine respectively, the Indian Muslims and the Indian Christians would not be able to conjoin *punyabhumi* uniquely with *pitribhumi*. The exclusion of these potential traitors was given simultaneously with a supreme internal tolerance towards the divergences of rituals and beliefs among Hindus. What was important was not religious conviction but commitment to the nation, that is, to (an arbitrarily and arrogantly defined) Bharatvarsha. Anybody – a theist, monotheist, polytheist, Buddhist, Jain, Sikh, adherent of the reformist Arya Samaj or Parthana Samaj or an advocate of the conservative Sanatan Dharma – for whom Bharatvarsha was *pitribhumi* as well as *punyabhumi* qualified, according to Savarkar, to be called a perfect Hindu. In fact, Savarkar's definition of Hindutva was to fulfil another very important function. Generations of Hindus who, during the course of the twentieth century, were to leave home and settle abroad, for either professional or personal reasons, could by a mere affirmation of their allegiance to the Hindu nation claim that they remained Hindus by faith. Hinduism's hierarchies, notably those of class and caste, did not bother Savarkar because, as he saw it, these hierarchies would become irrelevant once Hindu solidarity had been achieved.

The promise of Hindu solidarity so fired Savarkar's imagination that he soared above the frictions and the fractions that had traditionally divided the Hindu fold. But correspondingly there was a willingness in Savarkar to accommodate every Hindu sect, small and big, within Hindutva since Hindutva valorized the common civilization of Bharatvarsha. Thus, no Hindu institution – whether theology or pilgrimage or festival – could be deemed dispensable as each contributed to the inclusiveness of Hindutva. The inclusiveness of Hindutva did not, of course, extend to those who did not subscribe to Hindu institutions and, by corollary, to the Bharatvarsha of Savarkar's vision.

Savarkar's vision itself emanated out of a context of vicious communal polarization that engulfed northern India in particular during the mid-1920s. In the wake of the withdrawal of the Indian National Congress from the Non-Cooperation Movement against the British Raj that it had initiated, and its consequent let-down of support to the Khilafat agitation, an unprecedented wave of riots swept across the country from Kohat in the west to Dacca in the east. The relations between Hindus and Muslims were vitiated as never before, and continued to remain so through the rest of the decade. Between 1923 and 1927 there were no less than 91 outbreaks of communal violence in the United Provinces, the worst affected region in this regard.

Meanwhile, there was a hardening of stance among Hindu as well as Muslim groups on issues of communal identity. For instance, *tabligh* (propaganda) and *tanzim* (organization) evolved as Muslim communal counter-parts to *shuddhi* (purification) and *sangathan* (organization), strategies of Hindu communal consolidation promoted by the Arya Samaj protagonist Swami Shraddhanand and others. Shraddhanand's pamphlet, *Hindu Sangathan: Saviour of a Dying Race* (1926), combined the concerns of a perceived Hindu population decline due to conversions to other religions with the felt need therefore to end untouchability if the unity and integrity of the 'dying race' was to be saved. These anxieties on behalf of 'the Hindu race' were enthusiastically endorsed by the Hindu Mahasabha, the most important communion of Hindu communal interests till then. Yet the Hindu Mahasabha was only an annual conference, unable to confront the day-to-day challenges that were seen to besiege Hindutva. Hindutva votaries were now in search of disciplined cadres constituting a Hindu *sangathan*. The Rashtriya Swayamsevak Sangh (roughly translatable as National Self-helpers Association) was formed to fulfil this quest (Basu et al., 1993; Goyal, 2000; Kanungo, 2002).

The name was suggestive. This Hindu *sangathan* deliberately aligned itself with the cause of the Hindu nation rather than with the cause of the Hindu religion. In fact, the Hindu religion was relegated to the peripheries of the RSS's programme as the centre was occupied by endeavours to realize the Hindu nation as defined by Savarkar. In the first two decades of its existence, from the mid-1920s to the mid-1940s, the RSS engaged in the defence of Hindu rights within the multi-denominational milieu of an emergent Indian nation-state. As a result, it distanced itself acutely from the mainstream of the Indian national movement which, under the tutelage of the Congress Party, had developed a pluralistic orientation.

It was only as late as in the early 1950s that the RSS involved itself in a specific religious agitation by supporting the demand articulated by a number of Hindu *sadhus* (religious leaders) belonging to different orders for a ban on cow-slaughter to be imposed by the Government of India. The agitation against the slaughter of cows, a sacred symbol for Hindus, which was revived on a more massive scale in the 1960s by the *sadhus*, was again seconded by the RSS, on this occasion through the agency of its political affiliate, the Bharatiya Jana Sangh (BJS)

These episodes were but the prologue to Hindutva's tryst with Hindu religion which was formally inaugurated with the founding of the VHP, under RSS's sponsorship in the 1960s, and its phenomenal expansion and empowerment in the decades that followed. How and why the VHP was sponsored by the RSS remains a matter of speculation. All that can be stated with definiteness is that, in the

1960s, RSS activities attuned to the task of building a Hindu nation, which had been entrusted to its *shakhas* (branches), had arrived at a phase of passivity. The hegemony of Nehruvian socialism over the state, civil society and the intelligensia of India was still rather tight. The BJS, on the behalf of the RSS, had not made much of an impact on the public life of the nation either. In the event, the RSS sought to explore fresh routes to the achievement of its goal.

This was also the period in which a counter-cultural revolution threatened to turn the western world topsy-turvy: the high-point of the beat generation, and of the cult of the hippies, and of salvation-shopping by a materialist population in pursuit of spiritual medication from the Eastern world. Hindu *sadhus* were suddenly much much in vogue as gurus (mentors) to an angst-filled parvenu. Several of these gurus set up ashrams (retreats) in countries of Europe and America to cater to the needs of their foreign following which, year by year, came to include a substantial section of Non-Resident Indians (NRIs) – the semi-formal appellation for Indian emigrants. The RSS saw in these transnational gurus, whose influence in India increased in direct proportion to their growing constituencies abroad, a most appropriate medium for globalizing Hinduism as well as for hinduising India.

Not surprisingly, the vanguard of the VHP was provided by gurus such as Swami Satyamitranand, founder of the Samanvaya Parivar (Family of Harmony), Swami Chinmayananda of the Chinmaya Mission fame and senior swamis of the Divine Life Mission, whose mass discipleship in India was complemented by an elite discipleship from across the globe. A tacit division of labour marked the relationship between the global and the local disciples of these gurus. While the local disciples, cutting across divisions of region, caste and class, communicated a sense of Hinduism's pan-Indian religious appeal, the global disciples, dispersed over various countries, showed that Hinduism was not merely a parochial Indian religion.

For the VHP, which presented itself as the sole custodian of Hinduism, it was important that both these aspects of Hinduism be played up equally. This was evident in the declaration trumpeted by Swami Chinmayananda, president of the VHP to Lise Mckean, author of *Divine Enterprise: Gurus and the Hindu Nationalist Movement*, during the course of an interview:

> When your Pope [Paul VI] came to India [December 1964], he said he was going to convert 125 people to Christianity. Public opinion made him withdraw his plan but I was in Bombay and announced that I would convert 200 people to Hinduism and I did. Then I had the idea to start a group to work for conversions. I did not have enough people of my own so I asked the RSS for their help. Guruji [RSS head, Golwalkar] liked the idea and had thousands of workers everywhere. The VHP has grown into a mighty force. It is all over the world. After I stared the VHP, I returned to my own mission as spiritual teacher of Vedanta. Anyone can do the work of the VHP. I have been invited to the VHP's conference in Washington as the keynote speaker and will be given an award. Awards are good because they mean a press conference and publicity. Later in August I will speak at the Parliament of the World's Religions in Chicago. [a repeat of the 1893 Parliament addressed by Swami Vivekananda] (Kean, 1996, p. 102).

On its official website (http://www.vhp.org) the VHP designates itself as an organization of 600 million Hindus living in 80 countries. It claims to favour no one

Hindu creed or custom. Its aim, as the literature observes, is to bring together an array of religious denominations which call themselves Hindu and affirm their Hinduness by invoking Bharatvarsha as the *pitribhumi* and *punyabhumi* of all Hindus. The pioneer members of the VHP included 'Hindu' seers as diverse as those owning allegiance to the Sanatan Dharma, conservative Brahmanical Hinduism, Hindu reformist efforts like the Arya Samaj and the Prarthana Samaj, and even Buddhist, Jain and Sikh sympathizers.

Nevertheless, the structural apparatus of the VHP arrogates ultimate authority to the non-religious command of the RSS. RSS personnel dominate the 51-strong Governing Council of the VHP which controls VHP's policy-making at the very top. There have been hardly a handful of religious personages, at any point of its existence, in the Governing Council of the VHP. In an insightful essay, 'Soldier Monks and Militant Sadhus,' William R. Pinch has highlighted the dichotomy between the religious and the non-religious segments within the VHP leadership as a possible source of tension in the Hindutva movement:

> Historically, sanyasis have been fiercely independent and resentful of state control, even while benefiting from the land grants of emperors and regional rulers, even more so if confronted with the intractability of the modern bureaucratic machine. How they will respond to the desire of party-politicians to dictate behaviour over the long term remains to be seen (1996, p. 159).

As of now of course, this tension has not too often come to the fore, not often enough at least to disrupt the Hindutva movement's enormous aggrandizement at the national and at the international levels over the last few decades.

The Hindutva movement has brought the Hindu *sanyasi* (renunciant) into international and national limelight as defender of the Hindu religion, a role that, according to William R. Pinch, numerous Hindu *sanyasis* have enacted anyway through history without being implicated in defending the Hindu nation. The *sanyasi*, in turn, has been instrumental in bestowing upon the Hindutva movement the aura of being indistinguishable from a centuries-spanned seamless history of Hinduism.

Globalizing Hindutva and Non-Resident Indians

This invented tradition of Hindutva effectively camouflages its modern inspiration from nationalist rather than religious ideologies. The religious dimension has been foregrounded decisively at the turn of the twentieth century with the launch of the Ramjanambhoomi (Ram's birth-land) liberation campaign by the VHP. The VHP campaign in India successfully carried out a transition of tactics on the part of the RSS – a shift to mass-Hindutva (mass mobilization for Hindutva) from class-Hindutva (mobilization for Hindutva through training of a class of core volunteers). This shift paid tremendous dividends to the Hindutva movement, and enhanced the quantity and quality of popular participation in the Hindutva movement as never before. The popular participation in the Ramjanambhoomi liberation campaign in particular was prepared for by the VHP through meticulously orchestrated events such as *yatras* (journeys), *shilanayas* (foundation-stone laying) ceremonies and *kar seva* (voluntary service), all geared to the construction of a temple at Ram's purported birth-spot. The VHP's everyday enterprises, such as the instruction of Hindu *pujaris* (priests), promotion of Sanskrit studies and spreading Hindu *samskaras* (rites) among *vanavasis* (aborigines), *girijans* (tribals) and *harijans* (outcastes) in general received a boost after this shift.

At the onset of the 1970s, some 10 years before the initiation of the campaign for Ramjanambhoomi liberation by the VHP, the VHP hastily started to establish its chapters overseas. The overseas chapters were established with the intention of inviting Indian emigrants settled abroad or Non Resident Indians (NRIs), who were now a significant presence in several countries, to join the Hindutva movement. Through the 1970s, VHP chapters cropped up in American and European countries to begin with, and then in countries of Asia and Africa. The wooing of NRIs by the VHP was an acknowledgement of their growing affluence in their countries by adoption, as the VHP home-page on the website of the VHP puts it:

> Hindus are enterprising people and many of them have been going abroad for trade, business, propogation of religion, etc. During the past centuries, thousands went abroad as indentured labour and settled in large numbers. During the last few decades they have been going as engineers, doctors, teachers, etc., not only to developing countries, but also to advanced countries like U.S.A., Canada, West Germany, UK, Norway, Sweden, etc.

Some of these prosperous Hindu expatriates were eventually to become VHP's primary source of funding for its work in India, its everyday enterprises as well as its magnum opus, the Ramjanambhoomi liberation campaign.

The Ramjanambhoomi liberation campaign has been used by the VHP to mobilize expatriate Hindus from locations as far apart as Canada and South Africa for the Hindutva movement. The VHP home-page notes that on an appeal from B.P. Toshniwal, vice-president (Foreign Coordination), devotees of Ram located outside India performed a Sri Ram Shila *puja* (worship to pray for the laying of the foundation stone for the Ram temple at Ayodhya). The *puja* was performed by the consecration of *shilas* (bricks) slated to be used for the Ram temple's construction. According to the VHP home-page, bricks with the name of Ram etched on them arrived at the VHP headquarters from Canada, USA, UK, Spain, Germany, Belgium, Portugal, Sweden, Norway, Denmark, the Netherlands, Bangladesh, Nepal, Sri Lanka, Israel, Malaysia, Singapore, Hong Kong, China, Surinam, Zambia, Botswana and South Africa. The bricks were of different shapes and different sizes and composed differently. The brick from China was made of jade, from Zambia it was coated with copper, a few were engrafted in marble.

Through the image of a resplendent Ram temple at Ayodhya, which features in all the print and visual documents distributed by it, the VHP has sought to offer Hindus abroad an imaginary perfect homeland in lieu of the real imperfect homeland they left behind. The image of the Ram temple to-be, like the Hindu homeland of Savarkar's dreams, dispels all sources of potential conflict among Hindus. The temple, as Arvind Rajagopal has remarked, 'has a design incorporating a shikhara, a dome in the north Indian style; there are also two gopurams, domes in the south Indian style, although these are only a quarter of the shikhara's height' (2001, p. 245). Such syncretism, Rajagopal writes, is without precedent in Indian temple architecture, and is cast as an explicitly propagandist gesture at Hindus abroad across regional lines by the VHP. Additionally, the sheer opulence of the structure, as embossed on VHP literature, exorcizes the spectre of destitution and deprivation of fellow-Hindus back home from the minds of viewers.

For the Hindu diaspora, this spectacle symbolizes a resurgent India of the future and is indeed comforting. It is comforting for them, in their homes away from home, always wearing the tag of a minority community and afflicted frequently with feelings of anguish and anxiety about their status vis-à-vis the majority communities in their adopted countries, to contemplate the exalted destiny of Bharatvarsha, the Hindu utopia in which they and they alone will hold sway. The Hindu utopia does not automatically appeal to Hindus at home however, mired as they are in the messiness of an imperfect present. As beleagured subjects of a still backward India, they find it difficult to forget the grim actualities of their day-to-day lives. For them, the Hindutva movement manufactures a victim complex, a litany of wrongs perpetrated on them by Muslims and Christians, the 'invaders' of Bharatvarsha. Inevitably, this litany evokes a perfect past of Hinduism in India which compensates for the native Hindu's sorry self-perception.

The sufferings of the native Hindus are attributed by the VHP to the secular Indian state which, in its opinion, has ignored the interests of Hindus at home while giving preferential treatment to the minority communities of India. The minority communities, it is alleged by the VHP, have been systematically pampered by the secular state which hence needs to be overthrown by the Hindus.

This radical positioning of the VHP in India against the secular Indian state does not tally with the moderate positioning of its overseas units. The VHP abroad, while keeping up the rhetoric of Hindu nationalism, is careful not to choose a confrontationist trajectory towards the states under which they function. The principal pre-occupations of the VHP abroad are in the realm of culture: coaching children of Hindu families in the Hindu way of life, proselytization to Hinduism of Hindu renegades and non-Hindus interested in embracing Hinduism, protesting incidents of discrimination against Hindus elsewhere than in their homeland. The protests are aired in an accommodative rather than in an antagonistic spirit.

The VHP takes care to proclaim through its home-page that its overseas units do not shy away from interaction with people belonging to other faiths:

[The VHP] interacts with them with an open mind. In 1987, Dr B. Ramaraju, Vice-President, VHP International, attended the Second Conference of the Council of the World Religions held at Harrison Hot Springs Resort near Vancouver (Canada) [...] The VHP of UK, Denmark, West Germany, etc. have been participating in various inter-faith programmes.

The home-page also has snippets which put into perspective the character of its units overseas. The VHP of UK has very cordial relations with the local authorities. A Hindu conference convened by the VHP of the Netherlands was attended by the Lord Mayor of the city of The Hague, the Dutch Minister of Home Affairs and the Deputy Secretary-General of the Second Chamber of Dutch Parliament. The

VHP has petitioned the United Nations (UN) to grant it recognition as an advisory appendage to the UN. Clearly, the VHP abroad uses Hindutva as a bargaining ploy with the respective home governments to earn for diasporic Hindus there all the prerogatives and privileges that the VHP deems to be their due. In so doing, unlike the VHP in India, the VHP abroad has no extra-constitutional objective: it functions merely as a special interest lobby for the Hindu diaspora in different countries of the world and not as a no-holds-barred champion of the Hindu nationalist movement as in India.

Thus, the garb of nationalism that the VHP wears at home is exchanged for the garb of ethnicity while it operates in the countries abroad. The purpose of the VHP abroad is to make available for overseas Hindus their own niches in the multicultural mosaic of post-modern societies, even as the VHP at home stays committed to the goal of realizing the Hindu nation through the pre-modern evocation of Hindu religion.

References

Basu, T., Datta, P., Sarkar, S., Sarkar, T. and Sen, S. (1993), *Khaki Shorts and Saffron Flags. A Critique of the Hindu Right* (New Delhi: Orient Longman).

Goyal, D.R., ([1979] 2000), *Rashtriya Swayamsewak Sangh*, (New Delhi: Radhakrishna Parkashan).

Kanungo, P. (2002), *RSS's Tryst with Politics. From Hedgewar to Sudarshan* (New Delhi: Manohar Publishers and Distributors).

McKean, L. (1996), *Divine Enterprise. Gurus and the Hindu Nationalist Movement* (Chicago: University of Chicago Press).

Pinch, W.R. (1996), 'Soldier Monks and Militant Sadhus', Making India Hindu, 140–161 in *Religion, Community, and the Politics of Democracy in India*. Ludden, D. (ed.) (Delhi: Oxford University Press).

Rajagopal, A. (2001), *Politics After Television. Hindu Nationalism and the Reshaping of the Public in India* (Cambridge: Cambridge University Press).

Savarkar, V.D., ([1923] 1989), *Hindutva* [Who is Hindu?] (New Delhi: Bharti Sahitya Sadan).

Sharma, J. (2003), *Hindutva. Exploring the Idea of Hindu Nationalism* (New Delhi: Penguin Books).

Vivekananda, S. (1922), *The Indian Lectures of Swami Vivekananda. Being a Record of his Addresses in India after his Mission to the West* (Calcutta: Udbodhan Office).

Vivekananda, S. (2002), *Selections from the Complete Works of Swami Vivekananda* (Kolkata: Advaita Ashrama).

Yogananda, S. (1926), 'What I Mean by the Word Hindu', *East West*, **2**(1), 30–34.

Chapter 16

Negotiating the Shifting Boundaries of Nativeness and Modernity in Immigrant South Asian Women's Clothes

Vinay Bahl

Sociology, Pennsylvania College of Technology, Williamport, USA

Introduction

My objective in this chapter is to interrogate dress as an aspect of cultural identity in the context of Indian women in the diaspora, pulled as they are between two cultural frames of reference, India and the West. As immigrants, these women struggle to balance their desire to protect their individual identity while at the same time maintaining a sense of membership within the ethnic and national cohorts from which they derive (India) and to which they belong (the West) respectively. In doing this they contend with negotiating between ideologies of modernity, feminism, nationalism, and so on.

How does one define what is a 'modern' (as 'progressive') or a 'native' (as 'backward') dress? This question is difficult to answer because the same 'native' style of dress can be the most visible symbol of defiance, as for Iranian feminists and African-American Muslim women, as well as of conformity, as in the case of Afghani women under Taliban rule. In many societies the particular style of attire is used sometimes as a social control mechanism and sometimes as a ploy to change social norms (the banning of Muslim women's head-cover in schools is a case in point). Besides the political and social significance of women's dress, how a person uses her/his dress, and in what context, is equally important (Barnes and Eicher, 1992, pp. 202–207). For example, one generally finds that men's formal dress in most contemporary societies is Westernized. But it is not necessarily the same for women's formal dress. What does this mean? Are men being conformists to Western fashion or, are they being 'progressive' within their own societies? Are women being conformists to 'native' culture or resisting the pressure of Western culture by wearing so called 'traditional' dress or are they defying Westernization? Do women wear 'traditional' dress because of 'personal choice' or is it the consequence of ascribed social gender roles, the prevailing idea of beauty and style, as well as to hold on to the so called 'native tradition'? (In the 1960s feminists used the term 'personal choice' to go against the social norms. Today this term is used to follow and accept prevailing social norms: marriage, staying home with children, or going to work for wages.)

In the contemporary postcolonial context, dress as a symbol of establishing so-called 'authenticity', identity, and freedom (as 'progress') also raises very complicated issues. For example, the daily task of choosing a dress to fit into the prevailing norms of an adopted society is itself a tedious, oppressive and even frightening one for immigrant Indian women in Western societies. Moreover, dress gives contradictory messages depending on the gender, age, nationality, ethnicity, and class of the audience. For example, Indian males find an Indian female in Western attire less accessible than one in Indian attire. At the same time Indian females who wear Western dress assume that females who wear Indian dresses must be conservative in their outlook (therefore often dubbed *desi* – home grown/narrow minded – and *penji/bhenji* – sister – and considered not 'sexy'). Obviously, one cannot win the appreciation of both Indian males and females at the same time as gaining acceptance in American (or any other Western) society. This means Indian women in the USA have to perform a juggling act to please three categories of people: Indian males, Indian females (at several levels in turn – younger, older, in-laws, and peer groups – because Indian women in each age group judge women of other age groups differently) and American society.

The confusion of those Indian women who wear Indian-style dress within the USA is further complicated by the confusion that prevails within the Indian subcontinent about the definition of an authentic Indian dress. In the last decade or so within Indian society the meanings of so-called 'authentic' Indian dress have changed dramatically. For example, the North Western Indian regional attire called *salwar-kameez* has acquired a national status and most other kinds of regional ethnic clothes – even while ethnic styles are becoming more fashionable in the designing of *salwar-kameez* – are abandoned by urban young Indian women (Nandwani and Seth, 2001). Interestingly, this is happening at a time when the focus on local identity, 'authentic' ethnicity, and so on, is on the increase. *Salwar-kameez* is considered as 'progressive' and modern, whereas, other regional dresses are seen as 'backward' or 'exotic'. For instance, *mundu* and *vesti*, a south Indian regional dress for young women, has been relegated to a 'backward' status in comparison with *salwar-kameez*. But at the same time *salwar-kameez* is treated as less 'progressive' than blue jeans or other Western dresses.

Interestingly, the Indian educated elite are pushing the concept of indigenism and 'authenticity' through ethnic dresses. Mass media, especially television and popular cinema, have also contributed in important ways to the imagining of the new indigenism, which takes up elements from diverse and continually changing folk traditions and presents them as local, authentic, and specific. The internationalization of markets has played an important role in this process, as it demands the formation of new identities, which has resulted in the reinvention of all sorts of local dresses according to the new consumerist values. Interestingly, new consumerism is presented in the form of traditional or ethnic clothes, which are mass-produced. Thus, a neo-nationalism is being created for multinationals while the struggle to look 'modern' and 'progressive' is also increasing in two contrary styles: denim jeans, the American style, on the one hand; and *salwar-kameez*, which is also widely worn in Islamic countries, on the other.

It is interesting to note how in India these dresses have acquired a status of being 'progressive' even when they represent opposite values. It seems that there is a hierarchical progressive status between these two dresses: a woman wearing jeans is considered to be more outgoing than one in *salwar-kameez*. But *salwar-kameez* is considered more 'progressive' than the *sari* and other regional Indian dresses, thereby maintaining the notion of keeping Indian women in traditional dresses. In the USA, Indian women face many other pressures that create a constant need for balancing the contradictory demands of workplace and home, and ethnic, regional, and national identities. Thus, it now seems that geographically defined regionalist identities are closely linked to geographically defined markets (Rajadhyaksa, 1990). In other words, these hierarchical labels are products of a historical process that bestows superior status upon those women 'choosing' to wear Western or Indian clothes. India as we understand it today is itself a recently constructed entity, therefore, what really is an Indian traditional dress?

The discussion above shows that the labelling of particular clothing signifies a variety of social, economic, cultural, and political relationships between dress and social order in terms of power, authority, gender, status and class (Storm, 2000). Based on this understanding it is fair to say that dress is part of the custom of a society that is created and promoted in the historical process of social formation. Furthermore, it implies that freedom to buy and wear what one wishes is restricted by: a) economic condition of a society, b) the colonial/non-colonial/neo-colonial status of a society, c) control over personal choice, d) variety of alternative clothing styles available (and therefore availability of technology), e) the demand for conspicuous consumption, and f) the ability to experience satisfaction from one's choice.

As I discuss below, South Asian women's dress has been a site of conflict for a long time and the labelling of women's dress as traditional/modern and so on has evolved over an extended period.

Changing Attire of South Asian Women from Antiquity to British Colonial Rule

Historically, changes in Indian clothing styles can be attributed to the interplay of three factors. 1) Clothing styles changed by changing social needs, changing social institutions and changing customs within Indian society, in the process of social interactions. 2) Clothing styles changed under the influence of, and through interaction with, other societies – by invasion, or by trade and commerce, or by the initiative of a noble or a local king. 3) Clothing styles also changed through the creativity of individuals: tailors, women of upper class, women in villages who create styles in response to social customs, market forces, class and caste distinctions, religious influences and entrepreneurship.

The differences in dresses according to class and gender in India became more apparent after more surplus wealth was created in Aryan society. Between the sixth and third centuries BCE the clothing industry was highly developed in India due to the growth of commerce and the subsequent growth of large towns. But the growth of commerce also led to further social divisions of society based on 'class/caste' (for a discussion of these terms see Bahl, 2004), and the assignment of different kinds of garments for different sections of society. For the Gupta period, 335 ACE to 530

ACE, more information is available about dress and ornaments (Pandey, 1988, p. 91, 118). The images of goddesses in temples showed no garment for the upper part of their bodies and nuns were not permitted to wear saris or girdles usually worn by housewives. Other women wore upper and lower garments and sometimes a tunic. The upper garment was generally wound round the left arm (ibid., p. 114).

India's interaction with China, Bahlika, Pari Sindhu, increased the use of tunics, caps, trousers and coats. With greater division of labour and specialization of work and craft in society, class distinction through dress became more defined. But under Muslim rule (977–1526 ACE) the state started intervening in all aspects of people's lives and a new market mechanism was developed to transfer wealth from villages to the state. This new socio-economic process changed the social structure leading to the pauperization of lower class people while creating new social groups: money changers, usurers, traders, and transferring more power to *zamindars* (landlords). During this time a variety of sewn clothes started emerging with elaborate embellishments for the ruling class and royalties (ibid.).

Muslims introduced pyjamas and *kurtas*, and Muslim women wore wide, loose Persian pyjamas, which were gathered and fastened round the ankles. Later, the hems became narrow and the legs tight at the extremities, but the body remained loose. The early dress of Muslim ladies in Lucknow was pyjamas which were very tight at the hems, tight fitting *ungia* over the breasts with half sleeves, and a *kurta* covering the lower front and the back with a *duppata* over it. Towards the end of the *Navabi* rule a *shaluka*, or short sleeved tight blouse, was worn. It was first worn over the *ungia* in place of the *kurta*. Eventually, the ungia was replaced by a loose *kurta*. However, all these garments were later superseded one by one by British style jackets and blouses (Sharar, 1975).

The penetration of European goods during the nineteenth century and the end of royal patronage for India's weavers and spinners represented a crisis in economic history leading to the destruction of the Indian cloth industry. In this context, some Muslim women started wearing *saris* and discarded their old fashions. It is not surprising that by the late nineteenth century many educated Hindu families regarded stitched clothes as superior to the comparatively scanty *dhoti*. While in religious contexts they saw them as defiling, in secular contexts they saw them as proof of educational advancement and sophistication. This is when clothes acquired the status of being 'progressive' or 'backward', whereby the idea of 'progress' accompanied stitching rather than just wrapping.

During the final years of the Mughal political system, after 1740, the first English broad-clothes and cotton goods began to be imported into India. During this time, new regional consumer aristocracies were establishing themselves, notably in Lucknow, Bengal, and Hyderabad. European styles of clothes, which were introduced principally by European traders, missionaries, and colonial administrators, gained importance. European dress differed from most forms of Indian dress in the way it was cut, stitched, and shaped to the contours of body. Gender differences were also strongly demarcated in European dress, with women's skirts and dresses giving them a distinctive and exaggeratedly curvaceous outline in relation to the more linear forms of men's dress (Chaudhuri, 1976; Tarlo, 1996: xi).

Mughal rulers actively insisted on the adoption of Mughal styles by all officials in government employment and forced many Indian elites to wear Mughal dress in the public sphere. But the British did not try to force their own garb upon Indians (Tarlo, 1996, p. 24). On the contrary, they actively sought to discourage what they called 'meaningless imitation'. The British sought to reinforce their separateness from the 'Indian' population by rigorously adhering to British standards of dress and by encouraging Indians to dress in an 'oriental manner'. The British tried to control and discourage the Anglicization of Indian dress and ridiculed what they considered 'inappropriate dressing' (Chaudhuri, 1976; Cohn, 1989; Tarlo, 1996, p. 25). But the British were not very successful in their efforts because of the ready availability of imported machine-woven cloth from abroad.

Since British rulers were not very successful in stopping Indians from looking more like English men, they increased their efforts at controlling the clothing style and code of conduct for British Civil Servants. These new social values and codes of conduct were based on the assumption that the British were superior beings and Indians were inferiors. Therefore, British civil servants were expected not to wear Indian clothes in order to justify their 'civilizing' presence in India (Elwin, 1907, p. 43). As the British consolidated their political dominance in India in the early nineteenth century, the wearing of Indian styles among the British officers became increasingly unacceptable.

British rulers wanted to 'civilize' Indian dress but did not wish to make it completely European. In this process of 'civilizing' India the role of the Christian missionaries had been very important. For example, under the influence of Christian missionaries lower caste Nadar women attempted to wear a breast cloth, which led to a major controversy in Travancore in the first half of the nineteenth century. Members of the upper caste viewed the attempt of lower caste women wearing such a breast cloth as an infringement of their status (Hardgrove, 1968; Panikkar, 1998). Thus, while lower caste women under the influence of Christianity tried to imitate upper caste women's breast cloth, upper caste women were adding European accessories to their Indian dress. Upper class Indian women only added accessories such as shoes, blouses, petticoats, and jackets to their existing dress. They retained the distinctive sari but followed European fashion in fabrics, colours, and designs, thereby incorporating the latest trends from Europe and giving them a new Indian form (Tarlo, 1996, p. 39). However, by this time upper 'class/caste' Indian men were choosing to adopt the complete European dress as they found it useful for interacting with British rulers for gaining favours, getting well paid jobs and going to official parties and be accepted as 'progressive' and modern in their outlook.

Changes in Attire due to the Nationalist Movement

With the emergence and development of the nationalist movement some nationalist leaders realized the importance of Indian women's dress. Jyotirindranath Tagore (brother of Rabindranath Tagore) was one of the first Indians to suggest that a redefinition of Indian dress could bring about a sense of political unity. Thus, what to wear, especially among upper middle class Indian women, became a problem of national identity. The matter of national identity also entailed the issue of Bengali middle class women's education and their participation in social functions, at which British and other unrelated males would be present. These issues were matters of intense debate from the 1920s onwards both among Hindu reformers and conservatives. Earlier, elite Bengali women used to wear a *sari*, an expensive but semi-transparent muslin cloth wrapped around the body. But when they went out of the house they covered themselves with a *chador* (a shawl). While such a dress code was comfortable and adequate in a segregated and secluded society, this was not well suited to modern urban life. So far only prostitutes and poor labouring women, who wore scanty *saris* and worked outside the home, had an already established style of clothing for their work. The issue of clothing middle class Bengali women thus became important because now they were also participating in the public life outside their homes. An effort was therefore made to create a dress for middle class Bengali women that would distinguish them from prostitutes and labouring women, but which would at the same time not resemble European male attire, and would help in maintaining Indian national unity (Tarlo, 1996, p. 59).

The solution to this complex issue of national identity through women's clothes was found by adapting the Victorian dress – high necked long sleeve blouse, petticoat, and long chemise intact but disguised by draping the *sari* material over it. This meant that middle class women's clothing now needed an additional three to four more yards of cloth for the blouse and petticoat, which reinforced their class status. Peasant and tribal women could ill afford the extra fabric and continued to wear a thick cotton sari that was shorter in length and narrower in breadth, as they always had. From this time on the modest sari-clad middle class women, symbol of 'Hindu Indian national identity', became the everyday face of 'tradition'. Women got further confirmation of their modern *sari* style from the temples where goddesses were now wrapped in like fashion instead of being attired in the earlier scanty clothing (Mazumdar, 1992).

Thus, through the construction of a national dress for Indian women, and later promotion of *khadi* (hand spun cloth), Indian upper class men were able to create a social movement against the Westernization of Indian society. Upper class Indian men even allowed some elite family (including rural elite) women to join Indian politics, clad in *khadi saris*, a national symbol. But a large proportion of the female village population remained either in the cheaper, finer mill-cloth they had recently adopted, or wore other forms of regional dress (Tarlo, 1996, p. 320).

Changes in Attire due to Modernization and Global Cultural Forces

Soon after India's independence, Indian politicians once again changed their position on the issue of clothes. Indian women's dress also lost its earlier oppositional political role. Women's *sari* now acquired the status of representing 'authentic' Indian clothing and its aesthetic 'traditions'. But politicians chose to put India itself on the path of Western model of industrialization and modernization (ibid., p. 323). This path of modernization soon led to many attitude changes among the urban middle class and they quickly chose to switch their affiliation back to mill cloth instead of *khadi*. Many young urban Indian women of well-to-do families also adopted European styles, such as skirts, blouses and later trousers and denim jeans.

Many women (mostly city working women) while keeping the 'tradition' of *sari* intact started adopting synthetic fabrics. And many of them also switched to wearing *salwar-kameez* because of its functional usefulness and inexpensive maintenance as well as its so-called 'progressive' image (ibid., p. 328). The modernization of India helped the development of the film industry that promoted Western images, fashions, and styles through Hindi film stars.

During the 1960s and 70s, with changes in US immigration policies, many educated Indian elites had an opportunity to witness the ongoing civil rights movement as well as appreciation of the Indian tradition and art heritage in the US. The Beatles' George Harrison, for instance, became a disciple of sitar maestro Ravi Shankar and helped to arouse Western interest in the Indian sitar. Stimulated by this newly found pride in 'native' Indian clothes and art heritage, the educated Indian elite helped in the creation of a new Indian 'ethnic chic' that also came to be regarded as a resistance to Western aesthetics.

At the same time however the importation of second-hand discarded Western clothes, shipped as 'rags', started making their way into the daily life of many lower class urban people. Moreover, many rejected manufactured clothes (created in Indian sweatshops ostensibly for the Western world) also became available to common Indian people in the big cities. The increased availability of Western style clothes had two consequences. On the one hand, people became more tolerant of Indian women wearing skirts and long kaftans in their daily lives. On the other hand, in order to differentiate themselves from the common people, the Indian elite and Hindi film stars began to depart from a so called 'progressive' Western image and returned to 'ethnic chic' and the village women's dress. In this context, elite Indian women's choice of 'ethnic' clothes cannot be explained as anti-modern or anti-Western; it allowed them to express individual tastes (Tarlo, 1996, p. 328).

By the 1980s this exclusivity of 'ethnic' dress was diminished by mass produced machine made replicas of 'ethnic' clothes (Venkatesh, 1994; Belk, 1998). In reaction to this elite women opted for 'art-wear' (a dress is used as a canvas for special exclusive painting and the wearer of the dress becomes part of the painting), which is very expensive, to distinguish themselves from wearers of mass produced 'ethnic' dresses (*India Today* 6/30/89). At the same time, with increasing numbers of women joining the formal labour market (under the forces of liberalization and globalization) *salwar-kameez* rapidly began to replace the *sari*.

Changes in Attire due to Liberalization and Changing Global and Local Structures of the Labor Market

With the liberalization of the Indian market in the 1990s, once again the *sari* is emerging as an erotic wrap for some upper class, trendy women (*India Today* 2/25/02). The blouse is being discarded (in some cases), and the *sari* itself is changing in size, altering its form and being tied in a variety of new ways (sometimes so as to show the navel). By 2002 this trend, at least in the upper echelons, had gained strength and Indian designers began to think of this new kind of *sari* like fusion music. In contrast to the conventional draping style the New Age *sari* can be made to look like a divided skirt, flowing trousers, or even an ankle-length dress. Thus, the *sari* has once again become a functional, heady mix of sex appeal, feminine mystery, elegance, individuality and adaptability.

But there is growing resistance to Western influences and a renewed search for an 'authentic' Indian dress, which is both non-Western and fashionable, is on (Tarlo, 1996, p. 331). But Indian women have not abandoned native styles on a mass scale, they have successfully adapted Indian outfits such as *salwar-kameez* to the whims of contemporary fashion (Malwani, 2001). Interestingly, the removal of trade barriers in the 1990s also encouraged a new wave of 'international spirit', and an increased desire for things foreign – including clothes. When Princess Diana chose to wear *salwar-kameez* to a charity ball in London in 1996 it was considered as the arrival of *kurta* on the international scene (Malwani, 2001). By 2003 the *kurta* had become available in fashionable shops in Paris, New York and London, as well as in low cost marts. At the turn of the twenty-first century, as the service sector continues expanding, *salwar-kameez* remains popular with all age groups in all regions of India.

At the beginning of the twenty-first century the definition of 'native' Indian women's dress has changed fundamentally. A recent report (Malwani, 2001) suggests that most of the Non-Resident Indians (NRIs) use Bollywood (the Bombay film industry) style and fashions for their choice of clothes, believing them to be authentically Indian. Ironically, Bollywood is increasingly using taller, thinner, and more Caucasian looking girls with blue eyes and fair skin in Western style clothes (Malwani, 2001).

Attire as a Site of Struggle in the Context of Neo-Imperialism and Migration

The search for 'authentic' Indian clothes and exclusive fashions does not stop at the borders of India. In fact, it becomes more intense when Indian women migrate to the US or to the UK. In the wake of a new international division of labour, and opening of national borders, increasing numbers of Indian people are settling abroad. In the new environments of adopted societies Indian women face various types of pressures to choose their attire and they have to find their style of clothes within the context of traditions of two different (in many ways culturally opposed) societies. With the advent of multiculturalism (Goldberg, 1994) in the USA, the myth that 'it is hard to look deviant these days' is spreading (Kuper, 1973; Wilson, 1990). But this claim does not tally with the experiences of South Asian women within the USA. For example, 'Indians' living in New Jersey are well aware of the 'dotbuster' gangs (a hate group of white young men who are attacking Indian women for wearing a red dot on their foreheads) which shook the Indian immigrant community in 1987 with their violent acts, specifically targeting Indian women's 'native' dresses. There is a mounting demand for assimilation (in other words, to look like and be packaged like 'white' people) in North America. Since ties with the home country are generally strong, immigrant Indian women are also under pressure from people back home (including parents and in-laws) to maintain Indian femininity in the USA.

The question is, how are Indian immigrant women coping with the contradictory demands made on them: a) to maintain Indian tradition through wearing their *saris*?, b) to maintain regional images of being a South Asian?, c) to maintain the image of being an 'ideal minority' (*India Today* 12/15/1987; Lessinger, 1995; Haines and Mortland, 2001)?, d) to conform with work place demands to look efficient by wearing professional Western suits?, e) to protect themselves by hiding their Indianness from 'dot-busters' and other violent racist gangs?, and f) to try to be socially accepted in the larger American society (Uddin, 1996)?

These contradictory demands, while revolving around the issue of self-image and social acceptance, also impinge on the economics of maintaining a large wardrobe. But most Indian people do not wish to deal with these issues. Indian women, it seems, are asked to set aside Indian regimentation and adopt American regimentation without supposedly losing their Indianness, and their subjectivity. Most Indian women do not even question these pressures and accept them as necessary tools for survival. Under these circumstances Western dress is seen as a welcome change (Bhattacharjee, 1992), but whenever these women visit India they feel 'backward' amid the prevailing fashions in India. How can Indian immigrant women in the USA balance the demands of dress codes without going through a basic transformation of their own identity or becoming a victim of racism? The pressure of a daily eight hours identity change somehow is perceived as unproblematic, as if their sense of personal identity or desires takes leave of them for eight hours and comes back intact when they reach home.

It may be pointed out that there is nothing abnormal with this balancing act because people have to survive and they try to make the best of any situation. But in the context of multiculturalism and the opposing demand to assimilate, the struggle over 'native' dresses becomes important. Most Christian countries have adopted Western dresses both for working men and women. Indian male dress was Westernized a long time ago and men did not have to go through the similar indecisions and struggles. In that sense, it remains mainly an Indian women's problem. Indians who are labelled as a 'model minority' refuse to accept that Western culture is largely based on racism and that nothing changes their subordinate status in this country (Fisher, 1980; Sethi, 1993). They easily fall into the trap of thinking that if they work hard they will be amply rewarded. It would not be long before an increasing number of Indians will find it easier to shed their 'Indian-ness' to fit into the market and hence become more socially acceptable.

Indian immigrant women also experience choices of clothing differently depending upon the type of family they come from, what work they are involved in, what age group and which generation they come from, and their solidarity with the Indian 'community' (which involves patriarchal control) in the USA, or a 'community' back in India. Demonstrations of 'Indian-ness', including wearing the sari, are an important requirement for receiving any help from the immigrant Indian 'community' in the USA. The Westernization of dress and family values are also seen to be part of the increasing problem of domestic violence within the Indian 'community'. The Indian 'community' within the USA appears neither to be cognizant of the patriarchal structure of Indian society, nor of Western racism.

Instead it insists that Indian women adhere to 'Indianness' (which usually means wearing a *sari*) to resolve family problems (Lynch, 1994).

Conclusion

The above historical and contemporary considerations allow me to state my main point: South Asian women's clothes are not part of established 'authentic' Indian culture but are constructed in the process of the historical development of Indian society. This means that no style of dress is inherently either 'traditional' or 'modern'; each style is a product of the historical process within which such labels are assigned. In the context of such a historical process, many social relations are negotiated, including gender roles, in terms of which women creatively make their clothing choices. One cannot therefore understand the subjectivity, identity, and creativity of an individual without connecting the individual's life with the larger historical processes of her society. The focus in this chapter is on South Asian women's clothes to show how the individual choice of identity and self-expression is constantly changing, not only due to individual choices but also within the historical context in which these women find themselves. The customs of society – which are constructed historically in the day-to-day social interaction of people – equally influence the boundaries of the choices of an individual. If we wish to understand human creativity and subjectivity (personal experiences and identities), it is imperative to understand the larger historical and contextual processes that continuously exist in a dialectical relationship to the former. Focusing on one aspect of this dialectical process will provide us only with a partial picture of both society and individuals. It is necessary to assume such a comprehensive perspective on cultural issues like South Asian women's clothing and to eliminate the binary concepts of 'traditional/modern', and 'progressive/primitive'.

References

Bahl, V. (2004), 'Terminology, History and Debate', *Journal of Historical Sociology*, **17**, 2.

Barnes, R. and Eicher, J.B., eds. (1992), *Dress and Gender, Making and Meaning* (Providence, RI/Oxford: Berg).

Belk, R.W. (1998), 'Third World Consumer Culture', (Greenwich: CT Jai). Kumcu, E. and Firat, A.F. (eds.) in *Marketing and Development: Toward Broader Dimensions*.

Bhattacharjee, A. (1992), 'The Habit of Ex-nomination: Nation, Women and the Indian Immigrant Bourgeoisie', *Public Culture*, **5**(1), 19–44.

Chaudhuri, N. (1976), *Culture of Vanity Bag* (Bombay: Jaico).

Cohn, B. (1989), 'Cloth, Clothes and Colonialism: India in the Nineteenth Century' in *Cloth and Human Experience*. Weiner, A. and Schneider, J. (eds.) (Washington: Smithsonian Institute Press).

Elwin, E.F. (1907), *Indian Jottings: From Ten Years' Experience in and Around Poona City* (London: John Murray).

Fisher, M.P. (1980), 'The Indian Ethnic Identity: The Role of Association in the New York Indian Population' in *The New Ethnics: Asian Indians in the United States.* Saran, P. and Eames, E. (eds.) (New York: Praeger).

Goldberg, D.T. (1994), *Multiculturalism: A Critical Reader* (Oxford; Blackwell).

Haines, David W. and Carol Mortland (2001). *Manifest Destinities: Americanizing Immigrants and Internationalizing Americans* (Westport, Connecticut: Praeger).

Hardgrove, R.L., Jr (1968), 'The Breast-Cloth Controversy: Caste Consciousness and Social Change in Southern Travancore', *The Indian Economic and Social History Review,* **5**(2), 171–187.

Khan, N. (1992), 'Asian Women's Dress from Burqah to Bloggs: Changing Clothes for Changing Times' in *Chic Thrills: A Fashion Reader,* (*Berkeley: California University Press*). Ash, J. and Wilson, E. (eds.).

Kibria, N. (1998), 'The Racial Gap: South Asian American Racial Identity and the Asian American Movement' in *A Part yet Apart: South Asians American.* Dhingra Shankar, L. and Srikanth, R. (eds.) (Philadelphia: Temple University Press).

Kuper, H. (1973), 'Costume and Identity', *Comparative Studies in Society and History,* **15**, 348–367.

Lessinger, J. (1995), *From the Ganges to the Hudson* (Boston: Allyn & Bacon).

Lynch, C. (1994), 'Nation, Woman, and the Indian Immigrant Bourgeoisie: An Alternative Formulation', *Public Culture,* **6**, 425–437.

Malwani, L. (2001), 'What is Hot', *Little India,* June issue.

Mazumdar, S. (1992), 'Women, Culture and Politics: Engendering the Hindu Nation', *South Asia Bulletin,* **12**, 2, Fall.

Nandwani, D. and Seth, S. (2001), 'Salwar: Recolonizing India', *Little India,* June issue.

Pandey, I.P. (1988), 'Dress and Ornaments in Ancient India', (Delhi: Bhartiya Vidya Prakashan).

Panikkar, K.N. (1998), 'The "Great" Shoe Question: Tradition, Legitimacy and Power in Colonial India', *Studies in History,* **14**, 1.

Rajadhyaksa, A. (1990), 'Beaming Messages to the Nation', *Journal of Arts and Ideas,* **19**, 33–52.

Schlenker, B. (1980), *Impression Management: The Self Concept, Social Identity and Interpersonal Relations* (Monterey, California: Brooks/Cole).

Sethi, R.C. (1993), 'Smells like Racism: A Plan for Mobilizing Against Anti-Asian Bias', Karin Aguilar ed. *State of Asian American,* (Boston: South End Press).

Sharar, A.H. (1975), 'Lucknow: The Last Phase of an Oriental Culture', Tr. and edited by E.S. Harcourt and Fakhir Hussain (London: Paul Elk).

Storm, P. (2000), *Function of Dress: Tool of Culture and the Individual,* (N.J: Prentice Hall).

Tarlo, E. (1996), *Clothing Matters: Dress and Identity in India* (Chicago: University of Chicago Press).

Uddin, Sufia M. (1996), 'The Oral History Project of South Asia in the Greater Philadelphia areas', sponsored by the Balch Institute for Ethnic Studies, Philadelphia.

Venkatesh, A. (1994), 'Gender Identity in the Indian Context: A Sociocultural Construction of the Female Consumer' in *Gender Issues and Consumer Behavior*, *(Thousand Oaks: Sage)*. Costa, J.A. (ed.).

Wilson, E. (1990), 'Deviant Dress', *Feminist Review*, **35**, 67–74, Summer issue.

Index